SOCIAL COST - BENEFIT ANALYSIS

ABDUL QAYUM

LIBRARY OF CONGRESS
CATALOGUE NUMBER: 78-62056

ISBN: 0-913244-16-3

PREFACE

This treatise is designed as a text for senior and graduate students studying cost-benefit analysis, and as a handbook for research-workers in the field of project appraisal. I have used the material in teaching graduate students at Portland State University and have benefited from the disscussions with the students over the last several years.

I have included an extensive bibliography at the end of the book. The references are arranged by dates. This was done to facilitate the selection of more recent contributions for readers with limited time.

My colleagues, Professors Key Kim, Thomas Palm and John Walker, read and commented upon the first draft of the manuscript. Professor Bent Hansen of the University of California at Berkeley also read that draft and gave valuable suggestions for improvements.

Professor Leif Johanson of the University of Oslo gave detailed comments on a synopsis of the present draft, which were very helpful. Professor R. B. Halley, Acting Director of the Systems Science Ph.D. Program suggested several stylistic changes. Two of the graduate students, James Wilson and Terry Schumacher, of the Systems Science Ph.D. Program read the manuscript minutely and enabled me to improve the presentation.

I am grateful to all of these colleagues, friends and graduate students for their help and encouragement in the process of writing this book.

Professor Daniel J. Scheans, Head of the Anthropology Department, allowed the secretaries of his department to help with the final typing of this manuscript. The Dean of Graduate Studies and Research, Professor Stanley E. Rauch, and Assistant Dean and Director of Sponsored Research Activities, Dr. Richard B. Streeter, were kind enough to allocate funding to cover the typing cost of the bulk of the book. Ms. Chris Young of the Systems Science Ph.D. Program patiently and cheerfully typed the appendices and the bibliography.

I am grateful to Professor Joe Pierce, Executive Editor of Hapi Press for publishing this book in such a short time. I understand he plans to arrange publication of an Indian Edition and possibly another unhurried Western Edition. I wish him all success.

Finally, I wish to express my gratitude to the secretaries of the Economics Department, Ms. Mitsie Shinoda and Ms. Regina Lawson, for their consideration and politeness to me.

SOCIAL COST-BENEFIT ANALYSIS

Table of Contents

Appendices

Chapter One

INTRODUCTION

1. A SHORT HISTORY

1-1 The Origin

Social cost-benefit was probably never studied as an area of scientific enquiry until 1844 when a French economist, Dupuit, published an incisive paper on public utilities.[1] Though it may or may not be due to the momentum of this early start, today in France quantitative methods of cost-benefit analysis are applied routinely in the planning and management of road and water resource investments. These methods include the use of an accounting discount rate, and of a premium exchange rate for the allocation of available funds and foreign exchange.[2]

In other Western European countries and in the United Kingdom, cost-benefit analysis had a late arrival. In the U. K. cost-benefit analysis has been mainly applied in transport problems such as underground railways and the proposed Channel Tunnel.

Since cost-benefit analysis is essentially a micro-economic technique, it has not made much headway in the USSR. Until recently, Soviet planners were only concerned with consistency planning through commodity balances. However, the communist countries of Eastern Europe have been applying cost-benefit analysis, using accounting prices.

1-2 Important Developments in the United States

It was in the U. S. that the cost-benefit

analysis came first into priminence. In 1902 a board of engineers[3] reported on the cost of Army Corps of Engineers' river and harbor projects and upon the amount of benefit to commerce from these projects. In the mid-thirties, the New Deal ushered in an era of broader social justification for projects. The Flood Control Act of 1936 authorized Federal participation in flood control schemes. This was a key document in the development of cost-benefit analysis. It set forth as a standard in project evaluation the requirement that "the benefits to whomsoever they may accrue (be) in excess of estimated costs." The flood control Act, aside from implying distributional neutrality, did not state any criteria for defining benefits and costs nor how they were to be measured. Several of the public agencies in the area of water resource development formulated evaluation criteria which were favorable to their own programs. These criteria differed from one agency to another and disagreement arose among them. In 1950 an interagency committee attempted to reconcile differences which had arisen between the departments in an effort to introduce uniformity in the evaluation criteria. This attempt resulted in the publication of the committee's Green Book: Proposed Practices for Economic Analysis of River Basin Projects. The book never attained official standing but it was remarkable in that it was the first attempt to bring techniques of economic analysis to bear upon the problems of public investment.

In 1952 the Bureau of the Budget, which reviews all proposals for project authorization and appropriations before they are transmitted to Congress from the White House, adopted its own set of criteria for the appraisal of river development projects. These were published in Budget Circular A-47. This circular remained the basis for the Budget Bureau's appraisal throughout the sixties, despite opposition from various agencies and their congressional allies. These critics alleged that the Bureau took a narrow "accountant's" view of the contribution of river development projects to the nation.

In response to President Kennedy's February 1961 message to Congress, the director of the Bureau of the Budget invited a panel of economists to assess the existing criteria for river development. The report of this panel, referred to as the Consultant's Report, reflected a sophisticated analysis. The Bureau of the Budge, however, was not in a position to accept this. Subsequently, in 1962, a new inter-agency committee was appointed to recommend policies and procedures relating to cost allocations, reimbursement, and cost sharing in plans for the use and development of water resources. These recommendations were approved by President Kennedy for application by the agencies and the Budget Bureau.

1-3 Operations in the Deparment of Defense

There were also related historical antecedents also in the Department of Defense. Article I, Section 8 of the Constitution states that Congress shall have the power to "provide for the common defense." Military objectives and operations became increasingly more complex during the nineteenth century. And, during the World War I, it became evident that the vast increase in the military expenditure necessitated budgetary reforms. Congress responded by enacting the Budget and Accounting Act of 1921. This act concentrated the responsibility for preparation and transmittal of the budget in the hands of the President.

The movement toward a unified defense establishment which had grown stronger in the 1920's and 1930's, and the experience of World War II made it quite clear that Congress could not exercise effective stewardship over the defense establishment by parceling out hundreds of discrete appropriations. "Massive, world-wide, total war demanded integrated and coordinated planning, funding and execution."[4]

In 1961, President Kennedy abandoned the budget-ceiling as far as defense was concerned. He gave his secretary of defense, Robert McNamara, two general instructions: (1) Develop the military force structure necessary to support our foreign policy, without regard to arbitrary budget ceilings. (2) Procure and operate this force at the lowest possible cost. The mechanism developed by McNamara's Assistant Secretary of Defense, Charles Hitch was a three phase operation: Planning--Programming--Budgeting, (PPB).

Systems analysis played a central role in the development of PPB by the Defense Department. The term 'systems analysis' is used with varied and diverse meanings. The one relevant to PPB evolved in response to planning problems during World War II. Operations analysis during this period resulted in "the successful application of applied mathematics, physical science and systematic data collection to tactical problems of increasing complexity."[5] The Air Force in 1946 created Project RAND, later to become the RAND Corp.,to bring together people who had wartime operations analysis experience. The objective of this group was to advise the Air Force on its research and development activities.

1-4 Extension of the PPB System to the Executive Branch

Finally, in 1965, President Johnson announced his desire to introduce an integrated PPB system, similar to that of the Defense Department in other agencies of the Executive Branch. On August 25, he announced a new PPB system to his cabinet members and other agency heads. He asserted his conviction that the "system will improve our budgets rather than having them control us..."[6]

A basic part of PPB system is an emphasis on cost-effectiveness, a discipline which is now well-established throughout the Executive Branch of the Federal Government, and is being increasingly followed by the state and local governments.

II. VARIANT APPROACHES AND TERMINOLOGY

II-1 Introduction

Numerous terms which are in current use convey the same general meaning as PPBS. These include: (1) Planning, Programming and Budgeting, (2) Systems Analysis, (3) Operations Research and Operations Analysis, (5) Cost-effectiveness Analysis, and (6) Cost Utility Analysis, and Cost-benefit Analysis. Each of these terms roughly describes the same discipline with some variations, although a broad definition of any of these might cover others. However, these terms are not defined uniquely or unequivocally by the experts working in these disciplines. In fact over the years, there has taken place an erosion of their earlier meanings, so much so that they mean different things to different people. The following are capsule descriptions of the concepts of disciplines mentioned above. Hopefully these may be considered definitive.

II-2 PPBS

Although the introduction of PPBS has led to the regular usage of analytical tools common to the fields of operations research and systems analysis, both President Johnson and the supporters of PPBS intended to develop a systematized approach to decision making rather than merely to introduce new tools of analysis. Arthru Smithies argued that the PPB system involved:

"(1) Appraisals and comparisons of various Government activities in terms of their contributions to objectives;

(2) Determination of how given objectives can be obtained with minimum expenditure of resources;

(3) Projection of Government activities over an adequate time horizon;

(4) Comparison of the relative contribution of private and public activities to national objectives; and

(5) Revision of objectives, programs, and budgets in the light of experience and changing circumstances.

Program budgeting involves more explicit recognition of the need to perform them than has been traditional. It also involves the application of new analytical techniques as an aid to the exercise of human judgment on which choices must ultimately rest."[7]

II-3 Systems Analysis

The essence of systems analysis is to construct and operate within a model, that is, a simplified abstraction of the appropriate real situation.[8] Such a model may take various forms such as a computer simulation, an operational game or even a purely verbal scenario. A sustems model introduces a precise structure and terminology that primarily serve as an effective means of communication. This enables decision makers to exercise their judgment and intuition within a concrete context.

There are five elements present in every systems analysis: (1) The objective. The first and most important task of the analyst is to discover what the decision-maker's objectives are and then how to measure the extent to which these objectives are, in fact, attained by various choices. (2) The alternatives. The alternatives are the means by which it is hoped the objectives can be attained. These alternatives need not be obvious substitutes for each other or perform the same specific function. For example education, anti-poverty measures, police protection, and slum clearance may all be the alternative methods of combating juvenile delinquency, (3) The costs. The choice of a particular alternative implies that certain resources can no longer be used for other purposes. Thus the true measure of cost is in terms of the opportunity foregone. (4) A model. A model is a simplified representation of the real world that abstracts the cause and effect relationships specific to the problem under study. This representation may be in the form of a mathematical equation, a computer program or a verbal description of the situation. In systems analysis, the role of the model is to estimate for each alternative the costs that would be incurred and the extent to which objectives would be attained. (5) A Criterion. A criterion is a rule or standard used to rank the alternatives in order of desirability. It provides a means for weighing cost against effectiveness.

II-4 Operations Analysis & Research

Operations research is today largely identified with specific techniques such as linear and non-linear programming, Monte Carlo (randomizing) methods, gaming and game theory and so on. While there is no hard and fast division between operations research and systems analysis, a rough distinction can be made. The less that is known about objectives, the more they conflict, the larger the number of elements to be considered, the more uncertain the environment, the more likely it is that the work will be called a systems analysis. In systems analysis there is more judgement and intuition and less reliance on quantitative methods than in operations research.[9] Operations research, on the other hand, has more to do with the specific mathematical and statistical techniques used in solving models. Systems analysis is a broader and more comprehensive field of enquiry. It may require a good deal of art, intuition, and vision, in addition to its scientific underpinnings.

11-5 Cost-effectiveness

Cost-effectiveness analysis may be considered to be the core of PPB system. Its use is a contractual requirement imposed by the Department of Defense in the Project Definition of large scale development projects.

A cost-effectiveness analysis can be defined as the procedure by which the cost of alternative means of achieving a stated effectiveness, or conversely the effectiveness of alternative means for a given cost, are compared in a series of numerical indices. The objective of the analysis is to isolate the alternative or combination of alternatives that either gives the greatest expected effectiveness for a given expected cost or a given expected effectiveness for the least expected cost.[10]

Cost-effectiveness analysis uses most of the mathematical and statistical methods developed in systems analysis and operations research. In fact, cost-effectiveness can be considered as a specialized branch of Systems Science, the one that minimizes the cost of a given effectiveness or maximizes the effectiveness for a given cost.

The theoretical underpinnings of cost-effectiveness analysis are the same as those of micro-economic theory. However, in cost-effectiveness analysis, the elements of costs, time phasing, and probabilistic aspects are considered in more detail and more specifically than in general economic theory.

II-6 Benefit-Cost, Cost-Benefit or Cost-Utility Analysis

It is obvious that cost-benefit analysis and benefit-cost analysis are synonymous. Which term comes first is a matter of taste; costs are incurred first, though benefits are thought of first. Insofar as benefit measures utility and vice-versa, cost-utility analysis[11] is no different. We shall use the term cost-benefit analysis in the sequel. The following are the main characteristics of cost-benefit analysis.

1. Cost-benefit analysis studies alternative courses of action that might be taken to achieve specified objectives.

2. For each alternative, which we shall call projects as explained below, the outputs in successive years are estimated.

3. Next, the initial inputs and the inputs in each successive year is determined over the life time of the project.

4. Next, the values of outputs and prices of inputs in the successive years are estimated.

5. Then from the values of outputs in each year the total annual benefits are assessed and from the values of inputs in each year, the corresponding total annual costs are estimated. Deducting the annual costs from the corresponding

benefits, the net annual benefits are derived.

6. Finally the present value of each project is derived by using time discounting rate or rates, and those projects with the highest present value are selected.

7. The projects yield outputs and require inputs over several years. Their amounts and prices may change which may vary over time. Hence problems of risk and uncertainty arise which have to be dealt with in estimating costs and benefits.

The above are the main steps taken in cost-benefit analysis. The inclusion of specific costs and benefits varies with project ownership and management. A private entrepreneur will typically be interested in the profits; he will include only those outputs which can be sold. Thus the benefits will equal the revenues. In a similar manner the costs will equal the expenditures incurred. For a government department, the benefits may not be only the revenues it receives but the "excess of benefits" which the users of the output or service might gain. Similarly the cost may be more or less than the expenditures incurred.

Social C-B analysis uses the same steps as mentioned above. But all the costs and benefits are measured in terms of losses or gains of welfare to the society.

III. SOCIAL COST-BENEFIT ANALYSIS

III-1 PPBS and Social C-B Analysis

Planning--Programming--Budgeting, Systems and OPerations Analyses, and cost-effectiveness and cost-benefit analyses might well cover the bulk of the considerations that enter into social cost benefit analysis. However there are some important characteristics of social cost-benefit analysis which are not common to other approaches. Social C-B analysis is a more general, more uniformly applicable and more broadly based discipline than those mentioned above. The distinctive feature of social C-B analysis is the fact that all the costs and all the benefits are viewed from the social standpoint.

A PPB system and systems and cost-effectiveness analyses use diverse techniques and elaborate procedures. They are applied to achieve the best or optimal performance in one department or in a group of interrelated agencies. While there is no limitation on the choice of objectives or on the alternative means to achieve them, the objectives are confined to the areas under the jurisdiction of the agencies and the alternative means are restricted to their areas of operation. In most cases the objective or objectives need not be given any values, and in other cases resources used need not be imputed any values. While these procedures may be adequate for the agency or agencies concerned, they may be found wanting from the viewpoint of the society as a whole. Moreover, so long as all the objectives or products of all the projects are not uniformly valued from the social standpoint, a uniform integrated approach for the country or society as a whole cannot be evolved. Similar remarks apply to the valuation of resources and inputs.

The chief merit of the social cost-benefit analysis lies in the possibility of integrating factors that affect society and the well-being of individuals, but are of no direct consequence to the private or public agencies who start and run the projects. Most of these effects are not amenable to being dealt with by actual or surrogate markets. Hence they escape the usual methods of national accounting. In social cost-benefit analysis all the effects, direct as well as indirect, created by the installation and operation of a project are included.

Another crucial requirement of social cost-bnefit analysis to which little attention has been paid is that all projects have to be treated uniformly whether the project is in the public sector or in the private. Applying a different set of principles and rates to the projects in different sectors is to introduce a disequilibrium or maladjustment in the economy with unknown and uncertain consequences. In any case such a procedure will certainly deflect the social economy from the path of optimal movement. It is true that the social C-B analysis can be administered directly in the public sector and only indirectly in the private, but this dichotomy cannot be a justification for confining the analysis to one sector.

Social C-B analysis thus defined and understood interlinks all activities which affect social welfare into a unified procedure. Piecemeal application of C-B analysis to one department or to a few departments or to only one sector may lead to heterogeneous results. This will be the case so long as all the outputs, objectives, inputs, and resources are not valued using uniform standards or norms.

III-2 Definition of Project

Social C-B analysis is applied through the evaluation or appraisal of projects. The purpose of project evaluation is an analysis of its social costs and benefits. Hence the two disciplines are essentially the same.

The term project has been used earlier. It is worthwhile, however, to define it briefly. A project is any activity expected to achieve one or more objectives. Of course, the same objective or objectives can be fulfilled by different activities, and so these will represent alternative projects. The objective may either be the production of some outputs or of some services. The outputs and services may be at any stage of completion but they must be well-defined for reasonable valuation. Even though an activity can be defined for any stage of completion of a product or service, the stage chosen for the design of a project should be one which is convenient for evaluation. There need not be one project for each activity. Some activities which are "interpenetrating" and complementary can be combined into one project. For instance a multipurpose project may have several objectives, such as provision of electricity, flood control, irrigation, fishery, and so on; and there may be several activities related to each. These activities may be complementary and interdependent and it may not be possible to separate them out. It may be convenient or unavoidable, therefore, to treat them as components of one project. Thus even though each of these component activities may be very big, they cannot normally be treated as separate projects.

On the other hand, some small activities can be conveniently treated as separate projects. For example in manufacturing, some parts are often purchased from other suppliers who specialize in producing it. The production of these parts which might be quite small can be conveniently considered as separate projects.

A project is exactly defined when the levels of activities it comprises have been set. There may be instances where the activity levels are expressed in terms of the number of workers, the size of capital, or by the amount of some other resrouce. Generally, the most appropriate measure of the level of an activity ought to be the volume of output or outputs intended to be produced. Indeed this is the common practice in activity analysis and programming.

With the level of an activity, the corresponding volumes of one or more outputs is determined and the project is defined. For another activity level, another project is defined. Thus a number of projects may be considered for achieving different levels of the same objectives.

III-3 Phases of Social C-B Analysis

i. Estimation of Outputs and Inputs

The volume of direct outputs of a project are known by definiton. However, the byproducts of the project may not have been estimated. Besides the intended outputs and expected byproducts, there might be some unintended outputs. Both the direct intended and unintended outputs have indirect repercussions. In some circumstances, it may be necessary to estimate these indirect effects. Unintended outputs may be goods like better roads and industrial milieu, or bads like air and noise pollution.

The direct inputs of a project are easy to estimate since a well designed project details the inputs. However, there are some inputs which are not accounted for. These are the resources and inputs which are used free of charge by projects, but which have value to society. In social cost benefit analysis these unaccounted inputs have to be included among costs. The unaccounted inputs may be items belonging to the natural environment, like water, air, and natural scenery, or to the social atmosphere like law and order, peace and stability. (Loss of some of these items may have been counted as negative output; care will have to be exercised to avoid double counting.) In addition to direct inputs, indirect inputs will have to be estimated, corresponding to both accounted and unaccounted inputs.

ii. Valuation of Outputs

The next stage is valuation of outputs. In commercial projects, it is the market prices at which the outputs are valued. In social C-B analysis, market prices will be adequate if they are compatible with maximization of social welfare. Some other criteria, such as consumers surplus and world prices, have been suggested.

iii. Valuation of Social Goods

Some goods, particularly those produced by public projects, have no market and will have to be valued by means other than those of a market merchanisms. Also the unintended outputs and unaccounted inputs often do not have markets, hence their values have to be determined by indirect or non-market methods.

iv. Valuation of Inputs

The procedure for valuation of intermediate inputs will be the same as that for outputs. But the factors of production will have to be valued according to some criteria that will lead to the maximization of output over time. The appropriate factor prices to be used in social C-B analysis are shadow prices which can be quite different from market prices.

v. Choice of Projects

The purpose of C-B analysis is to enable us to make the optimal choice of projects. There are several criteria for project selection; the most commonly used are present value and the internal rate of return. The first of these involves the determination of a time discount rate. The second can be used only if it is assumed that the rate of time discounting remains constant.

vi. Uncertainty & Risk

Any analysis which extends over several years into the future involves risks and uncertainty. The main uncertainties and risks of social C-B analysis relate to: (i) the estimation of the values of outputs due to changes of taste and the availability of substitutes; (ii) the estimation of values of inputs especially factors of production; (iii) estimation of the rate of time discounting (iv) any other natural or man-made causes leading to the failure of projects.

III-4 Social C-B Analysis & Economic Planning

The objective of social C-B analysis is to make the optimal selection of projects, so as to bring about welfare maximization in a country over time. This is also the aim of economic planning. The difference between economic planning and social cost benefit lies in their respective approaches. Social C-B analysis is a micro-approach. Indeed, the micro-theory of a firm is no more than its simple cost-benefit analysis. Economic planning, on the other hand, is basically a macro-approach. Here the allocation of resources is mainly done by sectors in physical terms. For the implementation of the economic plan, policies and measures are designed so as to realize the planned allocation of resources.

In social C-B analysis, the allocation of resources is achieved through optimal choice of projects, based on social valuation of goods and shadow factor pricing. Social C-B analysis is, therefore, primarily decentralized planning in a much more comprehensive sense.

One great advantage of social C-B analysis is that it allows the inclusion of various social and environmental considerations which are difficult to deal with by the usual macro-economic planning approaches. It is less inconvenient to analyze externalities and economies of scale in social C-B analysis than in formal planning methods.

It must be recognized that social C-B analysis is not a substitute for macro-economic planning. Many of the indicators and indices can be derived only from macro-analysis. The future values of outputs and inputs, factor prices and rate or rates of time discounting are all estimated from macrodynamic studies. Social C-B analysis is, therefore, a supplement to macroeconomic planning and endeavors to meet the challenges at the micro-level which generally defy macro analysis.

SUMMARY

Except for the appearance of a French economist's paper on public utilities in 1844, and some recent applications in France and Britain, most of the developments in the social cost-benefit analysis have taken place in the United States. It started from the board of engineers report in 1902 and was broadened by the social justification for projects ushered in by the New Deal. The introduction of systems analysis and operations research in the Department of Defense during the World War II greatly expanded the technical scope and the applicability of the analysis. The Flood Control Act of 1952, the Consultant's report of 1961 and the approval by President Kennedy of a new interagency report in 1962 all finally culminated in the President Johnson's announcement of the Planning-Programming-and-Budgeting System of 1965.

The terms, PPB System, Systems Analysis, cost-effectiveness and cost-benefit analysis have been used interchangeably and indeed they share a common methodology to a large extent. Their basic purpose, i.e., the achievement of efficiency and optimality is also similar. However there are important differences in their scopes and approaches. The PPB System is more appropriate for government departments and interagency procedures for project evaluation, for which it was originally developed. Systems analysis is a more abstract scientific approach where the objectives are not well-defined and where the means to achieve them are complex and interlinked. The essential prupose of the PPB system and systems analysis is to study the cost-effectiveness of alternative means or projects and select the one which will achieve a given objective or objectives with the minimum cost.

In cost-benefit analysis, both the level of objectives and costs are kept flexible, and projects are studies for different combinations of objectives and cost levels in order to seek the project for which the anticipated return is maximumized.

Social cost-benefit anlaysis is a cost-benefit analysis in which the values of objectives and costs are estimated from the broader standpoint of social welfare. Moreover the consideration of the many external effects associated with projects, left out from ordinary cost-benefit analysis, forms a major element in social cost-benefit analysis. These effects can be represented by unintended outputs and unaccounted inputs which cannot be valued by market mechanisms. The main steps in social cost-benefit analysis are: 1) estimation of direct and indirect outputs (intended and unintended), and inputs (accounted and unaccounted); 2) valuation of ouputs; 3) valuation of social goods which include most of the unintended outputs and unaccounted inputs; 4) valuation of factors and production; 5) choice of projects and derivation of present values; 6) consideration of risk and uncertainty.

Footnotes

1 J. Dupuit, "On the Measurement of Utility of Public Works," International Economic Papers, vol. 2. (translated from French).

2 Accounting and other concepts regarding prices of labor, capital and foreign exchange will be discussed in Chapter Five.

3 This board was required to report by the River and Harbor Act of 1902.

4 Lt. Cdr. Steven Lazarus, USN, "Planning--Programming--Budgeting Systems and Project Prime," Defense Industry Bulletin, 3:1 (January 1967).

5 Fred S. Hoffman, "Public Expenditure Analysis and the Institution of the Executive Branch," The Analysis and Evolution of Public Expenditures: The PPB System, A Compendium of Papers submitted to the Subcommittee on Economy in Government of the joint-Economic Committee, Congress of the United States, Vol. 3, Washington 1969, p. 926.

[6] Fremont J. Lyden & Earnest G. Miller (eds.): Planning, Programming Budgeting: A systems approach to management, Markham Publishing Company, Chicago 1968, Preface.

[7] Arthur Smithies, "Conceptual Framework for the Program Budget" in Program Budgeting, David Novick, ed., Washington, D. C., GPO, 1965, p. 5.

[8] This brief description of Systems analysis is based on E. S. Quade, "Systems Analysis Techniques for Planning--Programming--Budgeting," Report P-3322 (Santa Monica, California: The Rand Corporation, March 1966).

[9] Aaron Wildavsky, "Rescuing Policy Analysis from PPBS" in the Analysis and Evaluation of Public Expenditures: The PPB System Op. Cit., p. 853.

[10] Karl Seiler, III, Introduction to Systems Cost-effectiveness, Wiley-Inter-Science, New York, 1969.

[11] The term cost-utility has been used by Gene H. Fisher "The Role of Cost-Utility Analysis in Program Budgeting in David Novick (ed.) Program Budgeting, New York: Holt, Rinehart and Winston, Inc., 1965.

Chapter Two

ESTIMATION OF OUTPUTS AND INPUTS

I. ESTIMATION OF OUTPUTS

I-1 Definitions and Classifications of Outputs

A project is undertaken in order to produce "intended" outputs. These include the main outputs and the by-products. The operation of a project, however, results in some other outputs which are not intended and for which there is no demand. These may be called "unintended" outputs. Part of these may be harmless or even advantageous but others may be injurious to the environment and damaging to life and property. The latter outputs may be called negative outputs. Various types of pollution and effluents are major negative outputs.

Direct outputs are the first or immediate outcomes of the operation of the project. These are followed by indirect outputs, or effects which may be positive and negative.

In the estimation of a project's outputs, the direct and indirect, positive as well as negative, have to be traced. A project yields output over the period it is in operation. Hence the estimate of its direct output has to be carried over its life time. The indirect effects may continue even after the project has ceased to be in operation. In the estimate of indirect outputs, all effects have to be considered.

I-2 Estimation of Direct Output

The identification of various types of direct output is the first step in the estimation process. Given the availability of factors of production and resources, the technical constraints and the existing infra-structure and facilities, and the gestation lag involved in the construction of the plant, the direct outputs of the project can be estimated. The size of the project is predetermined and so is its full production capacity. The project may not be able to or it may not be designed to operate at full capacity from the date of its completion. Even if it is technically possible to operate the project at full capacity from the very beginning, the demand conditions may be such that the project is planned to assume full capacity operation gradually as the demand expands.

With due replacement the project may, in most cases, produce its full capacity output throughout its life. However it may be that towards the later part of its operating life its productive capacity will begin to decline. Hence irrespective of the demand for the project output, it may not be technically possible to produce at constant full capacity towards the end of the project's life.

The production of by-products will generally vary with that of the main output. The main outputs and the by-products can be estimated fairly accurately with due allowance for risks of breakdowns and stoppages.

The utilization of some projects, particularly public projects such as recreational facilities and libraries, whose outputs are not marketable, will vary with the number of people availing themselves of these projects. The actual output of such projects have to be estimated on the basis of forecasts of such utilization.

The unintended direct outputs are not difficult to identify. The opening of a music school provides service to students who take lessons, but the neighborhood may enjoy, say, good music. An industrial complex may create an industrial milieu, a sense of responsibility and an ambitious attitude on the part of the people in the area. While these are less tractable direct unintended positive outputs, there are others which are more tractable. Construction of transportation and communication facilities yields as outputs the movement of men and materials and transfer of information. This makes the adjoining areas more accessible and consequently the properties over this area appreciate in value. The appreciation of the properties may have been foreseen by the project planner, but it could not have been one of their intended outputs. If this appreciation could in some way be appropriated by the project, it could then be treated as by-product. The difference between a by-product and unintended positive output essentially lies in whether or not it is possible for the project to control and dispose of such output.

The direct negative outputs of a project are mostly unintended. Industrial projects produce more negative outputs than non-industrial projects, like educational institutions, and recreational facilities, though in the construction phase, they may be no different. The most common negative outputs are various types of pollution caused by the effluents of industrial wastes and harmful chemicals. Air is polluted by the smoke and smog of fuel burned by industries and in big cities by automobiles. The atmosphere is also worsened by the noise created by some projects, particularly by high speed means of transportation like trains and supersonic jets. Some projects cause deterioration of landscape and natural surroundings or the destruction of historical monuments and religious or cultural edifices. River dams, strip mining, forestry, urban renewal are among such projects.

The negative outputs mentioned so far are physical in nature. There are some other negative outputs which may be called social in nature. These may be congestion, social strife, crimes and so on.

After the identification of various types of direct outputs, the next crucial step is the measurement of these outputs in terms of appropriate units. The main outputs of a good many industrial projects can be conveniently expressed in terms of commonly used units, such as tons of steel or grain, bales of cotton, kilowatts of electricity, cubic feet of water supply. These are one-component units. Some other outputs can be precisely measured but in more than one component unit. For example, the outputs of a transportation project may be measured in terms of passenger-miles or ton-miles.

However, not all main outputs have convenient units of measurement. These are generally the outputs which are not marketed and not marketable. The output of a library or a recreational facility does not have any convenient units of measurement. For such projects some rough unit or units will have to be devised. For a library the main output may be measured by the number of books borrowed and/or by the number of readers. For some other projects, a good deal more ingenuity will be called for. Some outputs may defy all efforts to arrive at a unit of measurement. In such cases, the output may be given some dollar value, a subject which will be taken up in the following chapter. The direct outputs of a project can be tabulated as follows:

TABLE 2.1

Direct Outputs of a Project

			Gestation Period	Fruition Period
		Years	(1) (2) (3) ...	(1) (2) (3) ...
Intended Outputs	Main Outputs			
	By-Products			
Unintended Outputs	Positive Outputs			
	Negative Outputs			

In Table 2.1, the various outputs have been separated in two periods, the gestation and the fruition. In the gestation period, a project is started, constructed, and completed to its planned capacity; the actual production of the main outputs start after the completion of the project when the gestation period comes to an end. Therefore, the main outputs are nil in the gestation period. They begin at the start of the fruition period and last till its end. The production level of main output may remain constant throughout the fruition period or it may vary. The by-products may follow the same pattern, but it may be that the by-products change in volume in a compensating way. However, few by-products may be forthcoming during the gestation period. Since the by-products are related to the main outputs, the duration of their yield, in general, coincide with the fruition period.

The unintended outputs, negative as well as positive, may appear as soon as the construction of the project is started and may continue through the gestation and fruition periods. Their magnitudes may vary greatly during the gestation period, but may stabilize during the fruition period.

1-3 Indirect Output

Indirect outputs are all the outputs which flow from the direct outputs over time. If each output of various categories were so specific that it produced in turn only one output or could be used as consumption (ignoring exports for the moment), then it would be possible to trace forward the profile of outputs and consumption originating from the annual outputs of the project. In reality an output is seldom so specific. Hence the flow of indirect outputs on the production side is technically determined, to only a limited extent. Most of the outputs can be used in alternative ways. Hence what secondary outputs will be produced from the direct outputs is subject to decision-making in successive production periods. When the possibility of exports and imports is considered, the alternatives become very large indeed. It can therefore be concluded that there is no unique path of the constellation of indirect outputs which is physically or technically determined on the supply side. The intended direct outputs may therefore have to be valued directly.

In the framework of a comprehensive national plan, it becomes meaningful to contemplate or conjecture a maximal path over a sufficiently long time horizon. The maximal path, however, is an extreme theoretical abstraction, and has little practical relevance.[1] Even if it had any, it would be impossible to persuade the policy makers to stake the welfare of the country on such an illusive and unreliable concept. To try to trace the outputs that would follow from the direct outputs is, therefore, an unrewarding and uninteresting exercise.

The indirect outputs (or effects) of the unintended direct outputs has to be traced, however. The market mechanism fails to handle these outputs and their effects. Moreover, the unintended direct outputs (positive and negative) are mostly such that they affect the environment and the inhabitants of a certain area or a certain group indiscriminately with consequent repercussions over periods of varying duration. These repercussions get more and more diffused with time; therefore, it is necessary that they be traced as far and as completely as possible. Some of the effects of unintended outputs are not restricted to a certain area, and reach very distant location. For example, mercury dumped by some industrial projects into the sea is consumed by fish. These may be caught and tinned to be sold not only all over the country but even to foreign countries. These may be poisonous when consumed by humans in sufficient quantities.

The unintended outputs can take place in the gestation period as well as in the fruition period as shown in table 2-1. The indirect effects of these outputs may start just after their appearance, and continue through the gestation and fruition periods of the project and even beyond. The indirect effects of the positive unintended outputs are by definition beneficial and those of negative unintended outputs harmful.[2] A stream of indirect effects emanates from unintended outputs in each period; the volume of this stream may become bigger or smaller in each successive period or it may remain constant over time. Thus the stream may terminate or taper off or may be perennial.

The design of units of measurement for indirect effects, both positive and negative, may be even more illusive than those of direct unintended outputs. For example, a number of industrial effluents can be measured in terms of volume or weight, but their indirect effects on environment, such as water pollution, are far more difficult to measure. If water pollution takes place in an isolated area, with little human habitation, few indirect effects may be felt and their intensity may be small. But if the same level of water pollution takes place in a densenly populated area, the indirect effects would be more in number and greater in intensity. Thus the indirect effects are not only difficult to express in convenient units, they change in intensity with location and timing.

Some intended outputs like cigarettes and liquors have indirect effects comparable to those arising from the unintended outputs. Cigarette smoking not only affects the health of smokers, but non-smokers exposed to the smoke. It also adversely affects the children born to smokers. Drinking does not affect just the drinkers, but others who come in contact with them. Drunken drivers are the biggest killers on highways. It would be advisable, therefore, to measure the indirect effects of intended outputs, which affect individuals other than the direct users of these outputs.

In some cases even if a product does not

affect non-users but is injurious to the user's health and welfare in the near or distant future, it may be argued that these effects be measured and accounted for. This is an area where questions of freedom of choice arise. It can be debated whether any other person or authority has a right (or is more capable) to decide what is good for the individuals using the product. For individuals below a certain age, it can perhaps be maintained that the society and the state have an obligation to prevent them from using products which may be sooner or later harmful to them. It is only a step from this to suggest and justify state or societal intervention in the consumption of products to which adult individuals get addicted. For in case of addiction, an individual does not think rationally. Beyond these cases, it does not seem justifiable to impute any other indirect effects of products whose consumption by an individual has no effect on other individuals.

II. ESTIMATION OF INPUTS

II-1 Classification of Inputs

There is a basic division of inputs: fixed inputs and variable inputs. Fixed inputs are all those inputs which do not vary with the main outputs, and variable inputs are those which do vary. The services of managers, and all overhead items fall in the first category. The services of ordinary workers, raw materials and all items that vary with the level of the operation of the project fall in the second. Fixed inputs can be called capital inputs and variable inputs current inputs.

During the gestation period, various inputs are used to build the plant and buildings, to install the machines and equipment, to construct infra-structure and facilities and to set up the organizational and administrative system. All the inputs used in this period go to build up the capital structure and other paraphernalia to start production in the fruition period.

During the fruition period, most of the inputs are used to produce the intended outputs. But some inputs are used for replacement of the depreciated capital items. The magnitude of these inputs is small in the beginning of the fruition period and becomes larger towards the end. Some inputs may be used also to expand the capacity of the project during the fruition period. These inputs lead to an increase in the current output in the following years over the remaining life span of the project, while the replacement inputs prevent the capacity of the project from falling.

There may be some <u>unaccounted</u> inputs used in the project: the use of already existing infrastructure, various means of transportation and communication, and other industrial facilities. Insofar as the installation of the project leads to a speedier depreciation or deterioration of these, an accounting should be undertaken to estimate their utilization. Some of these inputs may not be already existing, but may have become available during the gestation or fruition period of the project.

On the contrary, however, the project itself may involve construction of new railroads, airports, residential housing, schools and other facilities which might be utilized by firms and communities other than those connected with the project. Not all of these, therefore, should be accounted as input of the project; an appropriate proportion, should be excluded.

Besides man-made goods, projects also use

elements of the environment as unaccounted inputs. These include water, air, land, natural scenery, mineral and forest resources and so on. Some of those resources are now and certainly will be scarce in the future. A reduction in some environmental resources affects the current welfare of society not to speak of the future.

II-2 Estimation of Direct Inputs

The direct accounted inputs of a project are easily identified, since, in most cases, they are itemized and listed in the design or description of the project. Direct unaccounted inputs may require careful scrutiny, since they easily escape consideration during project planning. The utilization of the existing infra-structure is generally taken for granted and no cost is imputed to the depreciation caused by the construction and operation of the project. The inputs of environmental resources are seldom given any recognition and they are not listed as inputs.

In a social cost benefit analysis, these unaccounted inputs are as important as the accounted ones. In some cases, these unaccounted inputs may be more essential to human welfare than the accounted ones.

The problems faced in devising units of measurement and methods of estimating inputs are similar to those related to ouputs. There is little problem, however, in case of accounted inputs, since they are purchased from the market.

In case of unaccounted inputs, the problem of defining units of measurement may become actue. If a project is using the existing roadways, the unit of measurement of the usage of the road may not be easy. The same applies to other categories of infra-structure for which the project is not required to pay any rates.

The difficulties are no less in estimating the inputs of environmental resources. Efforts have been made, however, to measure various residuals and how they use up essential elements of the environment. Some of these attempts will be mentioned later. The bibliography to this chapter contains a number of references where attempts have been made to estimate environmental inputs to various economic activities.

TABLE 2.2

Direct Inputs of a Project

				Gestation Period	Fruition Period
			Years	(1) (2) (3).....	(1) (2) (3).....
Accumulated Inputs	Capital		(1) (2) ...		
	Current		(1) (2) ...		
Unaccounted Inputs	Capital	Positive	(1) (2) ...		
		Negative	(1) (2) ...		
	Current	Positive	(1) (2) ...		
		Negative	(1) (2) ...		

II-3 Indirect Inputs

Indirect inputs of the accounted direct inputs of a project is a regular field of estimation. Given the levels of output and the techniques of production, all the direct and indirect inputs can be estimated through the familiar techniques of input-output analysis. In the case of a project, the direct inputs have been studied and are known to begin with. The point of interest is to estimate all the indirect inputs required to produce the direct inputs. These will depend on the techniques used in their production. Since a new project is a net addition, the direct inputs into the project would require additional production, causing net additional investment in all the sector interlinked with the production of these inputs. Hence the techniques on the basis of which the indirect inputs have to be derived are the latest marginal techniques. Since the evaluation of a project precedes its installation and operation, the estimation of indirect inputs required to provide direct inputs will have to be based on not only the techniques used but those to be used in the future. The accuracy of the estimation of indirect inputs, therefore, will depend on the degree of accuracy with which the changes in technology are predicted.

There are several reasons for estimating the indirect accounted inputs corresponding to direct accounted inputs. First, it may help in estimating the value of outputs. Second, the production of indirect inputs may involve some unintended outputs as well as some unaccounted inputs which must be taken into account cumulatively. Third, the estimation of indirect inputs may help in the determination of income distribution and changes in the structure of the economy.

The unaccounted direct inputs also initiate

chains of indirect inputs and outputs. In a complete cost-benefit analysis, these streams, which may be positive or negative, will have to be taken into account. In input-output analyses, the unaccounted indirect inputs corresponding to direct inputs are usually not analyzed. This is partly due to the absence of data and the difficulty in measuring and evaluating what is available. This is because most of the unaccounted direct and indirect inputs do not pass through market mechanism and are not caught by the net of national income statistics.

Some of the unaccounted direct and indirect inputs do not show all their effects in the year in which they are used, but over an extended period of time. In these cases, a simple current accounting will be inadequate. Therefore a series of long term analyses, stretching over the lifetime of the project and possibly beyond will have to be undertaken.

The chains of intended and unintended indirect inputs linked to a direct input in a year during the gestation and the fruition periods are too cumbersome to be shown in a tabular form. This can be better depicted by means of a tree as below:

Tree 2-4 Indirect Inputs

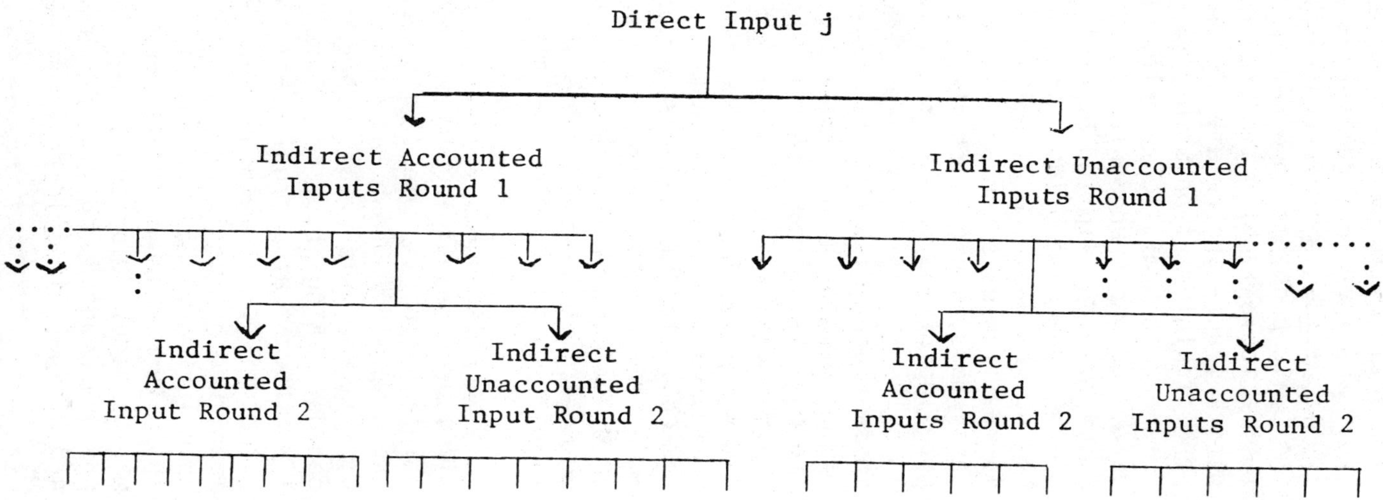

All the tedious iteration can be avoided if a table could be constructed with direct inputs as the final deliveries and indirect inputs as inputs in a usual input-output table. The basic problems involved in constructing such a table linking the indirect inputs to direct inputs are related to the absence of adequate information about the unaccounted inputs and the relationship they have to other accounted and unaccounted inputs. The difficulties are multiplied by the fact that some of the unaccounted inputs may not be known, or may not be known conclusively. A case in point is the fluoro-carbon propellent used in aerosol spray cans, a use which the U.S. Congress is debating at the moment of this writing. There is evidence, though not yet conclusive, that these fluoro-carbon propellents in spray cans may dissipate the atmospheric ozone, which prevents the ultra-violet rays of the sun from reaching the earth in undiluted form. The breaking down of the ozone layer could lead to an increased chance of skin diseases and other hazards. In this case ozone becomes an unaccounted indirect input of a project producing aerosal sprays using fluoro-carbon as an accounted direct input. This is a striking illustration of the concepts discussed here.

Such linkages, some hazardous, some beneficial, are present in almost any project. The point is that if some of the unaccounted inputs are simply not known and cannot be known, cost-benefit analysis or any other type of analysis can do nothing about it. But if there is some likelihood that a significant unaccounted input might occur, then an expected value of the magnitude of the input may be included in the calculations. For example, the probability that fluoro-carbon breaks down the ozone layer may be about 80 percent, then the magnitude of the unaccounted input of ozone may be taken as 4/5 of what it would be if it were known with certainty.

In order that all the indirect inputs are fully estimated, it is advisable to construct a direct-indirect inputs table, a blank for which is given in Table 2-5. In the gestation period, the direct inputs will be mostly capital inputs, in the fruition period, most of them will be current inputs. It is understood by definition that there will be no deliveries from the accounted indirect inputs to unaccounted indirect inputs; otherwise they will not remain unaccounted. Imported inputs may be included in the direct inputs or may be kept outside the table. If they are listed in the column of direct inputs, then the flows from the accounted indirect inputs may be from domestic transportation and banking and financing services, *etc*. In addition, there may be some flows from unaccounted inputs.

Table 2-5 Direct-Indirect Inputs

<table>
<tr><th colspan="2" rowspan="2"></th><th colspan="2">Indirect Inputs</th><th rowspan="2">Direct Inputs</th><th rowspan="2">Total Inputs</th></tr>
<tr><th>Accounted</th><th>Unaccounted</th></tr>
<tr><td rowspan="2">Indirect Inputs</td><td>Accounted</td><td></td><td></td><td></td><td></td></tr>
<tr><td>Unaccounted</td><td></td><td></td><td></td><td></td></tr>
</table>

III. SOME RAMIFICATIONS AND OBSERVATIONS

III-1 Unintended Outputs in Consumption

So far we have considered projects designed for productive activities and the unintended outputs and unaccounted inputs associated with them. But these outputs and inputs are connected not only with production but also with consumption activities. Cigarette smoking is one small example, but car driving is a major consumption item which results in external effects of great magnitudes. Excessive drinking, the use of detergents, the use of aerosol cans, picnicking, addictions to some medications, and many other consumption activities produce harmful physical and social effects in addition to satisfying the immediate needs of consumers. Of course, there are many consumption activities which produce beneficial effects. Education, vaccination, and beautiful landscaping are some of such examples.

In a macro-study, all these external effects of consumption activities will have to be considered along with the external effects (represented by unintended outputs and unaccounted inputs) of productive activities or projects. In social cost-benefit analysis each consumption activity which involves external effects will have to be considered as a project and analyzed along the same lines as other projects. Most of the consumption activities have little or negligible external effects. However, some consumption activities, such as car driving and use of aerosols and detergents have effects which must be seriously considered in analyzing external effects.

In case of those consumption activities which have substantial external effects, there are two approaches which may be adopted. Either the consumption activities may be themselves considered as separate projects, or the effects created by these consumption activities may be included in the analysis of projects producing the items of consumption. For example, the effects of driving may be considered in the analysis of projects producing cars or the effects of aerosol propellent containers can be considered in the analysis of projects producing such containers.

III-2 Duality Between Unintended Outputs and Unaccounted Inputs

There is a good deal of duality between unintended outputs and unaccounted inputs. For example, most industrial production is carried out by burning fossil fuels to create energy. This produces carbon dioxide which is unintended output. Carbon dioxide would be of no consequence or concern if it did not reduce or replace oxygen which can thus be considered an unaccounted input. Therefore carbon dioxide as an unintended output and oxygen as unaccounted input can be considered as dual of each other. It can be reasonably stated that this duality is present in almost all unintended outputs and unaccounted inputs. An intended output of a negative type must be such that it destroys or eats up some existing environmental resource which may presently be a "free" good, but the reduction in whose quantity may bring about harmful effects. In some cases this duality may not be easy to trace or establish. Some obvious examples of this type of duality include noise and quiet, polluted air and clean air, aerosol accumulation and ozone layers, polluted water and clean water, and social unrest and social tranquillity.

The main point to consider here is that in social cost-benefit analysis, this duality must be carefully noted to avoid the risk of double counting. If the cost of crime is included in the analysis, then the cost of police or prevention measures should not be added. Similarly if the cost of fatalities and accidents are included, then the insurance charges must be excluded from an analysis of road transportation. These examples are obvious but in many other cases the double counting may not be easy to detect.

III-3 External Effects

The term external effects has been used earlier; it seems necessary to describe it more precisely than before and to show how it is related to unintended outputs and unaccounted inputs.

An external effect is popularly known as an effect which causes a change in the utility of an individual or the profits of a firm independent of the actions of the individual or the firm, but due to the actions of other individuals or firms. The neighbors' utility is affected, if one burns his trash in the backyard or if one plays very loud music.

This definition is too general. An external effect is one which accrues to an individual or firm due to the activities of other individuals and firms but only when these activities are undertaken without any consideration for the affected individual or the firm. In other words, the other individuals' and firms' actions are completely independent of whatever effect they may have on the subject individual or the firm. That is, any effect on the utility of the individual or the profits of the firm must be unintended by those individuals and firms who cause these effects.

Another qualification which should be introduced is that in an interdependent economy, the actions of any firm or individual will affect the profits or utility of other firms and individuals via quantity and price adjustments. It is advisable and appropriate that these market adjustments be kept separate from the externalities as such. Traditionally these indirect equilibrating effects have not been included in the external effects or externalities.

From the point of view of an individual project, the external effects that it produces are <u>unintended</u>. It does not receive any revenues for them, nor does it sustain any losses, even though they may do some good or harm to others. In turn the external effects that an individual project receives or uses up are unaccounted; it does not incur any costs or receive any payments even though the external effect may do it some harm or good. All externalities are thus fully covered by unintended outputs and unaccounted inputs.

IV. SOME FORMAL METHODS OF ESTIMATION

IV-1 Estimation of Indirect Accounted and Unaccounted Inputs

Indirect accounted and unaccounted inputs corresponding to the direct inputs to a project can be traced by reiteration, but the procedure may become unwieldy and involved after a few rounds. Moreover iteration procedures do not yield exhaustive estimates. The indirect inputs of a project can be estimated more conveniently and exhaustively by imbedding the direct inputs of the project in the input-output matrix of the country.

Let x_i^{AD} be ith direct accounted input of the project, x_g^{UD} be the gth unaccounted input, and let x_i^{A} be the total accounted ith input and

x_g^U the total gth unaccounted input, then

$$x_i^A = \sum_{j=1}^{m} a_{ij}^{AA} x_j^A + x_i^{AD}$$

and $$x_g^U = \sum_{j=1}^{m} a_{gj}^{UA} x_j^A + \sum_{k=m+1}^{n} a_{gk}^{UU} x_k^U + x_g^{UD}$$

where a_{ij}^{AA} is accounted ith input per unit of jth input and a_{gj}^{UA}, unaccounted gth input per unit of accounted jth input and a_{gk}^{UU} is unaccounted gth input per unit of unaccounted kth input. By solving the above in terms of accounted and unaccounted direct inputs x_i^A's and x_g^U's can be estimated. The indirect accounted and unaccounted inputs x_i^{AI}'s and x_g^{UI}'s can be estimated: For $x_i^{AI} = x_i^A - x_i^{AD}$, $i = 1, \ldots m$ and $x_g^{UI} = x_g^U - x_g^{UD}$, $g = m + 1, \ldots n$. The solution can be shown using matrix notation.

Total inputs can be stated as:

$$X^A = A^{AA}X^A + X^{AD}$$

$$X^U = A^{UA}X^A + A^{UU}X^U + X^{UD}$$

where

X^A is the vector of total accounted inputs

X^U is the vector of total unaccounted inputs

X^{AD} is the vector of direct accounted inputs

X^{UD} is the vector of direct unaccounted inputs

A^{AA} is the matrix of accounted to accounted input coefficients

A^{UA} is the matrix of unaccounted to accounted input coefficients

A^{UU} is the matrix of unaccounted to unaccounted input coefficients

Solution gives the total accounted and unaccounted inputs of the project.

$$x^{A} = (I - A^{AA})^{-1} x^{AD}$$

$$x^{U} = (I - A^{UU})^{-1} [(I - A^{AA})^{-1} x^{AD} + x^{UD}]$$

Some of the unaccounted direct and indirect inputs may be such that their reduction is desired by the community. These are in effect negative inputs, and should be given positive values in evaluation.

The accounted and unaccounted indirect inputs are essential magnitudes in estimating the indirect effects of a project related to social objectives such as employment, income distribution, environmental quality, and social unrest. The vectors of indirect inputs are:

$$x^{AI} = x^{A} - x^{AD} = [(I - A^{AA})^{-1} - I] x^{AD}$$

$$x^{UI} = x^{U} - x^{UD} = (I - A^{UU})^{-1} (I - A^{AA})^{-1} x^{AD} + [(I - A^{UU})^{-1} - I] x^{UD}.$$

Here x^{AI} is the vector of accounted indirect inputs, and x^{UI} is the vector of unaccounted indirect inputs.

In the above formulation, no indirect accounted input flows to unaccounted direct inputs have been shown. The direct unaccounted inputs can be broadly classified into environmental elements and items of infrastructure constructed by projects other than the one being analyzed. There will be little indirect accounted input to the former, otherwise it would not be unaccounted. The accounted indirect inputs to the latter would be considered in analyzing the other projects which originally installed these elements of infrastructure.

IV-2 Leontief's Method

In a recent article Leontief developed a static input-output system in which pollution-related activities have been built. Since pollutants form only a part of unintended outputs, this system is less general. However Leontief's system includes abatement of pollution activities, which might help in pricing some of polluting effluents.

In Leontief's system, the first m goods are useful goods and the last n-m are pollutants. The technical coefficients are:

a_{ij} - input of good i per unit of good j (produced by section j)

a_{ig} - input of good i per unit of eliminated pollutant g (eliminated by sector g)

a_{gi} - output of pollutant g per unit of output of good i (produced by sector i)

a_{gk} - output of pollutant g per unit of eliminated pollutant k (eliminated by sector k)

The variables are:

x_i - total output of good i, $i = 1, 2, \ldots, m$

x_g - total amount of pollutant g eliminated

$g = m + 1, \ldots, n$

y_i - delivery of good i to households

With these notations, the balance equations are

$$x_i = \sum_{j=1}^{m} a_{ij}\, x_j + \sum_{k=m+1}^{n} a_{ik}\, x_k + y_i$$

$i = 1, \ldots, m$

$$x_g = \sum_{j=1}^{m} a_{gj}\, x_j + \sum_{k=m+1}^{n} a_{gk}\, x_k - y_g$$

$g = m + 1, \ldots, n$

In matrix notations, the above can be written

$$X_1 = A_{11}X_1 + A_{12}X_2 + Y_1$$

$$X_1 = (x_1, \ldots, x_m)', \quad X_2 = (x_{m+1}, \ldots, x_n)'$$

where

$$-X_2 = -A_{21}X_1 - A_{22}X_2 + Y_2$$

$$Y_1 = (y_1, \ldots, y_m)', \quad Y_2 = (y_{m+1}, \ldots, y_n)'$$

The above equations can be rewritten

$$(I-A_{11})\, X_1 - A_{12}X_2 = Y_1$$

$$A_{21}X_1 - (I-A_{22})\, X_2 = Y_2$$

or $$\begin{bmatrix} I - A_{11} & -A_{12} \\ A_{21} & -I + A_{22} \end{bmatrix} \begin{bmatrix} X_1 \\ X_2 \end{bmatrix} = \begin{bmatrix} Y_1 \\ Y_2 \end{bmatrix}$$

or $$\begin{bmatrix} X_1 \\ X_2 \end{bmatrix} = \begin{bmatrix} I - A_{11} & -A_{12} \\ A_{21} & -I + A_{22} \end{bmatrix}^{-1} \begin{bmatrix} Y_1 \\ Y_2 \end{bmatrix}$$

The amount of pollution of type g produced in sector i is $a_{gi}\ x_i$ of this x_g has been eliminated. But the elimination of x_g amount of pollution creates $a_{gg}\ x_g$ amount of pollution. Hence the uneliminated pollution g created by sector i is $a_{gi}\ x_i - x_g + a_{gg}\ x_g = a_{gi}\ x_i - (1 - a_{gg})\ x_g$.

IV-3 Some Other Models

There are some other models and methods which study the flows into and out of the environment. A few of these are very interesting for macro-analysis but are of little help in social C-B analysis. One of these is the general equilibrium-materials balance model introduced by Kneese and d'Arge.[4] The structure of this approach can be briefly summarized as follows.

The resources and materials utilized in the production of commodities is given by

$$r_j = \sum_{k=1}^{n} a_{jk}\ x_k \qquad j = 1, \ldots, m. \tag{1}$$

The relationship between commodity production and final demand is given by

$$x_j = \sum_{k=1}^{n} A_{jk}\ y_k \qquad j = 1, \ldots, n. \tag{2}$$

where A_{ij} are the elements of $[I-C]^{-1}$ where C is the usual Leontief-current input-output matrix.

Focussing explicitly on the flow of materials through the economy, we have,

$C_{kj}\, x_j$ physical quantity transferred from j to k

and $C_{jk}\, x_j$ physical quantity transferred from j to k

Flows into and out of the environmental sector Θ must be in the balance:

$$\sum_{k=1}^{n} C_{\Theta k}\, x_k = \sum_{k=1}^{N} C_{k\Theta}\, x_\Theta + C_{f\Theta}\, x_\Theta \qquad (3)$$

Material flows to and from the final sector must also balance:

$$\sum_{k=1}^{n} C_{kf}\, x_f = \sum_{k=1}^{n} C_{fk}\, x_k + C_{f\Theta}\, x_\Theta \qquad (4)$$

sum of all final goods	sum of all materials recycled	waste residuals (plus accumulation)

$$x_f = \sum_{j=1}^{J} y_j \qquad (5)$$

Substituting (5) in (2) in (4) we obtain an expression for the waste flow in terms of final demands:

$$C_{f\Theta}\, x_\Theta = \sum_{j=1}^{N} \sum_{k=1}^{N} (C_{jf} - C_{fj}\, A_{jk})\, y_k \qquad (6)$$

Kneese and d'Arge use the above captions based on the concept of environmental balance for deriving pareto-optionality conditions. This approach, though not directly helpful in social C-B analysis of a project, has led to other studies and empirical work which are very useful. For instance, some estimates given by Forsund and Strom[5] provide figures of residuals which might be used in social C-B analysis.

Residuals can be classified as: (1) material residuals such as solid, liquid, or gaseous; and (2) energy residuals such as heat, noise, and radiation. The natural environment serves as a sink for these residuals. The elements of the environment which receive these residuals are air, water, and land. The recipients are also suppliers of raw materials and recreational services. A residual acts as a pollutant if it negatively affects the quantity or quality of the raw materials or recreation services 'produced' by the recipients. The discharge of all residuals does not necessarily generate pollution. Parts of these are assimilated by the processes of dilution, decomposition and chemical transformation. Only the remaining parts cause harmful effects.

At a point of time, the total amount R_i of residual i discharged into recipient x is

$$R_i^a = \sum_j d_{ij}^a x_j + R_i^{ca} + R_i^{Ga} + R_i^{fa}$$

where $d_{ij}^a = \dfrac{W_{ij}^a}{x_j}$, d_{ij}^a is the discharge coefficient, W_{ij}^a is the discharge of residual of type i from production sector j to the recipient a (air, water, and land) and x_j is the volume of gross production in sector j. R_i^{ca} is the amount of residual i generated through consumption and R_i^{Ga} indicates residuals stemming from military defense and the use of the roads. R_i^{fa} is equal to the import of residual i to the national recipient minus the amount of residuals generated by national activities abroad. X_j's are determined from a multisectoral model first introduced by Johansen.[6] The development of R_i^{ca} and R_i^{Ga} over time is to some extent predicted outside the model.

The authors have been able to estimate various types of residuals by recipients and by sector.

The estimates of similar data projects is very valuable in social C-B analysis.

Summary

The estimation of outputs and inputs of a project is the first step in its social cost-benefit analysis.

The capacity to produce the planned or intended levels of outputs are given for a well-defined project. The expected levels of by-products are also known. However, a project produces some unintended outputs which benefit or harm other projects and individuals. The estimation of these unintended outputs may be bads, like the pollutions of air and water, noise, congestion, and crimes or goods like roads, schools, and recreational facilities.

The direct inputs of a project are also known; they are detailed when a project is formulated. However, projects use many inputs which are "unaccounted." These include elements from the environment such as oxygen, water, minerals, and so on, or infra-structure constructed by other projects or states. In a social cost-benefit analysis the unaccounted inputs must be taken into account.

Direct intended and unintended outputs have further repercussions and effects. In the case of most intended outputs, their values may reflect their indirect effects. But for valuing the unintended outputs, an estimate of their indirect effects will have to be made. This is particularly true of unintended outputs connected with the environment.

Direct accounted and unaccounted inputs are linked to the chain of indirect inputs. These indirect inputs may have to be estimated to assess their costs in the social cost-benefit analysis. The aggregates of these indirect inputs may be estimated by extending the usual Leontief's input-output analysis.

Appendix to Chapter Two gives details of the direct and indirect, intended and unintended outputs and accounted and unaccounted inputs associated with a timber clear cutting project.

Footnotes

1. The reference here is to J. Von Neumann's article "A Model of General Economic Equilibrium" Review of Economic Studies, 13, 1945, and the related literature on maximal growth path and turnpike theory.

2. This statement is true only in a general way. It is just possible that on the whole a negative unintended output may have some positive elements, beneficial to some individuals and there may be some negative elements in an unintended output which is on the whole positive. We shall not enter into these refinements here.

3. Wassily Leontief, "Environmental Repercussions and the Economic Structure: An Input-Output Approach." Review of Economics and Statistics, Volume LII, August 1970, Number 3. Note: The notation used in this subsection are slightly different from the preceding subsection IV.1.

4. Allen V. Kneese and Ralph C. d'Arge, "Pervasive External Costs and the Response of Society" in The Analysis and Evaluation of Public Expenditures Vol. I. The notation here is again slightly different from the preceding sections.

5. Finn R. Forsund and Seinar Strom, "Industrial Structure, Growth and Residual Flows" in J. Rothenber and Ian G. Heggie, (eds.), The Management of Water Quality and the Environment, New York: John Wiley & Sons, 1972.

6. L. Johansen, A Multisectoral Study of Economic Growth, (North-Holland Publishing Company, Amsterdam, 1960).

Chapter Three

VALUATION OF OUTPUTS AND INPUTS

I. INTRODUCTION

I-1 Valuation in Social Cost-Benefit Analysis

The purpose of social cost-benefit analysis is project evaluation. This is achieved by assinging a value to all the magnitudes involved in a project which affect social well-being. We have described the various types of outputs and inputs in Chapter Two. Another magnitude of critical importance associated with a project is time. The valuation of these magnitudes will be the subject matter of this and the following three chapters. The produced goods can be treated together, be they outputs or inputs. The same good should not be treated differently whether it is being considered as an output or as an input. Any given good should be given the same value in whatever state it is being considered. The valuations of inputs and outputs will be discussed in this chapter. However, there are some goods (or bads) which are either produced by the state or fall in the category of unintended outputs or unaccounted inputs. The valuation of these two categories of goods poses some special problems and will be discussed in Chapter Four.

The valuation of factors of production in countries with widespread unemployment and structural disequilibrium needs separate treatment. Here, the prevailing factor prices are not conducive to a rate of growth of their economies which is obtainable with their resources.

The valuation of factors in these countries will be discussed in Chapter Five.

Valuation of time, which is expressed by the rate of time discounting, is crucial to any inter-temporal problem. The determination of the rate of time discounting and its application in the derivation of the present value of projects will be considered in Chapter Six.

1-2 Principles of Valuation

The valuation of goods should be approached with reference to the principle to be followed, and the objective to be achieved. The objective of social cost-benefit analysis is the maximization of social welfare, and the principle to be followed should be one which achieves this objective. The welfare of a society is a function of the utilities of its individuals. Ideally, then, the valuation of goods ought to be related to the individual utilities. This principle is very difficult to implement. A second principle which is generally advocated is based not on individual utilitities, but on the market demand curve. This is known as the 'willingness to pay' or "consumers surplus" criterion. It appears that there are some basic difficulties in even applying this principle. The third principle or standard which might be ultimately resorted to is the market price. Valuing goods at market prices is convenient, but it can be debated as to how far they are compatible with the objective of maximization of social welfare. A fourth criterion recently suggested is that the goods should be valued at world prices. These four principles will be discussed in the following sections.

II. INDIVIDUAL UTILITY

II-1 Non-Measurability of Utilities

Ideally the values of goods should be determined with reference to the utilities that individuals derive from them. The idea of linking values of goods directly to individual utilities, though attractive,, faces insurmontable difficulties, which are well-known. Utility is non-measurable cardinally. An individual is not unable to state quantitatively how much he prefers one good to another. All that he may be expected to express is that he prefers one good to another, or that he is indifferent. Hence no relative values can be assigned to goods based directly upon individual utilities.

II-2 Impossibility of Interpersonal Comparison of Utilities

Individual utilities are not cardinally but only ordinally measurable. This determines the ordering of individual preference over goods and commodities. If interpersonal comparison of individual utilities were possible, the determination of social (or community) preference ordering over goods and commodities would be feasible. Since a reliable procedure for interpersonal comparison of utilities is not available, the valuation of goods through social preference ordering over goods is not an encouraging proposition. This has been abundantly whown by Arrow and others.[1] Therefore, it can be concluded that the valuation of outputs cannot be based on any direct aggregation or comparison of individual utilities or preferences.

III. WILLINGNESS TO PAY AND CONSUMERS SURPLUS

III-1 Demand Function and Individual Utilities

Individual preference ordering over goods and commodities allows us to construct indifference curves between pairs of commodities. The locus of points of tangencies between these curves and a spectrum of price lines, gives the demand curve. This standard discussion is contained in every introductory book on microeconomics.

The individual demand curve can, in general, be derived from maximizing individual's utility function under his budget constraint. Let U_j be the utility level given by goods x_{1j}, x_{2j}, ... x_{nj}, of the jth individual with his disposable income equal to y_j.

$$\max U_j = f(x_{1j}, x_{2j}, \ldots x_{nj})$$

$$\text{subject to } y_j = \sum_{i=1}^{n} P_i x_{ij}$$

$$x_{ij} \geq 0$$

gives $x_{ij} = x_{ij}\ (P_1, P_2, \ldots, P_n, y_j)$

$$i = 1, \ldots n.$$
$$j = 1, \ldots n.$$

Given the prices of the commodities and his income, the individual's demand for each commodity can be estimated.

III-2 Determination of Equilibrium Prices

If the total supplies of each good are

given for a period and the individual demand functions for each good and individual incomes are known then the equilibrium prices of goods can be derived. Let there be N individuals in the economy, then the demand of the jth individual for the ith good is given by

$$x_{ij} = x_{ij}(P_1, P_2 \ldots, P_n, \overline{y_j})$$

$$\sum_j x_{ij} = \overline{x}_i \qquad \begin{array}{l} i = 1, 2, \ldots, n \\ j = 1, 2, \ldots, N \end{array}$$

In the above there are $n \times N + n$ equations and there are nN xij's and n pi's. So the number of equations equals the number of unknown variables, hence the above can be solved for the P_i's and xij's, given values for $\overline{y}_j$'s and $\overline{x}_i$'s. If these can be predicted or planned than the equilibrium values of goods can be determined and these values would be such which maximize individual welfare in a Pareto optimum sense. This is to say that each individual would be as well off as he could, and that no individual could be made better off without making some others worse off.

III-3 Consumers' Surplus

The equilibrium prices derived in the preceding section do not reflect the total utility of the good to the individual, but rather the utility of the last unit he purchases. He will continue to purchase more units of the good until the utility of the good exceeds that of the price he pays. All the units of the good excepting the last one yield excess utility to him. The sum of excess payments he would be willing to make for earlier units is consumers' surplus.

A debatable question then arises as to whether the goods should be valued according to the utility of the last unit to the individual or according to the total utility of the units of the good he purchases. This is a crucial consideration in social cost-benefit analysis. The point at issue is shown by the following figure.

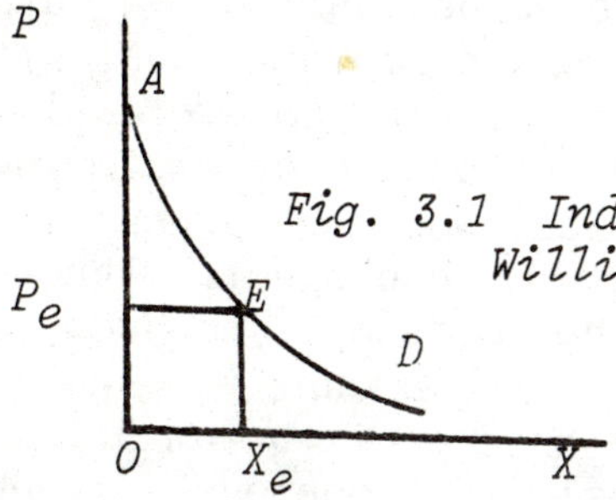

Fig. 3.1 Individual Willingness to Pay

AD is the demand curve of an individual for a certain good x, at a preassigned value of his income, $\bar{y}$. At equilibrium price OP_e, the individual purchases OX_e units of x, the utility of the last unit to him being equal to the price OP_e. He would be willing to pay higher amounts for the earlier units. The sum of the amounts he would have been willing to pay for the successive units is $OAEX_e$, whereas, in fact he pays OP_eEX_e. The difference between the two areas AP_eE is the consumers' surplus to the individual from this good. Many writers have advocated the inclusion of consumers' surplus in the valuation of outputs for social cost-benefit analysis of projects.[1] This implies that in such an analysis, the value of OX_e amount of good x is $OAEX_e$ rather than OP_eEX_e.

Consumers' surplus and willingness to pay are well defined for an individual; since his demand function can be constructed and the equilibrium price of the goods can be derived, the area $OAEX_e$ can be determined. However, the demand function of each individual will differ and so will the amount purchased by him and the area representing his willingness to pay. Hence the value per unit of output assessed according to the willingness to pay criterion will be different for each individual. Hence no unique value per unit of an output can be derived on the basis of individual willingness to pay criterion. In the evaluation process it may be impossible to estimate the willingness of individual would-be purchasers to pay for the outputs of a project. The equilibrium prices of the goods are, however, still needed to determine the amount the individual would purchase. These equilibrium prices are derived on the basis of exogenously given amounts of outputs, as outlined in the preceding subsection.

III-4 Aggregate Demand Function and Consumers' Surplus

It is impossible to base the valuation of outputs on the willingness to pay of each single individual. The next best approach would be to derive an aggregate demand function and to estimate the collective willingness to pay for an output. This aggregate demand function can be derived either through aggregating individual demand functions, or by fitting a demand function using cross-section or time series data. The aggregation of individual demand functions into an aggregate demand function involves problems which have been dealth with in the literature on aggregation. The derivation of a statistical demand functions may be more straight forward to derive, provided the data are availabl

Let us suppose the aggregate demand function for each output has been derived,

$$x_j^d = x_j^d (P_1, \ldots P_n, y), \; j = 1, \ldots, n$$

and the supply of each output is given

$$x_j^s = \bar{x}_j. \qquad j = 1, \ldots, n$$

In equilibrium $\quad x_j^d = x_j^s, \; j = 1, \ldots, n.$

$$\bar{x}_j = x_j^d (P_1, \ldots, P_n, y) \quad j=1, \ldots, n.$$

The above system has n equations and $n+1$ variables $P_1 \ldots P_n$ and y. It can be solved for Pi's, for a specific value of y.

Once the aggregate demand function and the equilibrium price for a commodity are known, the aggregate consumers' surplus and the aggregate willingness to pay may be determined. In the following diagram the horizontal axis measures the quantity and the vertical axis its price, and AD represents its aggregate demand curve, then the aggregate amount which all

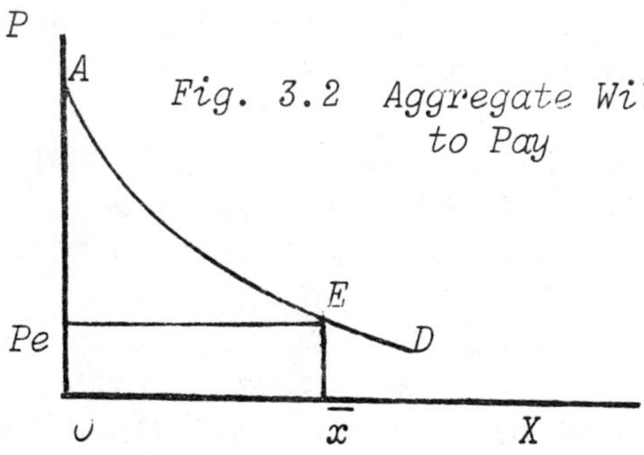

Fig. 3.2 Aggregate Willingness to Pay

the individuals are willings to pay for $\bar{x}$ amount of output is $o\bar{x}EA$ and the aggregate consumers' surplus is AEp_e.

Thus, given the aggregate demand function for, and the available amount of an output, the prices of all outputs, and the total income for a period, the aggregate willingness to pay for each output can be estimated. By dividing the aggregate willingness to pay for each output by its total supply, the value per unit of that output can be estimated. This estimation procedure, however, has several drawbacks.

First, insofar as the purpose of willingness to pay or consumers' surplus criterion was to value outputs according to individual satisfaction derived from them, it is substantially compromised in the process of aggregation or in the derivation of aggregate demand function. The extent of discrepancy introduced will depend on the procedure used in the aggregation of individual demand functions or the statistical method used in the estimation of aggregate demand function.

Second, it was mentioned in the preceding section that the individual willingness to pay criterion is inadequate for maximization of social welfare which is also a function of distribution of income. Aggregate willingness to pay criterion will therefore be deficient with respect to social welfare maximization.

Third, the values of outputs estimated according to the willingness to pay criterion (individual or aggregate) will certainly be higher than the equilibrium prices. Under certain perfect market conditions, these equilibrium prices would equal the market prices. The valuation of outputs according to willingness to pay criterion will deflect the benefit-cost ratio from that derived according to valuation of outputs at market prices.

This situation may not cause any problem in the public sector, but may be a source of disruption in the private sector. The private sector can be induced to invest in projects selected according to social cost benefit criteria through taxes and subsidies or through direct regulation and controls.

IV. MARKET PRICES

IV-1 Market Prices and Equilibrium

In the preceding sections equilibrium prices have been derived from systems containing individual or aggregate demand functions and given supplies of outputs. These supplies were assumed to be either planned or predicted. In determining market prices, the supply functions will also have to be introduced. Individual producers will supply the outputs in quantities that maximize their profits. In a frictionless competitive economy the determination of market prices can be represented by the following system.

The derivation of individual demand function was demonstrated in the preceding section. The individual supply function can be derived in an analogous way. Let x_{ij}^{s} be the ith output produced by the jth individual. Let the production function of the jth individual be expressed by

$$x_{ij} = x_{ij}\,(x_{1j}, x_{2j}, \ldots x_{nj}) \quad \begin{array}{l} i = 1, \ldots, n \\ j = 1, \ldots, N \end{array}$$

where x_{ij}'s within the brackets on the right hand side are the inputs used by the jth individual for producing the ith output. His profit from producing the ith output is

$$\pi_{ij} = p_i x_{ij} - \sum_{i=1}^{n} x_{ij} p_i$$

where p_{ij}'s are the n unknown prices. Maximizing π_{ij}'s with respect to the inputs x_{ij}'s, and solving in terms of n p_i's we get the supply function of the jth individual of the ith output,

$$x^s_{ij} = x^s_{ij}\ (p_1, \ldots p_n).$$

We have already derived the demand function for the th output of the th individual. Summing over the N individuals in our system, we have

$$x^d_i = \sum_{j=1}^{N} x^d_{ij} = \sum_{j=1}^{N} \Sigma x^d_{ij}\ (p_1, \ldots, p_n, y_j) \qquad i = 1, \ldots, n$$

$$x^s_i = \sum_{j=1}^{N} x^s_{ij} = \sum_{j=1}^{N} x^s_{ij}\ (p_1, \ldots, p_n) \quad i = 1, \ldots, n$$

In equilibrium,

$$x^d_i = x^s_i \qquad i = 1, \ldots, n$$

The equilibrium system (1), (2), and (3) has $3n$ equations but n unknowns p_i's, and n x^d_i's, n x^b_i's and N parameters y_j's. If the N parameters y_j's are given or known, the system can be solved.[1] These prices and quantities supplied and demanded will be Pareto optimal in the sense that no individual can improve his welfare as a consumer or a producer without causing a reduction in the welfare of someone else. However the Pareto optimal solution is not a unique one. In fact there corresponds one such solution to each constellation of y_j's, each representing a different level of social welfare.

IV-2 Market Equilibrium Prices and Social Welfare

The aim is to find a set of output prices which are compatible with or lead to maximization of social welfare. Therefore, we have to select that Pareto optimal solution which achieves this objective. Since Pareto optimal solutions differ with the configuration of y_j's, the set of output prices which maximizes the social welfare becomes a function of income distribution, given the society's taste and technology. The crux of the problem then is to find that configuration of y_j's which implies maximum social welfare. Only then can the equilibrium market prices can be derived, which might reflect maximum social welfare.

The determination of the optimal distribution of income is perhaps the most challenging problem facing the social sciences. If there were any possibilities, however remote, of interpersonal comparison of utilities, there could be some hope of solving the problem with a degree of objectivity. Since interpersonal comparisons are ruled out, the decisions about income distributions will have to be based on ethical judgments.

IV-3 Market Imperfections

In principle, competitive market equilibrium prices can be derived from a general equilibrium model describing the technical and behavioral relationships prevailing in the economy. However, the state of competition in any economy is far from perfect. A model which does not include representations of these frictions and imperfections cannot yield prices which might be close to those obtaining in the economy. It is difficult to construct a model in which all of the imperfections and frictions are fairly accurately represented. But even if they were, the relative prices obtained will not be even Pareto optimal, much less can they be used to maximize social welfare.

It may appear as though it would be easy to construct a model (rather a surrogate model) as if there were no imperfections present in the economy. Were that the case, the relative prices derived from the solution of the model could be used for project evaluation. Both the relative prices derived from the surrogate model might be so different from the prevailing prices that the model might become suspect and even incredible. And this might be rightly so. The fact of the matter is that the construction of a surrogate model as if imperfections were not present is not an easy task. The techniques and the systems of production and exchange are partly the outcomes of imperfections and frictions prevailing in the economy. Any model that incorporates only the techniques which are being utilized in the economy cannot remove the influence of imperfections. A model based on all potential techniques which allows a solution for prices which are in equilibrium with the optimal situation is not easy to construct. The use of the Cobb-Douglas production function or some other function as a catch-all for all techniques can be used to a limited extent but not to a degree that might substantially prevent the influences of imperfections.[2]

It seems that a set of competitive market prices which are free from the influences of imperfections has to be derived in most cases from adjustments and modifications of existing market prices. The imperfections whose influences have to be eliminated may have originated in several ways: (1) lack of adequate means of communication and information, (2) too few suppliers and (3) state regulations, control, and rationing.

Full information is one of the pre-requisites of perfect competition. Information about the supply and demand conditions and about the quantity and quality of outputs may be inadequate. This may occur because there are no adequate means of communications or there are sellers and/or buyers who restrict the flow of information. Inadequacy of information causes a considerable discrepancy between the existing price of an output and what it would be if there were adequate information. Individuals' demand might change for a good if they had adequate information about it. If during the life-time of a project no other project directly or indirectly provides better and greater information about the output, then the existing price and the existing trend will have to be treated as its market price. Inadequacy of information is due to the state of social and technical conditions. If there is not going to be any change in this condition over the life-time of the project, the demand conditions for the output may not change. However, if there are possibilities of greater information about the output, this will have to be taken into account in estimating the price of the output over the years.

When there are too few sellers of an output, it is typically the case of monopolies or oligopolies which represent serious market imperfections. The supply of an output produced by a monopolist is determined by the point at which the marginal cost equals the marginal revenue, which gives the monopolist maximum profit. If the production of the output is subject to diminishing returns, then the monopoly price would be higher than the price that would be obtained under the condition of free entry, that is, when there would be many sellers. When the output is subject to increasing returns to scale the monopoly price may be lower than what it would be otherwise.[3] The projects producing such an output are generally in the hands of state agencies. (The valuation of the outputs of state projects are considered in the next chapter). But if the production of such outputs is in the hands of private monopolists, the prices charged by monopolists may be the ones to be used in project evaluation. However, it should be pointed out that monopolists sometimes promote their sales by false advertisements and deceptive sales practices. If they do, then the unit values of these outputs will have to be adjusted upward or downward according to what would normally be the demand function and monopoly price in the absence of these unfair practices.

It is in the case of diminishing and constant returns, that the monopoly price of an output needs substantial downward adjustment. If the market for such an output is controlled by one producer, he may restrict the supply in order to raise the price and to reap monopoly profits. The same may be true of a duopoly or an oligopoly, when there is no free entry of firms. The duopolists or oligopolists may have various forms of collusion and arrangements among them, or they may react to each other in such a way that results in the reduction of supply and the raising of price. The size of the downward price adjustment can probably be determined by simulating a situation in which there is free entry and the market is shared by an appropriate number of producers. This raises questions concerning the size (possibly optimal) of the producing units and the feasibility of entry of new firms. The appropriate or optimal size of the firms is largely a technical question. Given the prices of the inputs, it is possible to find the size which minimizes the cost per unit of output. If the prices of inputs appear to have been formed in competitive markets, then the value of the output can be set at the unit cost corresponding to the optimal plant size.

In some cases, the optimal plant size may not be easy to determine. This is particularly so when the production of the output is subject to constant or increasing returns to scale. When the plant produces several outputs, its optimal plant size may not be possible to determine before the relative values of the several outputs have been established. Under this circumstance, the plant sizes of comparable industries which have not been operating under monopoly or oligopoly conditions will have to be considered. The optimal or modal size of a plant or project can also be indicated by the modal sizes in other equally advanced countries where there may be no monopolistic interference in the production of the output. Finally some efforts may also be made to predict how many firms would enter the market for an output if effective anti-cartel or anti-trust laws were enforced and other technical and financial facilities were made available. These efforts might indicate the size and the number of firms that would operate under competitive conditions. The total supply of the output may be derived from the estimates of the size and number of firms. Given the aggregate demand function for the output, the equilibrium price will be that at which the estimated quantity demanded equals the estimated supply.

In underdeveloped countries and at times in other countries, some goods become scarce and the governments resort to price control and rationing. In project evaluation the controlled prices will not be relevant values of the output. However, in this case, it is not difficult to determine what the price would be in the absence of controls and rationing, given the demand function for the output. If the total supply of the output for a certain year can be estimated by adding the amount produced by the existing plants and that produced by new projects, then the market price of the output in that year can be estimated.

Though market prices are not always appropriate for valuing outputs in social cost-benefit analysis, it is seen in addition that their use is not without problems. If it is decided to use market prices, they must be adjusted for imperfections and special circumstances, and conditions characterizing the demand and supply of the output.

V. BORDER PRICES

V-1 Introduction

Recently Little and Mirrlees have advocated the use of border prices in valuing the outputs and inputs in project evaluation. Border prices are the f.o.b. prices when they are exported and c.i.f. price of goods when they are imported. Thus, border prices are roughly the foreign trade prices. The principle of applying foreign trade prices was suggested more than two decades back by Professors Tinbergen and Hansen.[7] This section shall first discuss the Tinbergen-Hansen ideas regarding use of foreign trade prices, then the Little-Mirrlees approach and finally a critical review of this approach.

V-2 Tinbergen-Hansen Approach

Professor Tinbergen has suggested the use of foreign trade prices at several places and particularly in the context of his semi-input output method discussed in his Development Planning. Professor Bent Hansen has extended and built upon Tinbergen's approach. It is, therefore, appropriate to briefly summarize Hansen's discussion.[9]

Concerned with short-term and long-term planning in underdeveloped countries, Professor Hansen points to the insurmountable problem associated with the determination of a terminal capital stock in intertemporal planning. According to him, foreign trade neatly solves some of these problems. "With given foreign trade prices and the possibility of exchanging goods at these prices the only thing we need to know (in addition to technology and domestic resoures) in order to determine the efficient production path is the total value of consumption, or, alternatively, investments, but not their compositions, period by period, evaluated at the given foreign trade prices." Hansen suggests this "for efficient dynamic production planning in a completely open society under conditions of perfect trade." Under these assumptions any configuration of consumption and investment goods can be procured through international trade, whatever the composition of these goods produced domestically. In a perfectly free and competitive economy with no or negligible transportation costs the problem of fixing terminal capital stocks is avoided. Given the foreign trade prices, the problem of long-term planning is reduced to short-term efficiency.

In reality, no country is completely open and foreign trade is never perfect, nor are the transportation costs for the majority of goods negligible. There are always domestic sectors whose products cannot enter foreign trade. The demands for the outputs of these goods have to be met from deomestic production requiring investment allocations which cannot be determined by efficiency considerations according to foreign trade prices.

It was to sidestep the problem of domestic or national sectors that Tinbergen suggested the so-called semi-input-output method. The method rests on the division of the economy in two parts, one consisting of a number of "international" production sectors with prices given from abroad and characterized by perfect trade, and a number of "national" production sectors where trade is completely excluded. Tinbergen considers a "bunch" of projects consisting of one project in an international sector together with the corresponding investments in the national sectors.

The demand for outputs from national sectors which arise in connection with the production of a given project in an international sector consists of the input requirements of the bunch of projects and consumption requirements of those who earn income from the bunch of projects. The input requirements can be estimated from the coefficients of the projects themselves.

Consumption requirements for products from domestic sectors are a function of the income created by the investment project as well as its complementary investment. The value added depends on the prices fixed for domestic sector goods, given the foreign trade prices of international goods. These prices are not given in advance. If efficiency in production is to be achieved, some method of fixing them has to be introduced. It may be suggested that the price of the national sector output ought to equal the costs of all inputs. But this would involve prior knowledge of the prices of domestically produced inputs which are precisely what are to be fixed. Moreover the costs of labor and capital have to be calculated at their shadow prices, which are not known until the projects have been selected, since only then is the relative scarcity of factors determined. Hence the efficient prices of domestic outputs is indeterminate. Hansen concludes, "The niceness of planning - in particular the recursiveness - for efficiency in the completely open society is difficult to preserve without assumptions which are open to some doubt."[10]

When imperfections of trade such as quotas, bilaterial trades, tariffs and transportation costs, are introduced, the problem of achieving efficiency in the domestic sector becomes still more difficult. "Unfortunately, from the planner's point of view, there are good reasons for underdeveloped countries to embark upon exactly those bulky, crude commodities for which transport costs are high and where the chance for the commodity to become a national commodity, neither exported nor imported, is particularly big: if transport costs are high it is easier to become competitive. From our point of view this does not give rise to new problems, but it may imply that many seemingly international goods have to be treated like national sector products, and it may in all these ways happen that the truly international sectors become a minor part of the economy. In that case, little may be left of the recursiveness of the completely open society."[11]

Summing up, Professor Hansen states that "it would seem our arguments are mainly applicable to countries where the economy, in particular the new part of the economy, is dominated by international sectors, and where the government carries out a substantial part of the investments."[12]

V-3 Little-Mirrlees Extension[13]

In their recent book,[14] Little and Mirrlees have extended the procedure outlined by Tinbergen and Hansen. In particular, they have tried to solve the problem posed by Hansen in regard to the indeterminancy of output prices of national sectors.

Observing that domestic prices are very distorted in many underdeveloped countries, Little and Mirrlees seek price relatives "which reflect real opportunities open to the economy, then these can be used as sheet anchors" (p. 68). They propose "to measure all commodities in terms of <u>uncommitted</u> social income in terms of <u>convertible foreign exchange</u>" (p. 145). The choice of foreign currency seemed a better alternative to Little and Mirrlees for two reasons. (1) Foreign aid and loans account for a large part of new fixed public investment in many less developed countries, and the use of their numeraire makes the accounting rate of interest directly comparable with interest on loans payable in foreign currency, or with lending abroad. (2) They question the common practice of separating direct foreign exchange costs and receipts of a project from the rest to estimate the balance of payments effect. On the contrary, they find it nearer the truth to say that every output of the project is a gain of foreign exchange, and that _every_ input implies a rise of foreign exchange requirements. "Following the chain of production around, one must eventually end at commodities that are exported or are substituted for imports" (p. 142 Uncommitted social income is the income accruing to the government measured in terms of covertible foreign exchange.

Uncommitted social income is the numeraire in terms of which all commodities are to be valued. They call these values accounting prices or border prices. In the following discussion the latter term will be used except in quotations. In order to estimate the border prices, commodities are classified into traded and non-traded goods, more or less corresponding to international and national sector outputs of Tinbergen and Hansen.

According to Little and Mirrlees one can strictly say that a commodity is _wholly traded_ if its domestic production (if any) and consumption is unaffected by its increased demand and supply, ar that it is wholly non-traded if its imports and exports (if any) are unaffected. Otherwise it is partially traded. However, they advocate a loose definition and say "that if some of the demand for a commodity will be satisfied from imports, or some of the supply exported, it is a traded good. Other goods and services are referred to as non-traded" (p. 154-5). With some negligible exceptions,[15] all goods can thus be divided between traded and non-traded types.

The border price of an imported traded good is the amount of foreign exchange that has to be spent to buy it from the world market at a definite price which is virtually independent of the amount bought. It is suggested that purchase taxes and import duties are excluded from border prices in order to prevent the country from spending more foreign exchange on low tariff commodities to no advantage.

If the price the country pays for the commodity is not independent of the amount it wants to buy, then as a general rule the border price for an imported commodity will be the total foreign exchange cost including any increase in the cost of existing purchases, of increasing imports by one unit.

The border price of an exported traded good is the amount of foreign exchange earned per unit.

In the case of export or import quotas, the commodity, in general, may be treated as non-traded.

To find the border price of a non-traded good, say, an input, Little and Mirrlees suggest that "one should estimate the proportions in which extra demand for a unit of the commodity will increase production and reduce consumption elsewhere" (p. 164). The border price of the input is the weighted average of the marginal social cost and marginal social benefit, the weights being the proportion in which the production and consumption are reduced. The marginal social cost and benefit are to be estimated in terms of border prices. There is no circularity involved, however. Since all the commodities are to be expressed in terms of border prices, the number of prices are expressed by the same number of equations. They can be solved for the relative border prices, and given one numeraire, their actual levels can be determined. Little and Mirrlees claim to have succeeded in removing the indeterminancy pointed out by Hansen by decomposing through successive reiteration the non-traded goods of national sectors into traded goods of international sectors, for which foreign trade prices exist, and domestic factors for which they suggest the use of shadow prices.*

V-4 Critical Evaluation of Little and Mirrlees Suggestion

Little and Mirrlees suggestion that border prices as defined and described by them ought to be used for project evaluation is open to a number of objections. Border prices have been examined and discussed by various writers and in particular by the participants of the symposium published in the Oxford University Bulletin.[16] The following observation centers on one essential aspect, i.e., the claim by Little and Mirrlees that the border prices represent a set of opportunities open to an economy.

To start with, the two reasons given by Little and Mirrlees do not provide adequate justification for the use of boarder prices. Foreign loans and assistance are crucial to less developed countries but these may not be the only crucial factors. In fact the proportion of foreign loan and assistance to the total investment in underdeveloped countries in any year may not exceed ten per cent. Moreover the interest rates charged on foreign loans and assistance vary from almost zero to about 8 or 9 per cent. These interest rates are more the outcome of political situations and foreign relations than a representation of marginal efficiency of investment. The foreign loan market

* But the shadow prices of factors are not known until the projects have been selected as stated by Hansen. Hence L-M have really not succeeded in removing the indeterminancy.

is more imperfect and doctored than the domestic investment market would possibly be. Hence the need for foreign loans and assistance cannot be a good reason for valuing outputs and inputs in foreign currency.

The essential point of their argument for border prices is that "Border prices are used, not because it is thought that they are, in any sense, necessarily more 'rational' than domestic prices, but simply because they represent a set of opportunities open to a country, and the actual terms at which it can trade" (p. 161).

If the opening of this set of opportunities does not involve the closing of some other opportunities, the 'whole opportunity set' of the country will be enlarged and then the use of border prices will certainly be more rational. But if the resort to border prices closes up some other opportunities, then the 'opporuntiy set' of the country may be altered and it would not be possible to judge offhand whether the country can reach a higher level of welfare by operating through this altered opportunity (feasibility) set.

Since border prices replace the domestic prices, the opportunity set is not just enlarged but altered. The point at issue then is to see which opportunity set will lead to higher welfare, given the country's preferences in juxtaposition to its resources and technological possibilities. If the country has trading relations with other countries, then foreign trade represents one vector in the technological matrix of the country. The country tries to optimize its preference function under the constraint of its technological and resource constraints. Domestic prices formed in this process are duly affected by the vector (or vectors) corresponding to the foreign trade sector. Domestic prices are therefore not immune to the influences of opportunities opened by exports and imports.

Border prices, on the other hand, represent the interaction between the supplies and demands of all the trading countries and have less to do with the domestic circumstances of individual countries. Therefore, if the preponderant consideration is the domestic wellbeing of the individual country, it is the set of domestic prices which ought to be the guiding set rather than the set of border prices. The latter will serve as a sheet anchor when a world order is desired to be recreated. However, to an extent, they may be relevant to the countries belonging to a community such as E. E. C. whose goal is to create an economic union. Barring such special circumstances, for all other countries, the set of domestic prices are more appropriate than the border prices for economic evaluation.

The domestic prices of internationally traded goods will not be very different from the border prices, and it is immaterial whether one values them at border prices or domestic prices. As regards the non-traded goods, the domestic prices would reflect the preferences and welfare of the nations more than their estimated border prices.

The use of border prices in valuing outputs and inputs is unlikely to improve the analysis. If such criteria as 'the willingness to pay' are difficult to apply in valuing commodities and services, then the set of domestic prices will be more appropriate and rational than that of border prices.

Summary

Ideally the values of the outputs of projects should be determined according to the utilities individuals derive from consuming them. Utilities would differ from individual to individual and they cannot be measured cardinally.

Nor can the individual utilities be compared from one person to another. Hence it is not possible to value an output based directly on the utilities derived by it's consumers. Even if it were possible to measure individual utilities cardinally and strike interpersonal comparisons, it would be an almost impossible task to assess the aggregate utility of each output economy-wide and then to derive their relative prices.

An alternative would be to estimate the individual demand functions and given the supply of an output, to find the willingness to pay of each individual such that the given supply is cleared. To find the willingness to pay of the individuals will again be very unwieldy. In practice, it would be advisable to estimate the demand function of groups of individuals or the total demand function for the commodity and to estimate the total willingness to pay of all the individuals such that the given supply of the output is exhausted. The aggregate demand function will not reflect the individual utilities as much or as clearly as the individual demand functions, but it may be an acceptable or tolerable approximation.

Even the estimation of the aggregate willingness to pay for each output may be difficult to achieve. In that case, the outputs may be valued at market prices. It is generally accepted that competitive market prices are compatible with Pareto optimality. However, there are infinite Pareto optimality situations and only one or at most a few may correspond to the maximization of social welfare. The valuation of outputs at market prices, therefore, may not achieve the objective of welfare maximization.

The valuation of outputs at foreign trade prices appears attractive due to the fact that these prices are mostly independent of the volumes of outputs domestically produced. However, foreign trade prices would be advantageous only when most of the outputs produced are internationally traded. But border prices or foreign trade prices, cannot function as indicators of domestic social welfare as well as domestic prices can. Moreover in a country where international sectors are few and small, foreign trade prices may not be appropriate and the valuation of outputs at these prices may create more problems than it would solve.

Footnotes

1 Arrow, K. J., _Social Choice and Individual Values_, Cowles Foundation for Research in Economics at Yale University, Monograph 12, 2nd edition. New York: Wiley, 1963.

2 The "willingness to pay" or "consumers' surplus" criterion has been advocated by many of the recent writers on cost-benefit analysis. Cf. E. J. Mishan, _Cost-Benefit Analysis_ (New York: Praeger), 1976; and Partha Dasgupta, Amartya Sen, and Stephen Marglin, _Guidelines for Project Evaluation_ (New York: United Nation), 1972.

3 The conditions were shown decades back in more elegant and general form by A. Bergson, "A Reformulation of Certain Aspects of Welfare Economics," _Quarterly Journal of Economics_ (1938); O. Lange, "The Foundations of Welfare Economics," _Econometrica_ (1942); and Paul A. Samuelson, _Foundations of Economic Analysis_, Harvard (1947).

4 This statement is made here without any actual research or experimentation. If a Cobb-Douglas or a CES (Constant Elasticity of Substitution) production function is fitted for a country, the influences of imperfections may not be eliminated.

[5] Monopolies which arise due to increasing returns to scale are sometimes called natural monopolies.

[6] I.M.D. Little and J. A. Mirrlees: Project Appraisal and Planning for Developing Countries (Basic Books, Inc. 1974).

[7] J. Tingergen, Economic Policy: Principles and Design (Amsterdam, 1956); and B. Hansen, The Economic Theory of Fiscal Policy (London, 1958).

[8] Jan Tinbergen, Development Planning, World University Library (McGraw-Hill Book Co., 1967).

[9] Bent Hansen, Long-and Short-Term Planning in Underdeveloped Countries. Professor Dr. F. De Vries Lectures (North-Holland Pub. Co. 1967).

[10] Hansen, op. cit., p. 31.

[11] Hansen, op. cit., p. 34

[12] Hansen, ibid., p. 39.

[13] This section is heavily based on my article, "Evaluation of Public Sector Projects, Assessment Little-Mirrlees Manual," Economic and Political Weekly, vol. XI, no. 9, Feb 28 1976.

[14] I.M.D. Little and J.A. Mirrlees, Project Appraisal and Planning for Developing Countries (New York: Basic Books, Inc., 1975). All page numbers in parentheses refer to this book).

[15] This is in dire contrast to Hansen's view that 'many seemingly international goods have to be treated like national sector products.'

[16] Bulletin, Oxford University Institute of Economics and Statistics, Vol 34, Feb. 1972, no. 1.

Chapter Four

VALUATION OF SOCIAL GOODS

I. CLASSIFICATION OF GOODS

I-1 Principles of Exclusion and Rival Consumption

Goods can be classified in various ways. For the purpose of valuation, it is useful to introduce a classification related to the marketability of goods. A good is called 'excludible' when an individual's consumption is contingent upon his buying the good and paying its price and all individuals who do not pay are excluded. General items of food, clothing, and shelter are excludible goods.

Another distinction is based on the nature of consumption. The consumption of a good is 'rival' if, when it is consumed by one individual, it cannot be consumed by another. If the consumption of a good by one does not reduce its consumption by others, the consumption is nonrival. An example is a bridge or a park. If there is no overcrowding, their use by one individual does not reduce their use by others.

In most cases, the exclusion principle applies where the consumption of a good is rival. However, in some cases exclusion can be applied when the consumption is nonrival. The consumption of a broadcast is nonrival, since one individual's reception does not interfere with that of others. With the use of jamming devices, it can be made available only to those listeners who rent clearing devices.

I-2 External Effects

Another important distinction in valuation relates to the effect of goods. Some goods when consumed affect their consumer or consumers only. No non-consumers are affected. When consumption o goods affects individuals besides the consumer these goods are said to have external effects. Since external effects result in the consumption of some good or bad by others, we can call this external consumption. Thus while all goods are amenable to internal or direct consumption, some result in external consumption also. It is clear that the external consumption associated with a good is not identical with its direct or internal consumption. If it were so, it would be covered by the excludibility or nonexcludibility principle. Whether a good is excludible or not and whether its consumption is rival or not, external consumption may occur.

For illustration let us consider cigarette smoking. The consumption of cigarettes by an individual is direct and rival. However, smoking pollutes the air. If this air is enhaled by another individual, there is external consumption. The following table summarizes the distinctions mentioned here and shows the extent to which various categories of consumption are suited for market mechanism.

Table 4.1 - Classification of Goods

			EXCLUSION	
			Feasible	Nonfeasible
CONSUMPTION	Direct or Internal	Rival	Ideally suited for market mechanism.	Little scope for market mechanism.
		Non-Rival	Restricted scope for market mechanism	No scope for market mechanism.
	External		Nil	Nil

These goods whose consumption is rival and which are subject to the exlusion principle are the most suited for market mechanism. Some excludible goods whose consumption is nonrival can be valued through a market mechanism, as is the case with memberships in clubs, professional societies and other private instiutions. The goods whose prices are determined through the market mechanisms can be called private goods.

I-3 Public Goods

Public goods are those which are produced and/or supplied by state agencies, or those whose production and supply is controlled by state agencies. In Western economies a good which is excludible and whose consumption is rival rarely belongs to the category of public goods. The reasons for public agencies undertaking the production, control or regulation of a good are varied. The most important is a market failure in the case of nonexcludible goods whose consumption is nonrival. The most patent examples are national defense, public health, and law and order. However, it must be emphasized that there are many goods whose consumption is nonrival and yet they are supplied by private individuals or groups such as membership clubs, unions, and churches. In this case excludibility is applied through membership fees and annual charges. Barring some philanthropic activities, a private good is characterized by excludibility. Yet a public good is not necessarily one to which excludibility does not apply. Irrigation, utilities, housing and transportation, and many other publicly supplied or regulated goods are quite excludible. Moreover, in some instances, even a typical market good is supplied or regulated by state agencies.

Even when a good is excludible, its market may suffer from imperfections. The preconditions for an efficient market are viable competition, adequate information, and timely adjustments to supply and demand changes. In the absence of any of these the market may function so inefficiently that the state may step in to control the production and supply of the goods concerned.[1]

Even when the private exchange market for a good is feasible and can function effectively, states may prefer to regulate its production and/or supply. This may come from a desire to achieve some social objective, such as income redistribution, provision of equal opportunities, or just to secure revenues.

I-4 Social Goods

External goods are either unintended outputs or unaccounted inputs; their consumption is mostly nonrival and they are seldom excludible. These goods may be positive or negative. The negative goods can be called bads, as mentioned earlier. The external goods do not have a market. (If they did, they would not be external goods.) However, they do affect individuals. Some of these external goods can be evaluated indirectly by imputing values to their components or the changes they cause. Other external goods may defy all attempts at imputing objective values to their components or to the changes caused by them. Some public goods which do not have markets are such that no objective values can be imputed to their components or to the changes they bring about. These observations lead to the following classification

Table 4-2 Social Goods

As noted above, some public goods may be those which are also produced and supplied by private producers and sold in the market. These goods will have to be the values in the cost-benefit analysis at their market prices, if the principle of valuing goods at market prices is followed.

Social goods are defined to include all the remaining public goods and all external goods. Some of the public and external goods can be valued indirectly with reference to market prices but others will have to be valued through non-market procedures.

II. PRICING OF PUBLIC GOODS

II-1 The Valuation of Rival Public Goods

Before we discuss the valuation of social goods, it will be interesting to describe the valuation of a public good for which a market exists, but for which the market ceases to be competitive, because the good is subject to increasing returns or decreasing cost. In fact, a typical public good is of this type. For this reason the public authorities take over the production and supply of goods which they expect to be monopolized by large corporations. This prevents formation of monopolies and fixing of monopoly prices by such corporations.

If the good is one whose consumption is rival, there will exist a market demand for it. The public authority will have cost functions similar to those of a monopolist. The problem is what ought to be the price of the public good. The following figure describes the alternatives:

Fig. 4.1 Marginal Versus Full Cost Pricing

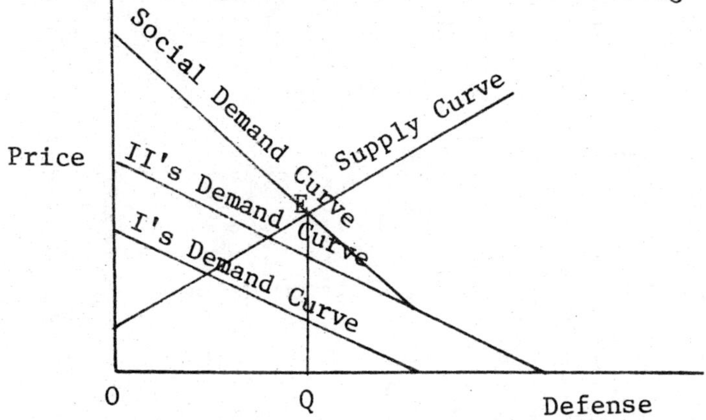

II-2 Marginal Cost Versus Full Cost Pricing

In Fig. 4.1, *MR* and *MC* represent marginal revenue and marginal cost curves and *AR* and *AC* represent average revenue and average cost curves. Monopoly output and price corresponds to the intersection of *MR* and *MC* curves.

If the public authority acts like a monopolist, as it might well do, the output-price combination will be given by (OE, OP_m). Since monopoly pricing is ruled out, OP_m is not the level at which the good should be valued. The other two alternatives are marginal cost pricing and full cost pricing. The first of these gives the output price combination (OA, OP_{mc}) and the second (OF, OP_{ac}). Obviously, the first of these yields a higher level of welfare than the second. But if the public authority supplies OA at price OP_{mc}, i.e., if it follows the policy of marginal cost pricing, it can do so only by sustaining a loss equal to $BCDP_{mc}$. On the other hand, if the authority follows full cost pricing, it will not incur any losses and will break even.

From the point of competive efficiency of resource allocation, marginal cost pricing is more appropriate than the full cost pricing.

However, the analogy of competitive efficiency is not quite relevant. While *AR* is unambiguously the demand curve, *MC* is defined to be the supply curve only after it intersects *AC*.

If the public goods are charged according to marginal cost pricing, it will result in greater social welfare than in the case of full cost pricing. But it will involve deficits which will have to be paid from general revenues. It seems appropriate that the payment of the cost of the public good be confined to the users. Various methods have been suggested to recover the full cost from the users besides fixing the price at average cost. One is a two tier fee or price: A flat charge for all users of the good, irrespective of the extent of the use and another charge to the extent of the use. An alternative method is differential pricing in which the user may be charged the marginal cost for the last unit, but higher rates for earlier units. The two methods can even be combined by charging a flat fee to all users and differential pricing for the rest of the cost. The costs of public goods are also covered through adjusting the rates for peak and off-peak buyers.

II-3 Some relevant considerations

The dilemma between marginal cost and full cost pricing of public goods is not easy to resolve. There are, however, other considerations which must be taken into account in valuing the goods supplied by public projects.

1. For the purposes of social cost-benefit analysis, the valuation of a public good with a view to covering its cost of production is not helpful. This is because if all the goods were valued according to this principle then all projects would be justified. For a meaningful cost-benefit analysis, therefore, the value of goods must be determined independently of their cost

of production.

2. In addition to supplying a good public authorities may want to achieve some additional social objectives which might require some price adjustments. The price of the public good should be expressed before these adjustments are introduced. The adjustments should be valued independently, and the price of the public good should be modified accordingly.

3. In valuing a public good, all the indirect benefits and disadvantages due to unintended outputs will have to be taken into account as far as possible.

4. In evaluating a public project, as in the case of any other project, not only the direct inputs but also the indirect and unaccounted inputs have to be taken into account. In costing the inputs, it is the accounting prices of factors that have to be used and not the market prices as discussed in Chapter Five.

III. VALUATION OF A SOCIAL GOOD OR BAD--INDIRECT MARKET INDICATORS

III-1 Introduction

A social good may be intended or unintended, but it is generally not characterized by rival consumption. In some cases, it may be characterized by rival consumption, but it may not be excludible. Since a market for social goods (or social bads) does not exist, the value of a social good cannot be determined directly. However, some indirect methods can be used. The procedure can be illustrated by considering noise pollution, a social bad.

III-2 Valuation of Noise Pollution

Suppose the construction of a new airport in a quiet area is proposed. Suppose further that the houses in the area are of uniform quality and are of the same value. The occupants of the houses in the area now want to move and begin to look for jobs elsewhere. Many of the houses are put on sale (or many of them become vacant if they were rented). The value of the houses falls, and it falls enough to attract new buyers who have either less income or else are not bothered by noise. The damage caused by the noise to be created by the construction and operation of the new airport is equal to the total numbers of houses in the area multiplied by the fall in their value.

This is a very simple example, yet it exposes some of the problems. One is that the damage value of the noise pollution will vary with the number of residential houses in the vicinity of the airport, for a given level of noise. Another is the fact that the damage value arrived at does not involve any subjective measurement of inconvenience to the residents of the area. The damage value is estimated indirectly from the fall in the value of the houses due to noise created by the airport. Thus even though a specific market for noise pollution or quiet does not exist, one for houses does exist, and the latter reflects most of the damage done by the noise pollution.

The fall in the market value of houses can be demonstrated by a simple diagram. Let OH represent the number of houses in the area. All the households may not be equally sensitive to noise; in fact, some of them may be quite insensitive. If all the households were insensitive, noise will cease to be a pollution or a social bad. But there are families which are sensitive to noise. Let these households be represented by *QH*.

Fig. 4.2. Equilibrium Cost of Damage

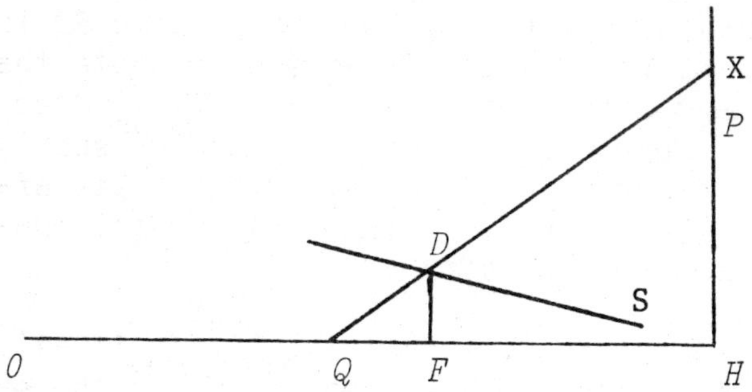

The families represented by points closer to *Q* are bothered less by noise than the families closer to *H*. For instance, the family represented by point *F* is bothered enough to pay *FD* amount to protect itself from noise pollution. *QP* which is a locus of points like *D* can be regarded as the demand curve for quiet after the construction of the airport. Let the supply curve for providing quiet either through moving or through sound-proofing be represented by *SD*. Then the equilibrium value of quiet in the vicinity of the airport is *FD* per unit of residence. Thus the fall in the market value of dwellings will be *DF* per unit.

Now the question is: what is the damage value of the noise created by the airport? Is it *FD* x *OH*, or *FD* x *QH*, or *FD* x *HF*? Of these the last will greatly underestimate the damage, hence it may be ignored.

As a first approach it would seem that *FD* x *QH* ought to be the damage value. This may exceed or fall short of the money value *QHP* the consumers would be willing to pay to prevent noise pollution. However, in practice, if all dwellings are located in the same area there is no way of knowing and thereby differentiating those dwellings whose residents are affected and those which are not. Moreover if all of the houses were affected by the noise, the fall in the value of the dwellings would be larger than shown above, so long as the supply curve *SD* is upward sloping. Hence it seems reasonable that the value of the damage ought to be estimated as $FD \times OH$. Depending on the slope of the supply and demand curves and the number of houses affected by noise, $FD \times OH$ is greater than, equal to or smaller than *QHP*.

The above describes a simplified situation. In reality the noise level would not be the same over all of the area affected by the airport. The occupants of the dwellings closer to the airport might feel the effect much more than those of the dwellings in the more distant areas. Beyond a certain distance the noise will be negligible. The decline in the market values of the dwellings in the more distant areas will be smaller than in the near-by areas. The total damage value will be the sum of damage values in different locations affected by the airport noise.

In reality it is not easy to estimate the damage value of noise pollution from changes in the market values of dwellings. Often the increase in noise level is accompanied by an increase in job opportunities, easier transportation services and availability and expansion of other facilities. Some of the studies on noise pollution, therefore, have failed to show a decline in dwelling values due to noise pollution. Others with more detailed specifications have succeeded in estimating damage costs.

Non-monetary and monetary damage functions have been derived for noise and other pollutions. For an example, according to the Roskill Commission Final Report,[2] the following demonstrates the effect on housing prices due to aircraft noise in Heathrow Airport areas.

Table 4.3

Average Percentage Depreciation of House Property Values in Heathrow Area [Houses Outside 35 NNI (Noise and Number Index)]

Price Range (£)	Noise Exposure		
	35-45 NNI	45-55 NNI	55-Up NNI
0-4,000	0	2.9	5.0
4,000-8,000	2.6	6.3	10.5
8,000-On Up	3.3	13.3	22.5

In the Metra Monograph,[3] one finds the following result of a regression analysis based on a survey of estate agents around London:

$$x_1 = 1.73 + .0017V$$

$$x_2 = 0.0295 + .00070V$$

where x_1 is the percentage depreciation of houses assumed to be in 45-55 NNI zone (compared to the <35 NNI zone), x_2 is the percentage depreciation of houses assumed to be in 35-45 NNI zone and V is the value of houses in the <35 NNI zone.

III-3 Valuation of Recreation Areas

Another example where indirect market indicators can be used for valuing a social good is provided by the case of recreation areas. Suppose a recreation area is proposed for a certain location, and that the supply costs for various sizes of the facility are known. These supply costs are assumed to be those that would be incurred in providing the various facilities for recreation and amusement, or these supply costs may be considered to be the opportunity costs estimated as the loss of value due to reserving the area for recreation.

The demand for recreational area can be estimated by studying the behavior of individuals who visit parks and other recreational facilities. The price that individuals pay for availing themselves of these facilities includes the transportation costs and any entry fee. The cost of transportation will vary with the distance travelled. In a study by Clawson[4] an estimate has been made of the cost of transportation to a recreation area from various distances.

Under certain simplifying assumptions, the demand curve for the recreational area can be derived from such studies, taking the transport cost and any other costs such as entry fee as the price which the visitors are willing and able to pay. Given the supply curve for the recreational area, the equilibrium price for recreational area can be arrived at. The value of a recreational area can be estimated by multiplying the equilibrium price by the number of visitors per year.

Fig. 4.3. Value of Recreational Areas

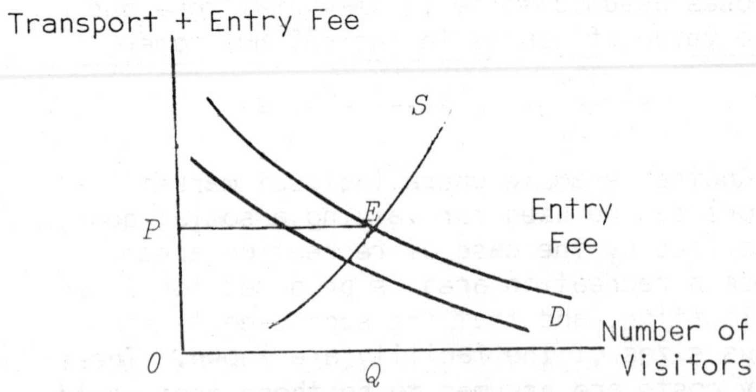

The above diagram shows that the equilibrium price of recreation per person is EQ. The social value of the recreational area would be the total number of visitors multipled by EQ, if the principle of market prices is adopted for valuation.

In this case, the value of the recreation has not been derived from the market of some other good. The demand curve for the recreation area which is not observable has been indirectly constructed from the transportation costs and entry fee which the visitors are willing and able to pay.

What about the individuals who do not intend to visit any parks and recreational facilities, yet want the provision of recreational area? It is assumed that they would like to live in a state which has recreational areas and amusement parks, and that they are willing to forego some income for this purpose. However, the amount of money they would be willing to pay is not observable, and there may not be any indirect means to translate their desire and readiness to pay in demand functions. The value to be imputed to the desires of these individuals has to be determined by political processes and by some form of collective decision making.

IV. PRESENT VALUE OF INDIRECTLY ESTIMATED MARKET VALUES

IV-1 Introduction

Many of the social goods (and bads) have several effects which last, in some cases, over several years. There is no market for social goods by definition, but there may be markets for goods which they affect in the present and in the future. If most of the goods affected by a given social good have (adequate) markets, then the values of these goods can be determined. From the values of these marketable goods, the value of the social good can be indirectly estimated. If the social good has effects on goods in the future, the present value of social good can be derived by aggregating the present values of the affected marketable goods.

The procedure may be illustrated by considering the valuation of air or water pollution. A number of studies have been conducted to estimate the various damage costs of air and water pollution.

IV-2 Air Pollution

The following are six categories of air pollution effects.

I. Health Effects
 --Productivity losses from accelerated mortality.
 --Incremental health care costs, including social overhead capital costs.
 --Productivity losses from morbidity, lethargy, and illness.

II. Soiling Effects
 --Incremental cleaning costs for clothing, person, building, autos, etc.
 --Costs imputed to soiling beyond that indicated by incremental cleaning costs.

III. Material Damage Effects
 --Incremental costs from accelerated replacement of metals, rubber, etc.
 --Incremental costs from damages to historical monuments and other irreplaceable objects.

IV. Damage to Animals and Wildlife

V. Damage to Vegetation
  --Incremental costs of additional plantings required to compensate for growth retardation induced by air pollution.
  --Incremental costs from damages to forests and landscapes.

VI. Damage to Cultural Assets
  --Incremental costs of preserving archaelogical assets, medieval and modern works of art, monuments, books and records.

This is by no means an exhaustive list of the effects of air pollution. This list has been selected from a larger list given by Haveman.[5]

The total cost of air pollution can be arrived at by estimating and adding the costs of the various damages caused by it. These costs may be determined by calculating the loss of specific values resulting from the disappearance or deterioration of human and material resources, or the expenditures incurred for their prevention. In many cases, the damages cannot be wholly prevented; hence the loss of values caused by air pollution will be the sum of expenditures necessary to prevent parts of the damages plus the loss of values associated with the rest of the damages which cannot be prevented or which have not been prevented. The money value of some of the damages which cannot be prevented can, in turn, be estimated by direct and indirect market indicators. This will be particularly true of damages due to cultural assets. Valuation of these damages may be based on some optional criteria.

The estimation of the monetary damage value of air pollution may not be easy or precise. In valuing the health effects of air pollution, the accelerated mortality rate and the incidence of infirmity and diseases related to air pollution will have to be considered. This is by no means an easy task. Some of the diseases associable with air pollution are: (1) cancer of the larynx; (2) cancer of the trachea, bronchi, and lungs, not specified as secondary; (3) other malignant tumors of the respiratory passages (except acute tonsillitis); (4) asthma (non-allergic); (5) congestive cardiac insufficiency; (8) lobar pneumonia; (9) bronco-pneumonia; (10) atypical primary pneumonia or non-specified types of pneumonia; (11) acute or sub-acute bronchitis and non-classified bronchitis; (12) chronic bronchitis; (13) abscess of the lung; (14) congestion and hypostasis of the lung; and (15) other diseases of the respiratory system.

Further, it is strongly suspected, though there is not yet enough scientific and epidemiological evidence, that other diseases can be associated with air pollution. These diseases include cancer of the stomach, some forms of anemia, some modifications of bodily growth, etc.[6]

After the extent of deaths, diseases and disabilities have been estimated, the monetary damage cost can be calculated. The loss of value due to premature death caused by air pollution can be calculated by capitalizing the present value of the expected future incomes of workers less the cost of subsistence. A similar procedure can be applied to housewives by substituting an imputed value of their services at the wage employed workers. As for diseases and disabilities related to air pollution, the damage cost can be considered to equal the sum of (actual or imputed) wages lost plus the cost of medication and treatment.

Damage due to soiling and damage to animal life and vegetation have to be estimated according to plausible assumptions based on whatever relevant information and research results are available.

Perhaps the toughest problems arise in the estimation of the monetary value of the damage done to cultural assets, in view of the lack of any previous study on the subject and the difficulty encountered in treating cultural assets in economic terms. The damage to cultural assets ought to be estimated by the difference between the expenditure necessary for restoration and prevention of damage and the expenditures required in the hypothetical absence of air pollution.

The cost of air pollution damage to cultural assets can also be roughly estimated by imputing the percentage of the total damage to cultural assets according to the damages to the component materials, such as stone, wall painting, canvas painting, wood painting, metals, leather, parchment, paper, fabrics, stuccoes, plasters, building materials and mosaics. Such percentages have been worked out in Italy, where pollution damages are substantial.

IV-3 Water Pollution

The economic damage caused by water pollution can be estimated in an analogous manner by analyzing its effects in various areas. The effects of water pollution can be broadly classified into the following categories: (1) agriculture and vegetation; (2) tourism and vacationing; (3) drinking and industrial use; and (4) fish population.

The damage to agriculture and vegetation can be estimated by the reduction in the quantity or in the deterioration of the quality of the products. The damage can also be estimated by the cost of preventing these harmful effects. The effect of water pollution on tourism, vacationing and recreation can be estimated by the reduction in the number of visitors to the polluted beaches and lakes or the reduction in the money they would have otherwise spent for their vacationing at these locations. On the other hand, the damage can also be estimated by the cost of pollution prevention.

The damage caused by drinking water may best be estimated by the additional cost of treating the polluted water to bring it up to standard. Similarly the damage caused by water pollution to industry can be estimated by the treatment cost, or the reduction in quantity and deterioration of quality of outputs.[8]

The effect of water pollution on the supply of fish in seas and rivers may be estimated by the loss of value due to a smaller catch and the lower quality of fish. Moreover, often the fish is contaminated which may cause serious diseases to consumers. In estimating the damage cost of water pollution connected with the fish population, the damage to human health has to be included.

IV-4 Higher Education

An illustration of a social good which has a long lasting effect on the welfare of individuals is provided by the case of higher education. In the United States there exists a sort of pseudo-market for higher education. One might roughly construct a supply schedule for college education, including the tuition, living, and other expenses in the supply price. The demand for college education can be estimated from the numbers of applicants which may differ from the number of persons actually registered and enrolled.

In the U.S., higher education is substantially subsidized but in most other countries it is almost wholly financed and supported by the states. Hence in these countries, not even a pseudo market for higher education exists.

Therefore, higher education cannot be valued by simulating a market for it directly. The value of various types of higher education can be arrived at by estimating the present value of expected annual earnings over the working life span of graduates over what they would have earned without that college education. Many estimates of earnings due to college education have been made and functional relations between years and intensity of schooling investment and returns have been established.[9]

The values of many other social goods can be estimated by various indirect methods, requiring a good deal of ingenuity and approximations.

V. VALUATION OF SOCIAL GOODS NOT TRACEABLE TO MARKETS

V-1 Introduction

In the preceding sections we have considered social goods whose values could be estimated by studying market prices for their direct and indirect effects. There are certain social goods for which a market approach fails. These goods include national defense, public education, museums of art and culture, national health service, and many others. With ingenuity and search, it may be possible to find markets and market prices for some of the effects of even these goods. The unmeasured effects would be so dominant that the values of these social goods cannot be estimated by invoking or simulating market mechanisms.

V-2 National Defense

A typical social good is a non-rival good which is jointly consumed. A good example is national defense. The size of national defense is remotely related to the size of a country's population. The defense of individual members cannot be separated. It has to be used collectively. Even though the consumption of national defense is non-rival, each individual may be willing to pay a certain amount for each size of defense, according to his ability to pay and concern. If this behavior were observable, a demand function for defense could be constructed for each individual. For simplicity, suppose there are two individuals whose demand functions for defense are given as below:

Fig. 4.4 Individual's Payment for Defense

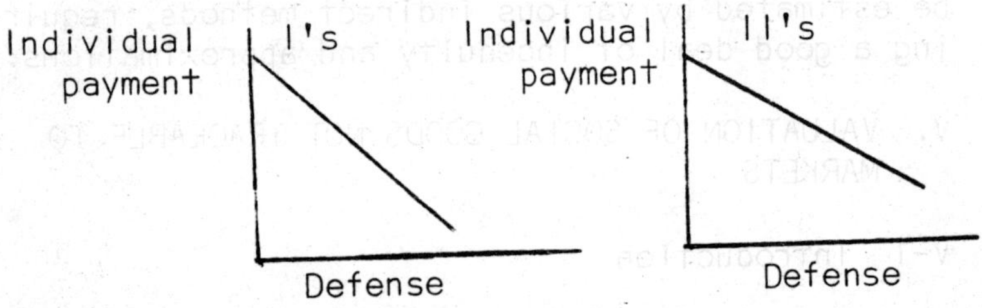

In political debate, it is generally the total expenditure which is under discussion, as if defense were a homogeneous good. This is a quite unrealistic assumption. However, if for simplicity, defense were treated as a homogeneous good, the supply curve could be constructed. The following diagram shows the sums of individual payments for each level of defense. The curve representing these aggregate payments may be called a social demand curve. The following diagram shows the individual and social demand curves along with the supply curve.

If individual demand functions were observable and a supply curve could be constructed, then the (imaginary) price of defense could be estimated as the amount *QE*. At this price, the size of defense *OQ* would be feasible, and it would appear that individuals are willing and capable of paying price *QE*.

The following problems, however, arise which prevent the pricing of social goods like defense from materializing. (1) As mentioned above, the individual demand curves for the social good are not observable and hence cannot be derived from statistical studies. (2) Even if the individual demand curves were known, there is no guarantee that each individual would actually pay the part of price he is willing and capable of paying. Since the consumption of the social good is non-rival and joint, each individual might be inclined to evade payment. (3) The intersection of the supply curve and the aggregate demand curves may not give the correct size of defense needed by the country. Individual preference for the non-rival social good may not indicate the right size. (4) For the market analogy to be true, each user of the social good must pay the same price. In the above diagram, the price that the different users would like to pay differs. This may be partly related to their relative income levels and partly to their taste. Since one of the aims of social goods provided by the state is the maximization of social welfare, the distribution of income may not be taken as given. This is because part of the purpose of supplying social goods by the state is to correct the distribution of real income. Moreover, when the state provides a social good like defense, the concern is not with what an individual is willing and able to pay, but with what he ought to pay. (5) If the price of a social good is determined <u>directly</u> by a cost-covering procedure as in the above diagram, then the provision of all social goods will be justified and there would be no need of any social cost benefit analysis.

It can, therefore, be concluded that the intersection of the supply and added-on demand curves does not provide an adequate guideline for the valuation of a social good.

The size of the social good such as defense has to be decided under considerations above and beyond those related to covering costs. For any size of the social good, however, it is theoretically possible to distribute the cost among the users of the good in such a way that conditions of Pareto optimality are satisfied. This was shown first by Erik Lindhal[10] as early as 1919 and has been recently demonstrated very lucidly by Leif Johansen.[11]

V-3 Some General Approaches

Many social goods cannot be adequately resolved into effects which can be priced through market mechanisms. The valuation of such goods will have to be accomplished through: (1) majority voting via referendum or legislative bills, (2) decisions of political leaders and (3) consensus or convergence of opinions of knowledgeable experts.

In practice referenda and legislative debates are not concerned with deciding the values of individual social goods, but rather with choosing among alternatives. Often the choice takes into account both the values of the alternatives as well as the costs. If a given alternative costs more (or the individuals and legislative members believe or are made to believe that it costs more) than other alternatives and still they choose it, it is certain that they value this alternative more than the other alternatives. The social value of the chosen alternative must be at least as much as the social value of any other alternative. If the values of other alternatives can be estimated by evaluating their effects which have market prices, then there will be some basis for the social value of the chosen item.

Unfortunately the above procedure provides a very weak guidance. First, the other alternatives may themselves be such that they cannot be valued through pricing their effects. Second, and more crucially, majority voting does not result into consistent and unambiguous choices. This fact was first pointed out by Condorcet and has become well-known due to contributions of Professor Arrow and his associates.

Despite the analogy between a market choice and a political choice, there are important weaknesses in the voting process with respect to social welfare effects. Often a voter does not extend the consequences of his votes to himself. He may vote for increased defense expenditure or U.S. participation in war, without being willing to pay higher taxes or to enlist in the army. An individual votes for a candidate only some of whose positions he accepts; in this situation a voter cannot vote for his own preferences in an exclusive manner. In the political process minority votes are largely wasted, but minority preferences exert an influence in the market. In voting, therefore, an individual who favors minority views, may avoid wasting his votes and vote for candidates who do not adequately represent his views. A _free_ political choice, however, provides equality of individual influence instead of reflecting an individual's command over economic resources as is the case in market choice. However, elections are infrequent and they seldom allow the expression of individual preferences for single items. Finally, political choices are generally related to the acceptance or non-acceptance of certain objectives often without very firm price tags attached. For social cost benefit analysis, explicit values of output are required; these values are seldom provided by normal political voting processes.

Some direct questioning of responsible leaders may be attempted to elicit information about the range of values they associate with certain specific outcomes under consideration. This range may be reduced by further questioning. Once it is realized that the range cannot be further decreased, a mean point can be taken as the value.[14] In some cases, social cost benefit analysis can be carried out in terms of the end-values of the range which can be used to estimate the lowest and highest values of the social goods.

Determination of the values of outcomes or outputs can also be carried out with a group of knowledgeable persons using the Delphi method.[15] This method has a number of desirable characteristics such as anonymity, controlled feedback and statistical averaging of opinions of the group members. It also avoids the influence of dominant personalities, semantic noise and pressure to conformity.

Both of these approaches are imperfect and inadequate in many respects. Some of the political leaders may be knowledgeable and may have a sincere interest in the welfare of people at large; however, every leader has a weakness for his own preservation which may only partly and only occasionally be coincidental with the general welfare. There is no wholly objective method of selecting the respondents in the Delphi method and they may have the same inadequacies as political leaders, although they may not have a stake in their self-preservation. The failure of the political process to take into account the minority interest may be partly corrected depending on the strength of the political leaders and the concern of the participants in the Delphi method. The fact remains that the valuation of social goods will have to be optional in nature. The magnitude of these values will be a function of the procedure adopted in arriving at them, the perception and motives of the persons involved in the decision making, and the finesse and strategy of the individual groups articulating and lobbying for their interests.

In this chapter, some rough procedures for the valuation of social goods have been indicated. This problem is so illusive and difficult that the above discussion hardly scratches the surface. However, this subject is so essential and basic to social cost-benefit analysis and to welfare studies that there is no alternative to continuing research. The literature in this and related fields is already enormous. The bibliography to this chapter is highly selective and may not be the most representative of the great many contributions in the various categories listed.

Summary

Goods can be classified in various ways. A good is called excludable when an individual's consumption is contingent upon his buying the good and all individuals who do not pay are excluded. The consumption of a good is "rival" if, when it is consumed by one individual, it cannot be consumed by another, otherwise it is non-rival. When consumption of a good affects individuals besides the consumer, it is said to have external effects.

Those goods whose consumption is rival and which are excludable are the most suited for market mechanism. The goods whose prices are determined through the market mechanism can be called market goods. Public goods are those which are produced and/or supplied by state agencies. Public goods which are also supplied by private producers and sold in the market can be valued at their market prices. Social goods are defined to include all the remaining public goods and all external goods representing the external effects. Some of the public and external goods can be valued indirectly with reference to market prices, but others will have to be valued through non-market procedures.

The valuation of a social good or bad can be attempted through the use of indirect market indicators. For example, noise pollution in the vicinity of an airport can be valued by estimating the fall in the values of residential buildings in the area. The value of a park can be determined by the cost of transportation and the entry fee that the people are willing to pay. However, these indirect market indicators are very often combined with other elements, which may neutralize the effects of market indicators. To illustrate, the market value of residential buildings near an airport may not fall, because of greater job opportunities.

The values of some social goods or bads can be derived by estimating the present values or their effects in the future. For example, for evaluation purposes, the effects of air pollution can be classified into six categories: Health effects, soiling effects, material damage effects, damage to animals and wildlife, damage to vegetation, damage to cultural effects. The effects of water pollution can be classified into: agricultural and vegetation, tourism and vacationing, drinking and industrial use, and fish population.

There will remain many social goods whose values cannot be determined through market indicators. The valuation of such goods will have to be accomplished through 1) majority voting via referendum or legislative bills, 2) decisions of political leaders, and 3) consensus or convergence of opinions of knowledgeable experts.

Footnotes

1. For a discussion and survey of literature on public goods, see Peter O. Steiner, "Public Expenditure Budgeting" in the Economics of Public Finance, The Brookings Institute, Washington, D.C., 1974, pp. 241-357.

2. Commission on the Third London Airport, Report H.M.S.O. 1971 (known also as the Roskill Report).

3. Plowden, S., "The Cost of Noise," Metra Monograph, 1970.

4. Clawson, M., "Method of Measuring the Demand for and value of Outdoor Recreation," Resources for the Future, Washington, D.C., 1959.

5. Haveman, "On Estimating Environmental Damage: A Survey of Recent Research in the United States," in OECD, Environmental Damage Costs, Paris.

6. Gilberto, Muraro, "Estimate of the Economic Damage Caused by Pollution: The Italian Experience Comments on the ENI-ISVET Research--1969-70," in OECD, Environmental Damage Costs.

7. Cf. Gilberta Muraro, "Estimate of the Economic Damage Caused by Pollution: The Italian Experience, Comments on the ENI, ISVET Research--1969-70," in OECD, Environmental Damage Costs, 1972.

8. For industrial uses the drawbacks caused by salinity, hardness, alkalinity and pH entail among other things, the replacement of equipment through which the water is

circulated. Soluble organic pollutants require continual chlorine or chlorine broxide dosing to eliminate them. When the dosing is insufficient or non-existant, various kinds of drawbacks may occur, such as the formulation of deposits, usually in connection with excessive biological growth, the clogging of equipment (filters, exchangers, etc.), the poisoning of active carbon, deposits in steam generators and so on.

9. A recent article by Arleen Leibowitz, "Years and Intensity of Schooling Investment," The American Economic Review, June 1976 gives some of the recent attempts in this field.

10. Lindhal, Erik: Die Gerechtigkeit der Besteuerung (Lund, 1919). The relevant section is printed in English in Classics in the Theory of Public Finance, eds. R.A. Musgrave and A.J. Peacock (New York--London, 1958).

11. Johansen, Leif, "Some Notes on the Lindhal Theory of Determination of Public Expenditures," The International Economic Review (1963), Johansen, Leif, Public Economics, Rand McNally & Company, Chicago.

14. Ragnar Frisch, "Numerical Determination of a Quadratic Preference Function for Use in Macro-Economic Programming," Memorandum, University of Oslo, Institute of Economics, February 14, 1957.

15. Norman C. Dalkey, The Delphi Method: An Experimental Study of Group Opinions, (Santa Monica, Calif.: RAND Corp., 1969).

Chapter Five

VALUATION OF FACTORS

I. INTRODUCTION

I-1 Preliminary Remarks

The markets for commodities in the developed as well as underdeveloped countries tend to adjust, and the excesses in their supplies and demands generally even out. However, the markets for factors have not adjusted over long periods, and excesses in their supplies and demands have persisted over decades. This is particularly true of underdeveloped countries where the maladjustment in factor utilization has resulted in an overabundance of labor and an acute shortage of capital. The market prices of factors which make the existing techniques of production profitable do not reflect the relative scarcities of factors. The valuation of factors, therefore, requires a separate treatment in underdeveloped economies.

I-2 Causes of Disequilibrium in the Factor Market

As stated above, most underdeveloped countries are characterized by a chronic structural disequilibrium which results in an over-abundance of labor and acute shortages of capital and foreign exchange. Over the long run, this disequilibrium has not diminished, but has increased. The main causes for this situation are: (1) The population rate of growth in most of the underdeveloped countries is very high. Every year more workers are added to the labor force than can be absorbed by expansion in job opportunities.

(2) Because personal incomes are extremely low, the rate of saving is very small, and the rate of growth of capital formation hardly remains above those for population and labor. (3) If wage and interest rates were flexible, all labor could be combined with the available amount of capital. But as things are, neither of them is flexible. This is because: (i) a number of wages are fixed by convention; (ii) there are minimum wage laws; (iii) wages cannot be allowed to fall below the subsistence level; (iv) labor mobility is very low due to widespread subsistence family farming; (v) the rate of interest is maintained below the equilibrium level by deliberate government policy, partly with a view to inducing investment through easy money policy; and (vi) at the same time, non-official rates in the rural areas is exorbitantly high allowing little private investment by farmers. (4) In the early stages of development, the need for foreign capital and highly specialized skills is very high and increases rapidly as the development proceeds; however, most of the underdeveloped countries do not allow the excess demand for foreign exchange to be reflected by alteration in the exchange rate. (5) In general, the economy of the underdeveloped countries is fettered with too many frictions, lack of mobility, restricted flow of information, and various cultural, social, and class rigidities.

I-3 Plan of the Chapter

This chapter is devoted to a study of the appropriate prices of factors in underdeveloped countries and the approaches that might be used to determine them. In section II, the accounting prices of factors are derived on the basis of full employment of factors as suggested by Tinbergen and Qayum [1960]. Section III outlines the approach presented by Agarwala [1966] which is based on agricultural food surplus. In section IV, the approach suggested by Marglin, Sen, and Dasgupta [1972] and Little and Mirrless [1968 and 1976] is discussed. Section V offers a derivation of accounting prices in the dynamic setting and includes a contribution by Johansen [1967], and another by Marglin [1976]. Section VI outlines a simple method of deriving accounting prices yielding a given marginal rate of savings.

In this book the terms of accounting prices and shadow prices are used interchangeably.

II. ACCOUNTING PRICES OF FACTORS

II-1 The Aim of Accounting Prices of Factors

It has been stated that the market prices of factors do not reflect their relative scarcities. The minimization of cost of production at these prices will not result in the minimum cost from the social viewpoint. In other words, if market prices of factors are used in selecting the most profitable techniques, they would not necessarily produce the maximum possible output. The purpose of accounting prices is the selection of techniques which will lead to the production of the maximum possible output.

The maximization of output from given resources is an aim to which no exception can be taken. However, there are two aspects to the maximization: the maximization of current output and the maximization of output over the long run. These two aspects often do not go together. The maximization of current output often involves a lower rate of increase of output in the future, unless some regulatory measures are taken.

Another problem to be faced in optimization is the fact that the availability of resources varies over time. The techniques which are most profitable according to the current scarcities of factors may not remain so according to the future scarcities. The longer a project lasts, the more pertinent this consideration becomes.

II-2 Derivation of Accounting Prices from Maximizing Current Output

As stated above, Tinbergen was perhaps the first to suggest that in the underdeveloped countries with abundant labor and scarce capital, the techniques and projects should be selected on the basis of a wage rate lower than the market wage rate and an interest rate higher than the market interest rate. He called these factor prices accounting prices.

Working under his supervision the present writer developed a simple and straightforward method for the derivation of accounting prices in 1960. Confining attention to two factors of production, the unskilled and moderately skilled labor (to be called labor) and the scarce and investible resources including advanced skills (to be called capital), an aggregate production function of the two factors can be derived for the economy as a whole. Let this function be $P = f(L,K)$, where P is the total value of output, L is labor, and K is capital, and f is a continuous function of L and K, assuming continuous substitution possibilities. It is also assumed that though capital is fully utilized, a part of labor is unemployed. Let $\overline{L}$ and $\overline{K}$ denote the amounts of employed labor and capital in the year under consideration, and L^* and K^* denote the total amounts available. In most of the underdeveloped countries $\overline{L} < L^*$, but $\overline{K} = K^*$. The marginal productivity of labor at the current levels of employment of factors is

$$\frac{\partial \overline{P}}{\partial \overline{L}} = f_{\overline{L}}(\overline{L},\overline{K})$$

and that of capital

$$\frac{\partial \overline{P}}{\partial \overline{K}} = f_{\overline{K}}(\overline{L},\overline{K}) .$$

The ratio of current prices of factors equals the ratio of their current productivities so that the following holds

$$\frac{\overline{w}}{\overline{r}} = \frac{f_{\overline{L}}(\overline{L},\overline{K})}{f_{\overline{K}}(\overline{L},\overline{K})} \tag{1}$$

where $\overline{w}$ and $\overline{r}$ are the market prices of labor and capital. The above implies that

$$\text{if } \overline{w} = \frac{\partial \overline{P}}{\partial \overline{L}}, \text{ then } \overline{r} = \frac{\partial \overline{P}}{\partial \overline{K}}.$$

The production function is continuous, allowing infinite substitution possibilities. A production function is by definition a maximal concept in the sense that for any combination of factors, the output given by it is the maximum possible. Therefore, the maximum output will be obtained when the production is carried out by utilizing all the factors fully, and the optimal technology is one that is given by the ratio of the total amounts of available factors. The ratio of the accounting prices will then be equal to the ratio of the marginal productivities of the factors when their full amounts are introduced in the production function. Thus

$$\frac{w^*}{r^*} = \frac{f_{L^*}(L^*,\overline{K})}{f_{\overline{K}}(L^*,\overline{K})} = \frac{f_{L^*}(L^*,K^*)}{f_{K^*}(L^*,L^*)}, \text{ since } \overline{K} = K^* \tag{2}$$

That is,

$$\text{if } w^* = \frac{\partial P^*}{\partial L^*}, \text{ then } r^* = \frac{\partial P^*}{\partial K^*}.$$

(1) and (2) can be solved for w^* and r^* in terms of $\bar{w}$ and $\bar{r}$. To illustrate, let f be the Cobb-Douglas Production function, so that $P = aL^{\alpha}K^{1-\alpha}$ where a is a constant efficiency parameter and α and $1-\alpha$ are labor and capital elasticities of production respectively, and let $\bar{L} = hL^*$. Substituting in (1) and (2) and solving for w^* and r^*, gives

$$w^* = wh^{1-\alpha};$$

$$r^* = rh^{-\alpha},$$

$$\text{and } \frac{w^*}{r^*} = \frac{w}{r}\, h. \tag{3}$$

The above simple result is due to the convenient form of the Cobb-Douglas function. For the constant elasticity of substitution[1], production function

$$P = A[\sigma L^{-\rho} + (1-\sigma)K^{-\rho}]^{-\frac{1}{\rho}}.$$

The current value of output with $\bar{L}$, the amount of labor actually utilized, is

$$\bar{P} = A[\sigma\bar{L}^{-\rho} + (1-\sigma)\bar{K}^{-\rho}]^{-\frac{1}{\rho}}. \tag{4}$$

Therefore, the market wage and interest rates are

$$\bar{w} = \frac{\sigma}{A^{\rho}} \left(\frac{\bar{P}}{\bar{L}}\right)^{\rho+1},$$
$$\bar{r} = \frac{1-\sigma}{A^{\rho}} \left(\frac{\bar{P}}{\bar{K}}\right)^{\rho+1}. \tag{5}$$

The total value of output with full employment of labor is

$$P^* = A\,[\sigma L^{*-\rho} + (1-\sigma)K^{*-\rho}]^{\frac{1}{\rho}}. \qquad (6)$$

Therefore, the accounting wage and interest rates are

$$w^* = \frac{\sigma}{A^\rho}\left(\frac{P^*}{L^*}\right)^{\rho+1} = \frac{\sigma}{\Lambda^\rho}\left(\frac{P^*}{\overline{L}/h}\right)^{\rho+1},$$

$$r^* = \frac{1-\sigma}{A^\rho}\left(\frac{P^*}{K}\right)^{\rho+1}. \qquad (7)$$

$$\text{Or,}\quad w^* = \overline{w}\left(\frac{P^*}{\overline{P}}\right)^{\rho+1} h^{\rho+1},$$

$$r^* = \overline{r}\left(\frac{P^*}{\overline{P}}\right)^{\rho+1}. \qquad (8)$$

The above derivation of the accounting prices of labor and capital implies some basic assumptions. First, it assumes that there exists a production function with given parameters which characterizes the production activities in a given economy. In short-term analysis, the parameters can be taken as given constants. But in the long run they may change. In successive years these parameters will have to be revised for deriving the short term accounting prices. Second, it is assumed that there are continuous possibilities of factor substitution. Over a sufficiently long period, this assumption may hold true. Over a short period, however, the substitution possibilities are probably limited. Therefore, it may be necessary to derive the short term accounting prices from discrete processes of production. This is discussed below. Failing to obtain the accounting prices from discrete processes of production, the accounting prices derived from aggregative production functions can be used. This is because the overall accounting prices of factors will reflect the overall scarcity of factors. While no project will exactly break even at these prices (because of limited substitution possibilities in reality), the projects closest to breaking even may be selected. Third, the above derivation has been carried out for two factors of production only. Resources, foreign exchange, and specialized and advanced skills were included in capital. It can be argued that land, natural resources and foreign exchange should be treated separately. Formally, a production function with four factors of production, land, labor, capital and foreign exchange, can be fitted and the accounting prices for each of the factors can be derived in the manner shown above. However, for most social cost-benefit analysis, the crucial accounting prices will be those of labor and capital.

11-3 Accounting Price of Foreign Exchange

The consideration of foreign exchange is somewhat problematic. Is foreign exchange a factor of production? Could there be an excess supply of foreign exchange with a shortfall in domestic savings or vice-versa? The problem can be analyzed by distinguishing between four cases: (i) excess supply of both foreign exchange and domestic saving; (ii) shortage of both foreign exchange and domestic savings; (iii) relatively smaller shortage of foreign exchange than that of domestic savings; and (iv) relatively smaller shortage of domestic savings than that of foreign exchange.

The first is not necessarily a sign of a prosperous economy. Many of the stagnant economies in the twenties and earlier had both a surplus in the balance of payments and a lack of absorptive capacity for the domestic savings. In recent decades this situation is rare. In fact, most of the developing countries have had shortages of both foreign exchange and domestic savings. To a large extent the demands for both foreign exchange and for domestic savings may be complimentary. If the supply of domestic savings increases proportionately more than the supply of foreign exchange, a part of domestic savings may not be used for investment. However, if the supply of foreign exchange increases proportionately more than the supply of domestic savings, it can always be used for domestic investment. This of course implies the convertibility of foreign exchange. Thus, the third case does not pose a problem in reality, because the savings gap can be filled by foreign exchange. It is the fourth case which is most crucial in that part of domestic savings cannot be invested because of lack of foreign exchange. Since domestic savings are in short supply relative to the supply of labor, the accounting price of capital would be higher than the prevailing rate of interest. If the introduction of the accounting prices of labor and capital reduces the scarcity of foreign exchange relatively more than that of capital, there may be no need to find and use the accounting price of foreign exchange. But if the relative scarcity of foreign exchange vis a vis capital is not likely to be removed, then the accounting price of foreign exchange may have to be estimated in addition to that of capital.

The short-term accounting price of foreign exchange, considering it as a factor of production, can be derived by using the same procedure as was used for capital. Alternatively, the accounting price of foreign exchange may be derived on the basis of the relative purchasing power of the currencies involved; or the free market exchange rate as against the official exchange rate may be taken as the accounting exchange rate.

II-4 Accounting Prices from Uncommitted Amounts of Factors

In practice it is, of course, the uncommitted amounts of factors which can be used in alternative ways. In general, once a capital item has been formed or manufactured to produce a specific good, it cannot be used to produce something else. Similarly, a worker after he has received training to produce one good cannot be easily transferred to produce another good. Hence, already installed machines, plants and equipment and already employed workers are committed factors. Their opportunity cost in the sense of their contribution in alternative uses may be nil or close to nil. It is the uncommitted amounts of factors which can be used in alternative ways and whose output can be maximized.

Uncommitted labor is considered to be all unemployed labor and all new entrants into the labor market. Uncommitted capital is all savings and depreciation allowances, i.e., gross domestic savings. Uncommitted foreign exchange is that amount which can be freely used to purchase imports. Given the estimates of the uncommitted amounts of factors in each year, the accounting prices can be derived for each year by maximizing a continuous production function of these amounts.

The estimates of the uncommitted amounts of factors of production for the initial year can be obtained from the performance of the economy in the previous year. Estimates of the uncommitted amounts of the factors in the second year of the project can be made from the performance of the economy in the first year and so on.

For the sake of simplicity and brevity, let labor and capital be the only two factors to be considered. Let $\tilde{w}_t$ and $\tilde{r}_t$ denote the accounting prices of labor and capital in year t, (t=1, 2, ...T). Let the uncommitted amounts of labor and capital be denoted by $\tilde{L}$ and $\tilde{K}$ in year t, $\tilde{L}_1$ and $\tilde{K}_1$ being known. Let f^1 represent the production function in year 1, then,

$$w_1 = \frac{\partial f^1}{\partial \tilde{L}_1} \text{ and } r_1 = \frac{\partial f^1}{\partial \tilde{K}_1} \text{ where } f^1 = f^1(\tilde{L}_1 \tilde{K}_1). \quad (14)$$

Let s_{w_1} be the rate of saving of wage incomes and s_{r_1} the rate of savings of non-wage incomes, then the saving from wage incomes accruing from projects started in year 1,

$$S_{w_1} = s_{w_1} \cdot \bar{w}_1 \tilde{L}_1, \quad (15)$$

and savings from non-wage incomes accruing from projects started in year 1,

$$S_{r_1} = s_{r_1} \cdot \bar{r}_1 \tilde{K}_1 . \quad (16)$$

Here $\bar{w}_1$ and $\bar{r}_1$ are the market wage and interest rates in year 1. The projects may be selected using the accounting prices of factors, but the factors have to be paid at their market prices. Private producers can be induced to install the chosen projects through taxes and subsidies equal to the differences between accounting prices and prevailing prices.[2] Uncommitted capital in the second year will equal the uncommitted capital in the first year plus the gross savings from the operation of uncommitted factors in the first year. Thus

$$\tilde{K}_2 = \tilde{K}_1 + S_{w_1} + S_{r_1} \tag{17}$$

The uncommitted labor in the second year is determined by the rate of growth of the population and the number of entrants into the labor force. $\tilde{L}_2$ can be estimated from demographic studies. In the second year, the accounting prices of capital and labor are

$$\tilde{w}_2 = \frac{\partial f^2}{\partial L_2},\ \tilde{r}_2 = \frac{\partial f^2}{\partial K_2} \text{ where } f^2 = f^2(\tilde{L}_2\tilde{K}_2). \tag{18}$$

Similarly, the accounting prices of factors for the successive years can be obtained.

In valuing the factors used by a project in successive years, the accounting prices of those years will have to be applied.

Two questions arise in using this approach. One is related to the accuracy of the derivation, and the other is related to the quality of the approach, i.e., how appropriate are these accounting prices and do they result in optimal values of output over time? The answer to the first question is that the accuracy of the derivation depends on the estimates of the quantity of uncommitted labor and capital and the production functions in the future years.

The second question is more difficult to answer. The accounting prices of factors in each year reflect the real relative scarcity of uncommitted factors in that year. If these prices are used for the amounts of factors utilized in successive years, then the resulting choice must be better than what the application of a single set of prices would bring about. But are there some other approaches which may yield better results? The answer to this question is that there may be such other approaches. Some of these approaches require the introduction of time horizon and the consideration of terminal conditions, such as terminal capital stock. The application of accounting prices that are derived satisfying these latter conditions will certainly give better results with respect to the fulfillment of these conditions. But the determination of the time horizon and terminal conditions itself requires optimal decision-making. Recent numerous efforts to study the optimal rate of economic development have not met with any significant success and have not provided any practical guidance.

II-5 Accounting Prices of Factors from Discrete Processes of Production

The accounting prices of factors can be derived from the discrete processes of production. This approach may be preferable if the substitution possibilities between factors appear to be too limited.

In order to derive the accounting prices, the value of the final output has to be maximized subject to the constraints of the primary inputs. Since the cost-benefit analysis is applied to new investment projects, the accounting prices ought to be derived by maximizing a linear function of the increments of final demand subject to availabilities of domestic savings, unemployed labor and that of foreign exchange. The model can be written as follows

$$\max \quad z = \sum_{i=1}^{n} \Delta c_i$$

$$\text{subject to} \quad \Delta x_i - \sum_{j=1}^{n} a_{ij} \Delta x_j - \Delta c_i = 0$$

$$\sum_{i=1}^{n} m_i \Delta x_i \leqq \tilde{F}$$

$$\sum_{i=1}^{n} l_i \Delta x_i \leqq \tilde{L} \tag{9}$$

$$\sum_{i=1}^{n} b_i \Delta x_i < \tilde{K}$$

$$\Delta c_i \geqq 0 \qquad i = 1, 2, \ldots, n.$$

In the above model Δc_i denotes the incremental amount of ith final output. Δx_j the incremental amount of jth output, $\tilde{F}$ the foreign exchange, $\tilde{L}$ the unemployed labor and $\tilde{K}$ the gross domestic savings. a_{ij} represents the input-output coefficients, m_i the import, l_i the labor input and b_i the capital input coefficients.

The solution of a simple model with three constraints may sometimes give an unrealistic result. For example, it may show that agricultural production will increase by, say, 10 per cent. But this may be impossible in practice, since there may be no additional land to reclaim to enable the country to increase its agriculture output by 10 per cent. In this case, either an additional constraint on land availability or on incremental agricultural output will have to be imposed on the model.

III. SHADOW PRICES IN TERMS OF CAPITAL COST

III-1 Introduction

In the preceding section, the accounting prices of factors are assumed to equal the marginal productivities of factors under the assumption that they are fully employed so as to maximize current output. In other words, the accounting or shadow prices are dependent on the demand for factors, given their supplies. The supply cost of factors has not been taken into account. Also some other considerations such as the dependence of employment in the industrial sector upon the amount of surplus from the agricultural sector has also not been incorporated.

An attempt has been made by Agarwala [1966] to derive the shadow prices of factors by expressing the cost of surplus food required by an additional industrial worker in terms of capital cost. In this way Agarwala has been able to express the relative shadow price of labor and capital as outlined below.

III-2 The Agarwala Approach

Agarwala has tried to estimate the shadow prices of labor and capital by explicitly introducing the elements of consumption per worker and agricultural surplus. His main concern is the study of technology in the industrial sector.

The demand for food surplus from the agricultural sector is given by the demand for food by the non-agricultural sector. This is equal to consumption per worker in the non-agricultural sector (c_i) multiplied by the number of workers (N_i).

$$S^d = N_i c_i. \tag{1}$$

The supply of food surplus is assumed to be given by

$$S^s = a + bN_i. \tag{2}$$

Here a is the autonomous amount of food surplus independent of the size of population in the agricultural sector, and b is a parameter associated with the number of industrial workers. In equilibrium,

$$S^s = S^d = S. \tag{3}$$

From (1), (2) and (3) we get

$$S = a + \frac{bS}{c_i} = \frac{a}{1-\frac{b}{c_i}} \tag{4}$$

Thus for increasing the employment by one unit, it is not necessary to increase the surplus of food by c_i, but only by $c_i/(1-b/c_i) = k$ (say). This is presumably because each worker who moves to the industrial sector carries b amount of food with him from the agricultural sector as equation (2) would suggest.

The autonomous amount of food surplus, a, that is independent of the size of population, may be in the form of taxes, imports, production on state farms, etc. When imports or taxation are not considered, and when N_i is constant, the increase in the income of the agricultural sector which would bring about a unit increase in surplus is given by

$$S = Y - C$$

$$\frac{dS}{dy} = 1 - \frac{dC}{dY}$$

or
$$\frac{dY}{dS} = \frac{1}{1 - \frac{dc}{dy}}$$

$$= h \text{ (say)}$$

with $C = cN$ and $Y = yN$ and N constant.

Here Y is total agricultural income, C total consumption and N total population of the agricultural sector. Thus, for increasing the autonomous surplus by k amount, production has to be increased by kh.

If the capital-output ratio in the agricultural sector is g, then for producing hk amount of extra food, hkg amount of extra capital must be introduced into agricultural production. However, by assumption, this capital will last forever, and it cannot be treated as the cost of labor over a particular period. In order to reduce these quantities to the same dimension, the annual cost of capital, which is given by $rkgh$ where r is the shadow rate of interest per annum, (Agarwala [1966] p. 122) is used. By this method Agarwala expresses the cost of labor in terms of the cost of capital. The shadow prices of labor and capital are given by

$$\frac{\text{Shadow price of labor}}{\text{Shadow price of capital}} =$$

$$\frac{\text{marginal productivity of labor}}{\text{marginal productivity of capital}}$$

$$= \frac{rkgh}{r} = kgh$$

Agarwala has thus managed to obtain the relative shadow prices of labor and capital without going into the difficult task of calculating the shadow rate of interest.

III-3 Some Comments on Agarwala's Approach

The somewhat elegant approach presented by Agarwala is open to some basic criticisms. The amount of surplus food, hk, required per worker for employment in the industrial sector, may be considered the price of labor. But its production in the agricultural sector requires both capital and labor; its cost of production in the agricultural sector cannot be equal to the rental value of capital alone, unless, the marginal productivity of labor is assumed to be zero. Agarwala assumes the marginal productivity of labor in agriculture to equal zero, thus he can impute the total value of hk amount of food to capital. If so, his shadow price of labor is the capital cost of producing the amount of surplus food required for employing one worker in the industrial sector. Since the capital cost is the only cost of producing the incremental amounts of food, the shadow price of labor is the simple total cost of producing the surplus food required per worker employed in the industrial sector.

This definition of the shadow prices of labor and capital is not irrelevant to policy making purposes. One wonders, however, if it leads toward the optimal choice of specific technologies. The cost of employing a worker in the industrial sector is estimated on the basis of existing technology, and there is no knowing how optimal would be the techniques selected according to these shadow prices. Given h and k, the choice of techniques depends in fact on g, the capital-output ratio in the agricultural sector. If g is high, then these industrial projects which are relatively labor intensive will be less preferable than those which are capital intensive and vice-versa. By itself this appears to be a sound policy, but it ignores the marginal productivity of workers in the industrial projects.

Another point that can be raised is that even though the marginal productivity of labor in agriculture is zero, the cost of his subsistence is not zero. This objection, however, need not detract from Agarwala's approach, since it is the purpose of shadow prices to reflect the marginal productivity rather than the unavoidable cost of subsistence which would be incurred irrespective of whether or not a surplus is produced.

The basic problem with Agarwala's approach is that the shadow prices of factors are based on the existing technology. The lifespan of projects, however, covers several years extending in some cases 50 years or more. Hence the shadow prices of factors that might be relevant for the initial year may be quite irrelevant in future years. This is not because the capital cost of producing surplus food in agricultural sector might change, but mostly because the capital cost of production in the industrial sector might undergo substantial change.

IV. LONDON-OXFORD-MIT APPROACH

IV-1 Introduction

Recently an alternative method of deriving the shadow prices of factors has been developed by Dasgupta and Sen of the London School of Economics, Little and Mirrlees of Oxford, and Marglin of MIT. The basic element in this approach is the shadow price of investment, which is defined as the discounted stream of consumption emanating from a unit of investment. The shadow wage rate is defined as the net cost of employing a worker in terms of shadow price of investment.

This line of approach can be traced to Marglin's 1963 publications. It was further developed in the Guidelines[3] by Dasgupta, Sen and Marglin [1972] and in the Manual[4] by Little and Mirrlees [1974]. Here the derivation of Shadow Prices as given in the Guidelines will be discussed.

IV-2 The Shadow Prices of Factors

Suppose that the number of jobs created by a unit of investment is l and the annual increment to net output is y. Let w be the wage rate in the industrial sector. Then the non-wage income from a unit investment equals $y-wl$. If a fraction s is saved from the non-wage income and the rest is consumed, then the direct annual (non-wage) consumption from unit investment is $(1-s)(y-wl)$, and reinvestment is $s(y-wl)$. Let the shadow price of investment be denoted by P^{inv}. Since P^{inv} represents the present value of streams of consumption originating from $s(y-wl)$, the portion of non-wage income reinvested, is $P^{inv}s(y-wl)$. This is the indirect annual consumption in perpetuity originating from the unit of investment in the initial period.

The workers are assumed to save nothing. Let z be the opportunity cost of labor, i.e., the amount of consumption per worker, if that worker had not been employed in the industrial sector. Then the increase in the direct annual consumption value from a unit of investment is $(w-z)l$. Aggregate annual consumption, the value originating from unit investment is

$$B = \underbrace{P^{inv}s(y-wl)}_{\text{indirect annual consumption}} + \underbrace{(1-s)(y-wl) + (w-z)l}_{\text{direct annual consumption}} \qquad (10)$$

The present value of B at the social discount rate, i, is the shadow price of investment

$$P^{inv} = \sum_{t=1}^{\infty} \frac{B}{(1+i)^t} = \frac{B}{i} \quad \text{since} \quad \sum_{t=1}^{\infty} \frac{1}{(1+i)^t} = \frac{1}{i}$$

$$P^{inv} = \frac{P^{inv} s(y-wl) + (1-s)(y-wl) + (w-z)l}{i}$$

$$= \frac{(1-s)(y-wl) + (w-z)l}{i - s(y-wl)}. \qquad (11)$$

The shadow wage rate is derived on the assumption that the wages paid to the workers are obtained from taxing the non-wage earners, viz., the capitalists. Of wages, w, transferred from them, the capitalists would have saved and invested sw resulting in the present value of aggregate consumption due to this investment equal to $P^{inv}sw$. The residue of w transferred, $(1-s)w$, would have been consumed by the capitalists. In addition, a worker employed in the industrial project foregoes his opportunity wage or subsistence wage equal to z. Thus, the total loss of consumption is $P^{inv}sw + (1-s)w + z$. From this, the worker's wage w which is assumed to be wholly consumed, is to be deducted to get the net cost of employing a worker in terms of net aggregate consumption value lost. Thus defined the shadow wage rate is

$$w^* = z + P^{inv}sw + (1 - s)w - w \qquad (12)$$

$$= z + s(P^{inv} - 1)\,w.$$

Since P^{inv} is likely to be greater than unity in most underdeveloped countries, the shadow wage rate accordingly is likely to be greater than the opportunity cost of labor and the subsistence wage rate.

It is evident that if $P^{inv} = 1$, the shadow wage rate becomes equal to z, the opportunity cost of labor or the subsistence wage rate, and the higher the shadow price of investment, the higher the shadow wage rate.

The shadow exchange rate is derived separately, and is quite unrelated to the derivation of the shadow prices of investment and labor. It is defined as the weighted average of the domestic clearing prices of imports and exports to their *cif* and *fob* prices respectively. That is to say, the shadow price of foreign exchange

$$P^f = \sum_{i=1}^{n} f_i \frac{P_i^D}{P_i^{cif}} + \sum_{i=n+1}^{n+h} x_i \frac{P_i^D}{P_i^{fob}} \qquad (13)$$

$$\sum_{i=1}^{n} f_i + \sum_{i=n+1}^{n+h} x_i = 1.$$

where P_i^D is the domestic clearing price of the ith good, $i = 1, 2, \ldots, n$ for import goods, and $i = n+1, n+2, \ldots, n+h$ for export goods, f_i's and x_i's are the respective weights attached representing the fraction of total value of trade that the value of import or export good i forms.

IV-3 Comments

The main contribution of the authors is the derivation of the shadow price of investment; on this hinges the whole rationale for the Guidelines. Since all human activity is motivated by the ultimate end of consumption, it is perfectly in order that investment be evaluated in terms of the present value of all consumption imputable to that investment.

In Guidelines no assumption is made about the social rate of discounting; it is considered an unknown in the procedure, thus avoiding the pitfall of optimum saving models. However, in deriving the shadow price of investment, the saving rate is assumed to be given exogenously. This is unacceptable. The problem can be looked at in two ways. First it can be assumed that the introduction of shadow prices does not affect the marginal rate of savings and thus it can be assumed to be given exogenously. It would, then, be advisable to maximize current output in order to maximize the volume of saving in each year and hence the growth rate. In that case the earlier approach of section II would be perfectly in order. Alternatively it can be assumed that the introduction of shadow prices does affect the marginal rate of savings. Under this condition, the marginal rate of saving cannot be assumed to have been given exogenously. Thus, there is a circularity in the method adopted for the derivation of the shadow price of investment. Furthermore, the labor-investment ratio is also assumed to be given exogenously. But if the labor-investment ratio is already given, there is little need for project evaluation. The whole purpose of cost-benefit analysis is to arrive at the most appropriate, or possibly the optimal, combination of factors. A preassumed labor-investment ratio cannot be used for arriving at the optimal combination of factors. This involves circularity as well as arbitrariness. The authors of the _Guidelines_ acknowledge these weaknesses.

V. ACCOUNTING PRICES IN THE DYNAMIC SETTING

V-1 Introduction

In the two preceding sections, the problems of arbitrariness and circularity involved in the derivation of shadow or accounting prices have been confronted. These are partly caused by the fact that the life of projects using the technique varies from a few years to 30 or 35 years or more. In addition, it would be inappropriate to apply the accounting prices of factors associated with one single year to factors utilized in different years. This practice would be appropriate only when the relative scarcity of factors remains constant for successive years during the lifetime of the project in question. Since this will seldom hold true, the accounting prices for factors ought to be estimated for each year of the project.

We have already discussed the incremental or marginal accounting prices of factors for each year of the life of a project in section II. The procedure there was static. We turn now to dynamic procedures.

Three approaches will be outlined here. One was suggested by the present writer [1960]. The other was put forward by Professor Leif Johansen [1967]. A third has been recently presented by Marglin [1976].

V-2 Cumulative Accounting Prices

This approach stresses the fact that from the vantage point of the present year, gross domestic saving and unemployed workers in the current year and the gross domestic savings and the new entrants into the labor force in each subsequent year are uncommitted. Hence in selecting techniques of production in the current year, the advantages latent in this condition should be fully exploited. This can be done by deriving the associated accounting prices in such a way that the techniques employed are appropriate to the uncommitted amounts of factors as they accumulate.

Denoting the amounts of uncommitted labor and capital in a year t by $\tilde{L}_t$ and $\tilde{K}_t$ as before, the accumulated amounts of uncommitted labor and capital in year t from year 1 are

$$ {}_1\tilde{L}_t = \sum_{t=1}^{t} \tilde{L}_t, \text{ and } {}_1\tilde{K}_t = \sum_{t=1}^{t} \tilde{K}_t. $$

The cumulative accounting prices of labor and capital in year t with respect to a project to be started in year 1 are

$$ {}_1\tilde{w}_t = \frac{\partial f(\sum_{t=1}^{t} \tilde{L}_t, \sum_{t=1}^{t} \tilde{K}_t)}{\partial \sum_{t=1}^{t} \tilde{L}_t}, \quad {}_1\tilde{r}_t = \frac{\partial f(\sum_{t=1}^{t} \tilde{L}_t, \sum_{t=1}^{t} \tilde{K}_t)}{\partial \sum_{t=1}^{t} \tilde{K}_t}. \tag{21} $$

According to this approach, labor and capital utilized in year t by a project started in year 1 should be valued at prices ${}_1\tilde{w}_t$ and ${}_1\tilde{r}_t$ respectively. The idea behind this approach is that before the construction of the projects is started in a year, the cumulative amounts of gross domestic savings and unemployed labor in future years may be treated as uncommitted, and the projects can be evaluated and selected on the basis of pricing the factors of production utilized in successive years at their cumulative accounting prices. Since this possibility is considered exante, there is no hitch in using the cumulative accounting prices of factors derived above.

The central question: will the projects selected according to cumulative accounting prices give better results, that is, will they yield higher values of output? In Appendix I to this chapter, it is shown that they will.[5]

Cumulative accounting prices can be derived from discrete processes as well. The production constraints of the linear program described in

Section II will have to be replaced by the cumulative amounts of factors ${}_1\tilde{L}_t$ and ${}_1\tilde{K}_t$, $t=1, 2, \ldots, T$, etc.

The main flaw in this approach is that it involves circularity. The incremental, and hence the cumulative amounts of labor can be estimated from demographic studies. These amounts are more or less independent of other economic factors. The incremental and hence the cumulative amounts of capital, however, depend upon the projects and techniques utilized, and the associated accounting prices to which they are adapted. Therefore the accounting prices cannot be derived from cumulative amounts of capital which in turn depend on these same accounting prices. But if the incremental amounts of capital, i.e., gross investment in successive years are given exogenously, then the above approach can be applied, without any circularity.

V-3 Intertemporal Factor Pricing - Johansen's Approach

Intertemporal optimal growth and factor pricing models invariably encounter problems due to indeterminacies and/or arbitrariness in the terminal conditions. By introducing some restrictive conditions Professor Johansen has succeeded in presenting a model which can be solved for factor prices associated with efficient allocations of resources over time. He divides the economy in three segments. Of these segments 1 and 2 are primary sectors producing outputs all of which are used as inputs in the third segment of the economy. This represents the secondary sector. It is denoted by x and produces final consumption goods. The number of primary and secondary sectors can be increased without affecting the model.

The crucial assumption which Johansen makes is that the amounts of output of the secondary sector for each year are given. These amounts may be either planned or forecast. Another less restrictive assumption is that all of the outputs from the first two sectors are fully used as inputs in the third secondary sector. All three sectors use labor and capital. A rather restrictive assumption is that the total supply of investment capital in each year is given. Under these assumptions an efficient allocation of resources among the three sectors can be made, and efficiency prices associated with labor and capital can be derived. A sketch of the model is given in Appendix II to this chapter.

V-4 Marglin's Dynamic Accounting Prices

In his recent book,[6] Marglin conceptualizes an economy with a single sector producing a homogeneous output under constant returns to scale by means of non-depreciating homogeneous capital and homogeneous labor. Outside this sector which is called F, there exists a reserve army of un- or under-employed workers, with marginal productivity equal to zero. The industrial wage rate is assumed to be institutionally fixed in terms of industrial output and independent of the level of industrial employment. The supply of labor to industry is assumed to be infinitely elastic at the exogenously fixed real wage until the labor force is fully employed. Workers consume all their wages; the capitalists consume an exogenously given fraction of their profits, the remainder being invested. There is an upper limit on the fraction of profit income beyond which the capitalists cannot be forced to save.

The basic model describing the above assumptions is as follows:

$$Q = F(K,L) \qquad L \leq N \qquad (1)$$

$$C = WL + (1-\alpha)\pi \qquad \pi \leq Q - WL \qquad (2)$$

$$I = \alpha\pi \qquad \alpha \leq \alpha \qquad (3)$$

Q is a homogeneous production function of degree one in capital (K) and labor (L) services - with all the regular characteristics of neo-classical production function. C is total consumption which is the sum of total wages WL and consumption by capitalists $(1-\alpha)\pi$. I is the amount of investment which equals a fraction α of profits π. The government cannot coerce the capitalists to raise α above an upper limit $\bar{\alpha}$. Profit π is the excess of total output over total wages. Number of workers employed L is less than or equal to the number of workers available N.

The optimal allocation between consumption and investment in a static framework is stated as below.

$$\max_{I,C} = (V(I,C) \tag{4}$$

subject to

$$C = (1-\alpha)(Q-WL) + WL \geq 0 \tag{5}$$

$$I = \alpha(Q-WL) \geq 0 \tag{6}$$

$$Q = F(K_0,L) \tag{7}$$

$$0 \leq L \leq N \tag{8}$$

$$0 \leq \alpha \leq \bar{\alpha} \tag{9}$$

$V(I,C)$ is a utility function representing the social ordering between I and C. The solution to the above yields the familiar marginal conditions:

$$\frac{V_I}{V_C} = \frac{(1-\bar{\alpha})Q_L + \bar{\alpha}W}{\bar{\alpha}(W-Q_L)} \quad \text{for} \quad \begin{matrix} L < N \\ \alpha = \bar{\alpha} \end{matrix} \tag{10}$$

$$1 \leq \frac{V_I}{V_C} \leq \frac{(1-\bar{\alpha})Q_L + \bar{\alpha}W}{\bar{\alpha}(W-Q_L)} \quad \text{for} \quad \begin{matrix} L = N \\ \bar{\alpha} = \bar{\alpha} \end{matrix} \tag{11}$$

$$\frac{V_I}{V_C} = 1 \quad \text{for} \quad \begin{matrix} L = N \\ \alpha < \bar{\alpha} \end{matrix} \tag{12}$$

The ratio of marginal utility of investment to marginal utility of consumption defines accounting price of investment. This price depends on the value of L and α at the point of time under consideration.

The dynamic values of L and α at each point of time are derived from dynamic optimization. The present value of marginal utility of investment at a point of time τ is denoted by $\psi(\tau)$ and by $u'(\tau)$ the present value of consumption. Let the rate of investment be increased by one unit at a point of time t, which increases output Q_K at each moment of time. The extra output is divided between investment and consumption in the ratio $\alpha:(1-\alpha)$. The intertemporal consistency requires that the utility of a unit of investment at a point of time t be equal to sum of the discounted values of marginal utilities of consumption and investment at each moment over the time horizon. This is to say,

$$\Psi(t) = \int_0^{t_0}\{u'(\tau)(1-\alpha(\tau))Q_K(\tau) + \Psi(\tau)\alpha(\tau)Q_K(t)\}d\tau + \Psi(t_0). \quad (13)$$

Differentiating the above, the instantaneous intertemporal consistency requirement becomes

$$-\Psi(t) = u'(t)(1-\alpha(t))Q_K(t) + \Psi(t)\alpha(t)Q_K(t). \quad (14)$$

(14) makes the intertemporal consistency requirement a moment-to-moment relationship between variables rather than a relationship covering the whole time horizon. The static maximization of (4) to (9) combined with (14) provide the necessary conditions for the optimal paths[6] of L and α.

The dynamic solution will depend on the terminal conditions. There is no wholly objective way of fixing the terminal conditions or the time horizon. Hence the solution values of L and α will imply subjective judgments.

The important point to note is that Marglin's dynamic optimization model is in substance as well as in appearance an optimal savings model. This is the crux of the matter. The accounting factor prices and optimal rate of savings are two facets of the same problem. Dynamic accounting prices cannot be determined without determining the optimal rates of saving. The optimal rates of saving implies optimal techniques of production. Dynamic accounting prices are the factor prices associated with the optional technology. Once the optimal rates of saving has been determined, it is an easy matter to derive the dynamic accounting prices. In the following section, the accounting prices of factors are derived on the assumption that the optimal rates of saving are known.

VI. ACCOUNTING PRICES COMPATIBLE WITH A GIVEN RATE OF SAVING

VI-1 Continuous Processes

The maintenance of a certain marginal rate of saving has been a desired goal in many underdeveloped countries. Unfortunately, there is no sure method to determine an optimal rate of saving. Researchers in this field have not yet provided any reliable results. Therefore, the target for the average or marginal rate of savings will have to be the result of a decision made by policy makers or politicians.

Suppose that the politicians decide upon a minimum acceptable marginal rate of savings, $\underline{s}$. The accounting prices of factors should be such that a marginal rate of savings $\underline{s}$ is achieved,

given the propensity to save of the wage and non-wage earners, s_w and s_r respectively. Let $f(L,K)$ be the production function. Capital being the factor in short supply, it is fully utilized. But if a certain given marginal rate of savings is to be achieved, then all the uncommitted labor cannot be employed fully. Let the amount of uncommitted labor which can be employed so as to yield the desired marginal rate of savings be denoted by $\overset{u}{L}$ then,

$$\underline{s} = \frac{\tilde{S}}{\tilde{y}} = \frac{s_w \tilde{w}\overset{u}{L} + s_r \tilde{r}\tilde{K}}{\tilde{w}\overset{u}{L} + \tilde{r}\tilde{K}} \tag{35}$$

where

$$\tilde{w} = \frac{\partial f(\overset{u}{L},\tilde{K})}{\partial \overset{u}{L}} \quad \text{and} \quad \tilde{r} = \frac{\partial f(\overset{u}{L},\tilde{K})}{\partial \tilde{K}} \tag{36}$$

Substituting $\tilde{w}$ and $\tilde{r}$ in (35), the value of $\overset{u}{L}$ can be obtained given the magnitudes of $\tilde{K}$ and the values of w, r, s_w, s_r, and $\underline{s}$. After the value of $\overset{u}{L}$ has been obtained, the accounting prices of labor and capital can be derived by substituting back in the expressions for $\tilde{w}$ and $\tilde{r}$ in (36).

VI-2 Discrete Processes

It is possible to derive such accounting prices through discrete processes as well. This can be done by adding some constraints to the program stated in section II. The program can be revised as below,

$$\max z = \sum_{i=1}^{n} \Delta c_i$$

$$\Delta x_i - \Sigma a_{ij}\Delta x_j - \Delta c_i = 0$$

$$\sum_{i=1}^{n} l_i \Delta x_i \leq \tilde{L}$$

$$\sum_{i=1}^{n} b_i \Delta x_i \leq \tilde{K}$$

$$\Delta c_i = 0 \qquad i = 1, 2, \ldots, n$$

$$s_w \overline{w} \overset{u}{L} + s_r \overline{r} \tilde{K} \geq \underline{s}(\overline{w} \overset{u}{L} + \overline{r} \tilde{K})$$

where $\overset{u}{L}$ is the amount of uncommitted labor that is utilized in the optimal solution of the program.

In social cost-benefit analysis, one of the aims may be higher employment. In that case, there may be a conflict between the twin objectives of a minimum marginal rate of savings and a certain level of employment. It may, therefore, be advisable to maximize the value of annual output and to limit consumption through monetary, fiscal and other regulatory measures such that a certain minimum marginal rate of savings is realized.

Summary

Many underdeveloped countries suffer from chronic disequilibrium with long term persistent unemployment and shortages of capital. This disequilibrium is caused by a rapid rate of population growth, peasant subsistence farming, minimum wage laws, an easy money policy, frictions and lack of mobility in the economy. The prevailing market factor prices, therefore, do not reflect the relative scarcity of factors. Hence, these prices cannot be used for social cost-benefit analysis.

The derivation and application of shadow factor prices have been suggested in two recent publications. The procedure involves assumptions which may not hold true and implies decisions about future consumption in perpetuity which may not be possible to predict. The main defect of the method, however, is that it involves circularity. It assumes a given rate of saving and a given investment-labor ratio, but these are the objective of the derivation of the shadow factor prices; they cannot be assumed to be given exogenously.

The derivation and application of accounting prices of factors suggested in this chapter aims at maximizing the value of output. The short-term marginal accounting prices are derived through maximizing annual outputs. Cumulative accounting prices aim at maximizing outputs over time. Under some restrictive assumptions, accounting prices in a dynamic setting can be derived. The application of accounting prices can be derived through a continuous production function or through discrete processes of production.

The use of a continuous production function in the derivation and application of accounting prices may lead toward full or nearly full employment. But it may adversely affect marginal savings. In order to prevent the marginal rate of saving from falling, it would be necessary to introduce some monetary, fiscal and other regulatory measures, or the accounting prices may be derived in such a way that they yield a predetermined rate of saving.

The developed countries with long term full employment do not suffer from structural disequilibrium in the factors market. In social cost-benefit analysis in these countries, the prevailing factor prices may be used. The focus of attention in these countries will be on the estimation and evaluation of direct and indirect,

intended and unintended inputs and outputs.

Footnotes

1 In the constant elasticity of substitution production function, *A* is the constant efficiency parameter, is the distribution parameter and is the substitution parameter.

2 For details of the system of taxation and subsidization see A. Qayum, Theory and Policy of Accounting Prices, Amsterdam: North-Holland Publishing Company, 1959.

3 Dasgupta, P.S., Marglin, S.A., and Sen, A.K. Guidelines for Project Evaluation, New York: UNIDO, 1972.

4 Little, I.M.D. and Mirrlees, J.A. Project Appraisal and Planning for Developing Countries, New York: Basic Books, Inc. Publishers, 1974.

5 Refer to A. Qayum, Numerical Models of Economic Development, Rotterdam University Press, 1966, chapter on "Life of Capital and Economic Growth or Processes of Factor Combination and Economic Growth."

6 Refer to Stephen A. Marglin's Value and Price in the Labour-Surplus Economy, (Oxford: Clarendon Press 1976) for details and fully fledged analysis.

Chapter Six

SOCIAL CHOICE OF PROJECTS

I. INTRODUCTION

I-1 Absolute and Comparative Choice

After all the inputs and outputs of a project have been identified and estimated and all the items have been properly valued, the annual benefits and costs of the project can be derived. The value of annual benefits less the value of corresponding annual costs constitutes annual net benefit. At this stage, the main question arises as to whether or not the project should be selected for execution. The relevant decision rules are related to two types of choice: absolute and comparative. In absolute choice, a project is selected when its aggregate benefits exceed its aggregate costs or when the aggregate net benefit is positive. In comparative choice, all projects are ranked according to their aggregate net benefits, and the project with the highest aggregate net benefit is selected.

The aggregation of net benefits and the choice of projects would be an easy matter if society were indifferent to the timing of benefits and costs. In that case the aggregate benefits would be the sum of annual benefits, the aggregate cost the sum of annual costs, and the aggregate net benefit the sum of annual net benefits. However, it is generally agreed that society is not indifferent to the timing of benefits and costs. This makes the choice of projects, either absolute or comparative, anything but straightforward.

Some of the methods used in commercial cost-benefit analysis suppress considerations of the timing of benefits and costs. These methods are briefly stated in section II. It will be noted that none of these methods exclude timing completely. On the other hand, the rate or rates used to discount the benefits and costs occurring in different project years need not reflect social time preference. In commercial cost-benefit analysis, a market rate could be quite adequate.

One of the methods used for comparative choice of projects in commercial cost-benefit analysis is based upon an internal rate of return. This method can also be used for comparative choice of projects in social cost-benefit analysis. However, the use of an internal rate of return faces tremendous difficulties in actual application.

Present value criterion is the most widely used method for absolute as well as comparative choice of projects in social cost-benefit analysis. This involves the prior determination of social time preference or the social rate of time discounting. Does a social rate of time discounting exist? If so, is there any way of deriving it precisely or even approximately? These are decidely the toughest problems in intertemporal social analysis.

I-2 Some Obvious Choices

In some comparative cases, the choice is obvious. When two projects have the same initial capital outlay and have the same life span, and if the net benefit of one project is larger than or equal to that of the other project in each year, then the first project is clearly preferable to the second project. This is a situation where one project dominates the other continuously and the problem of choice hardly arises. However, if the initial outlay of the first project which dominates the second project is larger than the second, then the choice is not obvious. To explain, consider two projects each of which has a lifetime of four years. Let their initial capital outlays and the yearly net benefits be given as below.

Table 6.1 Net Benefits

	Initial Capital Outlay	*Net Benefits in*			
		Yr. 1	*Yr. 2*	*Yr. 3*	*Yr. 4*
Project One					
Project Two					
Project One Normalized					

Net benefits of project one are greater than those of project two in each year. Apparently project one dominates project two. But the initial outlay of project one is three times that of project two. Project one can be normalized so that its initial outlay equals that of project two and its annual net benefits become comparable to those of project two. Dividing the row of project one by 3, it can be seen that project one does not dominate project two. The rest of this chapter discusses problems related to situations in which one or some of the possible projects <u>do</u> <u>not</u> dominate the others.

II. COMMERCIAL PROJECT SELECTION

II-1 Some Rough and Ready Criteria

Several methods are used in the commercial selection of projects. These can be broadly classified among the following categories: (1) Cut off period, (2) Pay off period, (3) Rate of return, (4) Present discounted value, and

(5) Internal rate of return. The cut-off period criterion can be used in the absolute choice of projects. According to this criterion a project is selected if its capital cost can be recouped before the end of a certain number of years; if not, the project is rejected. The cut-off period is an appropriate criterion for projects using new techniques which are expected to be known to competitors by the end of this period. This criterion may also be reasonable for projects producing new products which are expected to be produced by other producers by the end of the cut-off period. In some cases, the demand for a certain product may be expected to last for only a certain period. The capital cost of projects to be installed to produce this product must be recovered before the demand falls off. It is seen that this criterion does not give any weight or make any adjustments for the timing of benefits and costs within the cut-off period, and no value is attached to benefits occurring beyond that period.

The pay-off period is an extension of cut-off period criterion, and is suited for the comparative selection of projects. By this criterion each project is ranked according to the period in which its initial capital outlay is paid off. The project with the smallest pay-off period is selected first and then the one with the next smallest pay-off period and so on, till the available investment funds are exhausted or some other resource limits are reached. This criterion also does not consider the benefits and costs occurring in different years within the pay-off period, but it does imply that the sooner the benefits are realized the better the project would be. In other words, a positive time discounting of benefits is recognized. As in the cut-off period criterion, the benefits and costs occurring beyond the pay-off period are ignored.

Another crude method used for project selection is that of the average return. According to this criterion all the net benefits, excluding the initial capital outlays, over the lifetime of the project are summed, this sum is then divided by the number of years over which the summation has been carried out, giving the average return. The average return is then expressed as the percentage of the initial capital outlay. This criterion can be used for absolute choice as well as comparative choice. For an absolute choice of the project, the average return must be at least 100 per cent of the initial capital outlay plus the rate of interest at which the capital outlay has been borrowed. In a comparative choice the projects with the highest average percentage return will be selected first. A variant of this criterion is the net average return where the initial capital outlay is also deducted from the sum of benefits and costs occurring over the lifetime of projects. In this case, a project will be selected in an absolute choice only when the net average return is above the interest rate charged on the capital. It will be selected in a comparative choice when, as in the case of average return, the net average return as a percentage of the initial outlay is the highest. The average or the net average criterion does take into account all the benefits and costs over the lifetime of the projects, but it treats all the benefits and costs uniformly irrespective of the time when the benefits are realized and costs are incurred. In other words, the criterion does not involve any time preference or time discounting.

The three criteria suggested above can be formulated in the following way. Let B_{it} represent the value of benefits from project i in year t, C_{it} the amount of costs, and let the lifetime of the project be T_i. For simplicity assume that all the capital outlays K_{io} are incurred in the initial year 0, and all other recurrent costs and benefits are realized in the following years. The cost and benefit stream of the *i*th project can be stated as below.

Table 6.2 Costs and Benefits

Years	*0*	*1*	*2*	..	*T*
Costs	K_{io}	C_{i1}	C_{i2}	..	C_{iT}
Benefits	*0*	B_{io}	B_{i2}	..	B_{iT}
Net Benefits	$-K_{io}$	$B_{i1}-C_{i1}$	$B_{i2}-C_{i2}$	..	$B_{iT}-C_{iT}$

Cut-off period criterion: let F be the number of years of the cut-off period. Then a project will be selected according to this criterion if $A_i = -K_{io} + (B_{i1} - C_{i1}) + (B_{i2} - C_{i2}) + \ldots + (B_{iF} - C_{iF}) > 0$ in absolute choice. Or A_i is max $\{A_i\}$, $i = 1, 2, \ldots$ in comparative choice.

Pay-off period criterion: let P_i be the number of years such that $-K_{io} + (B_{i1} - C_{i1}) + (B_{i2} - C_{i2}) + \ldots + (B_{iP_i} - C_{iP_i}) = 0$, then the *i*th project will be selected if P_i is min $\{P_i\}$, $i = 1, 2, \ldots$.

Average return criterion: let AR_i denote the gross average return of the *i*th project, then

$$AR_i = \frac{1}{K_{io}} [(B_{i1} - C_{i1}) + (B_{i2} - C_{i2}) + \ldots + (B_{iT} - C_{iT})]$$

In absolute choice, the project will be selected if $AR_i \geq 1 + r$, where r is the rate of interest at which K_{io} has been borrowed or financed. In comparative choice the project will be selected if $AR_i = \max\{AR_i\}$. And if NAR_i denotes the net average return of the *i*th project, then

$$NAR_i = \frac{-K_{io}+(B_{i1}-C_{i1})+(B_{i2}-C_{i2})+\ldots+(B_{iT}-C_{iT})}{K_{io}} = -1 + AR_i.$$

So in absolute choice the project will be selected if $NAR_i \geq r$ and in comparative choice if $NAR_i = \max \{NAR_i\}$.

II-2 Net Present Value

None of the above rough-and-ready methods gives proper weighting to the timing of costs and benefits. In commercial cost-benefit analysis, earlier cash receipts are more valuable than later ones, since they can be used to defray the initial capital borrowed or reinvested to earn additional cash flows. The discounting of future benefits, therefore, is an essential prerequisite for project evaluation. What ought to be the rate at which the future benefits be discounted? In commercial cost-benefit analysis, the answer appears to be easy. It is the rate at which the initial capital has been borrowed or could have been borrowed. Under this reasoning, the rate of discount may be taken as a constant and equal to the market rate of interest on capital financing. However, this method would be correct only when all of the positive cash flows are used to pay back the initial capital borrowed. But parts or all of cash flows could be reinvested, and the rate of return on these investments might be different from year to year. In general, if the rate of return on these cash flows is higher than the interest on the initial capital loan, it would be more profitable to reinvest these cash flows. This means that for an accurate project evaluation the rate at which the net benefits are to be discounted for a year must equal the market rate of return in that year. And the rate of discounting may be assumed constant only when the market rate of interest is expected to remain constant over the lifetime of project or when the variations are expected to roughly cancel out.

In order to evaluate projects, the net benefits in each year must be expressed in terms of the present value in the initial year. The present value of the net benefit in year *1* of the ith project is $NB_{i1}/1+r_1$ where r_1 is the rate of discount applicable in year *1*. The present value of the net benefit in year *2* is $NB_{i2}/(1+r_1)(1+r_2)$ where r_2 is the rate of discount applicable in year *2*, and so on. If we denote the present value of the net benefit in year t by tPV_i, then

$$^{t}PV_i = \frac{NB_{it}}{(1+r_1)(1+r_2)\ \ldots\ (1+r_t)} = \frac{NB_{it}}{\prod_{\tau=1}^{t}(1+r_\tau)}$$

where r_τ is the rate of discount applicable in year τ, $\tau = 1, 2, \ldots t$. The present value of the net benefits in all the years of the ith project over its lifetime is

$$PV_i = {}^{0}PV_i + {}^{1}PV_i + {}^{2}PV_i + \ldots {}^{T}PV_i =$$

$$\frac{NB_{io}}{1} + \frac{NB_{i1}}{(1+r_1)} + \frac{NB_{i2}}{\prod_{\tau=1}^{2}(1+r_\tau)} + \ldots + \frac{NB_{iT}}{\prod_{\tau=1}^{T}(1+r_\tau)}$$

In most cases, $NB_{i0} = 0 - K_{i0} = -K_{i0}$, where K_{i0} is the amount of capital invested in year *0*.

When the rate of discount applicable in each year of the project's life is assumed to remain constant so that $r_1 = r_2 = \ldots r_\tau = r$, then

$$PV_i = NB_{i0} + \frac{NB_{i1}}{1+r} + \frac{NB_{i2}}{(1+r)^2} + \ldots + \frac{NB_{iT}}{(1+r)^T}.$$

In the special case when the net benefits in each year excepting year *0* are equal, i.e., $NB_{i1} = NB_{i2} = \ldots = NB_{iT} = NB_i$, then

$$PV_i = NB_{i0} + NB_i \left[\frac{1}{1+r} + \frac{1}{(1+r)^2} + \cdots \frac{1}{(1+r)^T}\right] =$$

$$NB_{i0} + \frac{\frac{1}{(1+r)^T} - \frac{1}{1+r}}{\frac{1}{1+r} - 1} = NB_{i0}$$

$$+ NB_i \left[\frac{-(1+r) + (1+r)^T}{r(1+r)^T}\right].$$

In the exceptional case when the life of the project extends to infinity, and the applicable rate of discount and the annual net benefits are constant, then,

$$PV_i = \frac{NB_i}{r} + NB_{i0}.$$

Though the neat formula above is valid only under very exceptional conditions, it can be used as a rough approximation to the present value of a project with a life of fifty or more years, and with a more or less constant annual rate of net benefits and when the discount rate is expected to be fairly stable.

In absolute choice, the th project will be selected if $PV_i \geq 0$.

The comparative choice cannot be made by directly comparing the PV_i's, because the bigger projects may have larger PV_i's and yet at the same time may yield lower rates of return. For comparative choice, the present value of benefits and costs of the project must be estimated. Denoting the present value of benefits by PVB_i and that of costs by PVC_i, we have

$$PVB_i = B_{i0} + \frac{B_{i1}}{1+r_1} + \frac{B_{i2}}{1+r_2} + \dots + \frac{B_{iT}}{1+r_T}$$

$$PVC_i = C_{i0} + \frac{C_{i1}}{1+r_1} + \frac{C_{i2}}{1+r_2} + \dots + \frac{C_{iT}}{1+r_T}$$

In most cases $B_{i0} = 0$ and $C_{i0} = K_{i0}$. Now the benefit cost ratio of the ith project is

$$BCR_i = \frac{PVB_i}{PVC_i}.$$

In comparative choice, the ith project will be chosen if $BCR_i = \max \{BCR_i\}$, $i = 1, 2, \dots,$. This is to say that the project with the highest benefit cost ratio will be chosen first.

The present value criterion seems to provide a foolproof method of selecting projects in commercial cost benefit analysis. However, even in such an analysis, the criterion is not free of problems. The market rate of interest differs with the size of the capital loan as well as its duration. In evaluating and comparing projects with different capital requirements and lifetimes, it is not clear which market rate of interest should be used in deriving present values. It is evident that for uniformity of treatment and comparability one common rate should be used for appraising each of the projects. But the ordering of present values of individual projects as well as their ranking according to cost-benefit ratio will alter with different <u>common</u> rates of interest used for the appraisal. This can be shown by the following diagram in which the two curves represent the present values of two projects corresponding to <u>common</u> interest rates.

Fig. 6.1. Present Values and Rates of Discount

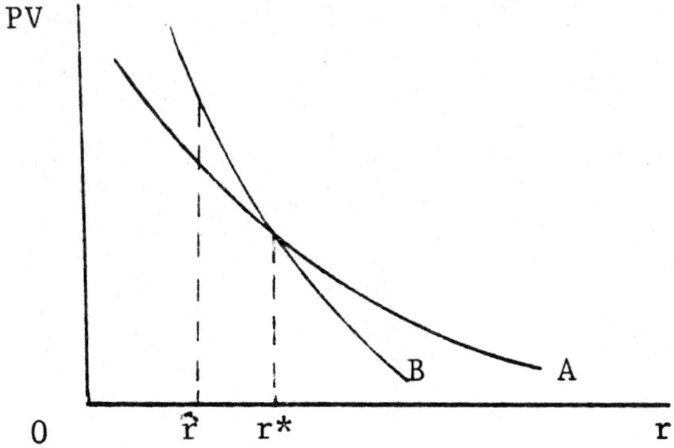

The present values of the two projects *A* and *B* are represented vertically, and the corresponding rates of discounting are represented horizontally. It can be seen that for all the rates less than r^* the present value of *A* is higher than that of *B*. But for all rates greater than r^*, the present value of *A* is higher than that of *B*. At r^* the present values of the two projects are equal. Suppose *B* is a bigger project than *A*, such that the discounted benefit cost ratios at $\hat{r}$ are equal. If the actual rate of discounting is around $\hat{r}$, then a little variation in the rate of discounting used might reverse the selection in comparative choice. The actual rates to be applied need not hover around $\hat{r}$. If they do, the damage done by the choice of one project instead of the other may not be too great, so long as the range of the market interest rates from which the rate of discount has to be derived is not too broad.

If the rate of discount is expected to vary over the years, similar observations will apply to each year.

Finally, it is worth considering that the difference between the market rates of interest on big, long-term loans and the small, short-term loans may be due to the degree and nature of the risks involved. The market rates of interest on capital loans for projects of the same size may also differ because of differences in risks associated with them. It may be suggested then that the benefits and costs of projects should be discounted at the respective market rates at which capital funds become available for financing them. This seems a reasonable suggestion, since if the same rate is used for all types of projects, then the less risky projects will be prejudiced against if the rate of borrowing capital for risky projects is used for discounting and vice-versa.

Some further complications arise when the perfect capital market assumed in the above discussion does not exist, in particular, when lending and borrowing rates differ. In this case, a decision will have to be made as to which rate ought to be used for discounting the net benefits of the project. The analysis becomes even more complicated when capital can be secured only at an increasing marginal borrowing rate.[1]

II-3 Internal Rate of Return

The above discussion shows that even in the commercial choice of projects, the determination of the correct rate of time discounting is not unequivocal. A much-debated alternative method for project choice is the use of an internal rate of return. This supposedly avoids the need for a specific rate of time discounting at least in the comparative choice of projects.

The internal rate of return for a project is the discounting rate ρ which reduces its net present value to zero. ρ_i, the internal rate of return of project i with life of two years is

$$NB_{i0} + \frac{NB_{i1}}{1+\rho_i} = 0.$$

The internal rate of return of a project i with life of n years is

$$NB_{i0} + \frac{NB_{i1}}{1+\rho_i} + \frac{NB_{i2}}{(1+\rho_i)^2} + \ldots + \frac{NB_{i,\,n-1}}{(1+\rho_i)^{n-1}} = 0.$$

In absolute choice a project i should be selected if the internal rate of return is higher than the rate of discounting r, i.e., when

$$NPV_i = NB_{i0} + \frac{NB_{i1}}{1+r} \geqq 0$$

or

$$\frac{NB_{i1} + NB_{i0}}{-NB_{i0}} \geqq r$$

or

$$\rho_i \geqq r.$$

In comparative choice a project i will be selected over another project j according to the internal rate of return criterion if

$$\rho_i > \rho_j.$$

In case of two year projects, again, the two criteria are identical. For $\rho_i > \rho_j$ whenever $NPV_i > NPV_j$ as can be easily verified.

For projects of more than two years duration the correspondence between the two criteria becomes tenuous at best and ceases to be of any practical significance in most cases. Only in the exceptional case when the rate of discounting, however determined, is assumed to remain constant over the lifetime of the projects and the projects have unique internal rates of return will the correspondence between the two criteria be valid, and that too only for absolute choice. The following figure shows the relationship between the net present values of projects i and j represented along the vertical axis and rates of discounts represented along the horizontal axis. The internal rates of return ρ_i and ρ_j are located on the horizontal axis where the

Fig. 6.2. Net Present Values and Internal Rates of Return

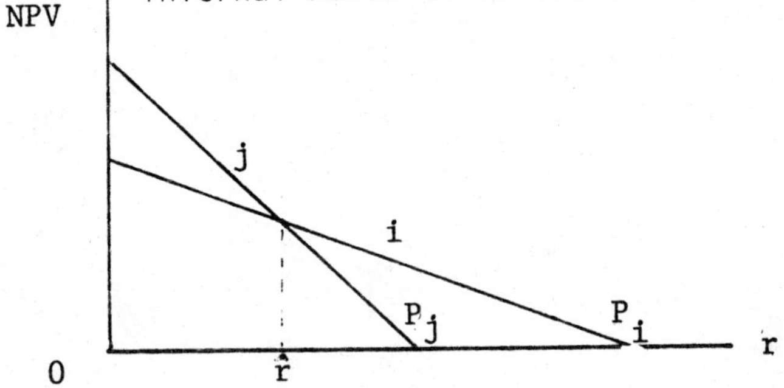

NPV_i and NPV_j are reduced to zero. It is seen that at any rate of discounting less than ρ_i, project i has a positive net present value. Hence in absolute choice

$$NPV_i \geq 0 \quad \text{whenever} \quad \rho_i \geq r \quad \text{for any } i, j, \ldots .$$

Under these restrictive assumptions then the net present value and the internal rate of return criteria coincide for absolute choice of projects.

In comparative choice, however, this is not true. According to the internal rate of return criterion, project i will be selected if $\rho_i \geq \rho_j$ as is the case in the above figure. But the net present value of project i is greater than that of project j only for rates of discount lying to the right of r^*. For rates of discount lying to the left of r^*, the net present value of project i is smaller than that of project j. Therefore the two criteria give opposite results for these rates. Therefore the internal rate of return criterion is liable to give incorrect choice if the rate of discount lies to the left of r^*, i.e., is smaller than r^*. For cases in which the exact rate of discounting is not known with certainty, the choice indicated by the internal rate of return criterion cannot be trusted.

In a more realistic case, when the rate of discounting is assumed to change between successive two-year periods there is no way to know about the correctness of the choice according to the internal rate of return criterion. This is because the comparability between the net present value and internal rate of return criteria is possible only when the rate of discounting is assumed to be constant over the lifetime of the project. The internal rate of return criterion, therefore, cannot be used for absolute or comparative choice of projects where there is a fair presumption that the rate of discounting will not remain constant.

Aside from the question of the constancy of the discount rate, the internal rate of return is seldom unique for a project with a lifetime of more than two years. For a three year project i with NB_{i0}, NB_{i1}, NB_{i2} equal to *-1*, *2*, *1* respectively ρ_i = *1.414* and so it is unique. And if the rate of interest is constant over the three years the internal rate of return criterion can be used for selection of projects. But consider the sequence of net benefits of another 3 year project j, *-1*, *5*, *-6*. Solution gives values for the internal rate of return ρ_j = *1.00* or *2.00*, i.e., the internal rates of return are 100 per cent or 200 per cent. For a four year project with net benefits equal to *-1*, *6*, *11*, *-6*, the internal rates of return are *0.00*, *1.00* and *2.00*, i.e., zero per cent, one hundred per cent and two hundred per cent. These solutions are depicted in the following figure.[2]

Fig. 6.3. Multiple Internal Rates of Return

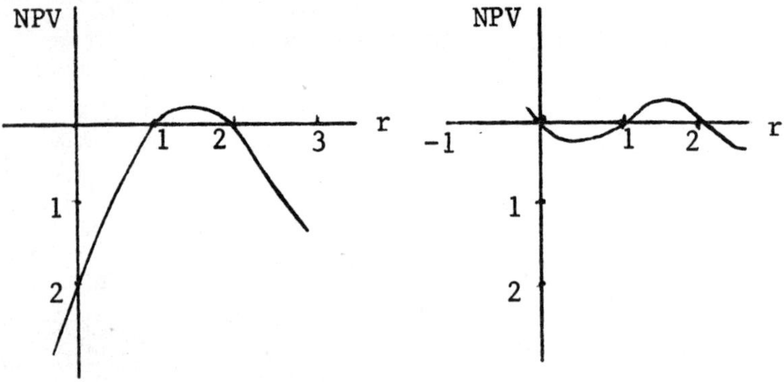

Moreover, a project may have no real internal rates of return. For example, the project with a net benefits sequence *-1, 3, -2 1/2* has imaginary solutions.

In particular, as stated by Bailey[3] and others, if the sequence of net benefits has any negative terms after the first positive one, the solution may give multiple values or no real values for the internal rate of return.

Hirshleifer has pointed out a somewhat subtle but fundamental flaw implied in the derivation of the internal rate of return. He has shown that the idea that the internal rate of return is a purely internal rate is not true. Consider the sequence of net benefits *-1, 2, 1* of a three year project as before. "The intermediate cash throwoff of $2.00 must clearly be reinvested <u>externally</u> of this option. How does the calculation of ρ handle this? The answer is that the mathematical manipulation involved in the calculation of ρ implicitly assumes that all intermediate receipts, positive or negative, are treated as if they could be compounded at the rate ρ solved for."[4] There will not be normally other investment or lending and borrowing opportunities for the intermediate cash proceeds (or net benefits).

Bailey has, however, shown that the flaw indicated by Hirshleifer can be given some plausible reinterpretation. He has also indicated that the criterion of net present value is not without some degree of circularity. This is due to the fact that the market rate of discounting is itself influenced by the choice of projects.

III. THE SOCIAL CHOICE OF PROJECTS

III-1 Introduction

The basic procedures in the social choice of projects are not different from those used in the commercial choice of projects, except that in the social evaluation of projects benefits and costs and the rate of discounting are not based on market valuations as such. Many of the benefits and costs are such that the market fails to put any values on them, and the social rate of time-discounting may be very poorly reflected by market rates of interest. The valuation of costs and benefits from a social viewpoint has been considered in chapters three, four and five. The determination of the social rate of time discounting has not yet been considered; this will be taken up in the following sections.

Of the commercial criteria discussed in the preceding section, the pay-off period, the cut-off period, and the simple rate of return are of little importance in the social choice of projects. The special circumstances characterizing these criteria may be present in the social choice of projects but they would be submerged in so many other weighty considerations that they can be ignored. Moreover the remaining two criteria, viz, the internal rate of return and the net present value criteria when properly used do take into account the special circumstances implicit in the other criteria.

III-2 The Internal Rate of Return and Social Choice of Projects

The internal rate of return criterion does not require any modification when applied in the social choice of projects. As noted above, the essential differences between commercial and social choices lies in the coverage of the elements of costs and benefits and their valuation. The net present value criterion would, in addition, require information about the social rate of time discounting. The derivation of the internal rate of return does not require the social rate of time discounting. The internal rate of return can be derived from the annual values of the net social benefits of the project. The net social benefits are, of course, the difference between the annual social benefits and social costs covering all the intended and unintended outputs and accounted and unaccounted inputs valued from the social viewpoint. Further, the stream of social net benefits may not be coterminus with the lifetime of the project, it may extend beyond. The internal rate of return of a project in social choice can be obtained, as before, by solving for ρ in

$$NSB_{i0} + \frac{NSB_{i1}}{1+\rho} + \frac{NSB_{i2}}{(1+\rho)^2} + \ldots + \frac{NSB_{iT}}{(1+\rho)^T} = 0,$$

where NSB_{it} is the net social benefit in year t.

In comparative social choice of projects, the project with the highest internal rate of return will be chosen first and that with the second highest rate next and so on. In absolute choice, however, a project will be chosen when its internal rate of return is larger than the social rate of time discounting. In this method of choice, therefore, the advantage of the internal rate of return criterion, that it does not require the determination of the social rate of time discounting, is no more there.

Just as in the case of the commercial choice of projects, the internal rate of return criterion can be applied only when the projects' internal rates of return are unique. For projects of more than two years duration, the internal rate of return is likely to be unique only in exceptional cases. Moreover, the application of this criterion in the social choice of projects is open to the same criticisms as mentioned in the context of commercial choice.

It must be noted that the social time preference and social rate of time discounting will vary from year to year. The internal rate of return implies a constant rate of time discounting. The internal rate of return criterion, even when there is a unique solution, will be relevant only in the exceptional case when it can be assumed that the social rate of time discounting will remain stable over the lifetime of the project. Since the knowledge available regarding time preference is meager, as will be seen in the following sections, it will be difficult to determine time periods during which the social rate of time discounting may be fairly constant. In practice, therefore, the internal rate of return criterion has little applicability.

III-3 Social Net Present Value

The most useful criterion for the social choice is the net present value, just as it is for the commercial choice of projects. In this case, the criterion may be called the social net present value, as it is applied to social net benefits. However, the derivation of the social net present value requires the determination of the value or values of the social rate of time discounting. But the determination or derivation of this rate or rates poses tremendous difficulties. In fact it has been questioned whether such rates in fact exist. If it is shown or believed that they do, then the problem of finding the most reliable and relevant indicators and parameters is faced. Another argument on which there has been a good deal of debate is whether the social rate of discounting is higher or lower than long-term market rates of interest. In the following section these and some other problems which have arisen in the search for social rate of time discounting are discussed.

While the search for a social rate of time discounting will continue, it is reasonable to believe that a foolproof analytical method for determining it will not be available in the foreseeable future. Ultimately and in the last resort, the political decision-making process will have to be brought into play to spot the rate when econometric analysis fails to provide reliable clues.

After the social rate of time discounting has been arrived at through economic analysis or political determination or a combination of the two, the social net present value can be calculated in the usual way.

The social net present value of project whose social net benefits extend up to year T is

$$SNPV_i = SNB_{i0} + \frac{SNB_{i1}}{1+sr} + \frac{SNB_{i2}}{(1+sr)^2} + \dots + \frac{SNB_{iT}}{(1+sr)^T}$$

where sr is the constant social rate of discounting. When the annual social rate of time discounting is variable the formula changes accordingly

$$SNPV_i = SNB_{i0} + \frac{SNB_{i1}}{1+sr} + \frac{SNB_{i2}}{(1+sr_1)(1+sr_2)} + \dots + \frac{SNB_{iT}}{\prod_{t=1}^{T}(1+sr_t)}.$$

As before, in absolute choice project i will be selected if $SNPV_i$ is non-negative. In comparative choice, project i will be chosen first if $SNPV_i = \max \{SNPV_i\}, i = 1, 2, \ldots$.

IV. THE SOCIAL RATE OF TIME DISCOUNTING

IV-1 Does Social Time Preference Exist?

The social rate of discounting must be related to social time preference in some way. In order that there be a social rate of time discount, there must exist a social time preference. There is no consensus among economists who have considered this problem. In fact some very distinguished economists have cast doubt on the existence of such a preference. Pigou wrote that "our telescopic faculty is defective, and ... we therefore see future pleasures, as it were, on a diminished scale, ... [This] does not imply that any economic dissatisfaction would be suffered if future pleasures were substituted at full value for present ones."[5] Since social time preferences must be a positive function of individual time preferences, if the individuals prefer present consumption to future consumption, then the same would hold for society as a whole. What Pigou seems to be saying is that individuals have inadequate foresight, hence social time preferences cannot be wholly based on individual time preferences. Society as a whole might be wiser and act wiser. Similar thoughts have been expressed by others. Ramsay, whose 1928 article on savings has played a pivotal role in recent researches, wrote that pure time discount is something that "arises merely from the weakness of imagination."[6] Harrod who can be regarded as the father of modern dynamic economics uses more colorful language to describe pure time preference as "a polite expression for rapacity and the conquest of reason by passion."[7]

However weighty these statements may be, if a given social time preference is to reflect individual time preferences, then individual time preferences have to be taken as they are. Hence the imperfections and inadequacies of individual preferences are largely irrelevant. One cannot but agree with Eckstein that "a social welfare function based on consumers' sovereignty must accept people's tastes including their intertemporal preferences."[8]

The great majority of economists, however, recognize on the basis of their observations of individual behavior, that time preference does prevail and that individuals do prefer present to future consumption.

It is theoretically possible, however, to show that under certain assumptions an individual might prefer future to present consumption. Indeed Samuelson has demonstrated, though under very special and rather abstract assumptions, that such a possibility does exist.[9] It is not rare to find in some rather stationary societies, individuals actually making payments to have their money stored, till a time when they would need them more.

Barring some very special cases, there are good reasons to believe that, in general, people prefer present to future consumption. First, an individual knows he will not live forever and that his capacity to enjoy consumption will decline. Second, the future is always more uncertain than the present and a sure thing is preferred to a less sure thing. Third, in general, a person's concern for the welfare of successive generations dwindles. Fourth, so far historically it has been true that per capita real income has been increasing, and it is expected to continue to rise; hence the marginal utility of a unit of future consumption to an individual is less than that of a present unit of consumption.

These indicators notwithstanding, it is very difficult to construct a social time preference due to the well-known problems associated with interpersonal and intertemporal comparisons. While these comparisons shall not be discussed here, some comments which question the reasonableness of the concept of the social time preference as such, will be dealt with.

Following Pigou, there has been a group of economists, including many contemporaries, who advocate that the social rate of discounting ought to be lower than the market rate of discounting, implying that the market discount rate does not reflect the social discount rate. It may not even reflect the private discount rate due to various market imperfections and state interventions in the money and financial markets. The various arguments related to this debate are discussed in section V.

In the following subsection it is assumed that a social time preference map exists. The equilibrium rate of social discounting is treated along the lines of Fisher's contributions.

IV-2 Social Rate of Discounting and Social Time Preference

Recent discussions of the social discount rate involving a social time preference map start from the basic contribution by Irving Fisher.[10] Hirshleifer, Bailey and Feldstein[11] have made a definitive presentation and extension of Fisher's ideas. Their analysis starts with the assumption that it is possible to construct a social time preference map.

For convenience, consider a two period analysis which can then be extended to more periods. Social time preference is the measure of the degree of preference which society attaches to a unit of consumption in year t as compared with that in year $t+1$. This can be estimated by the amount of consumption in year *t+1* which will compensate the society for one unit of foregone consumption in year *t*. In other words, social time preference is the marginal rate of substitution consumption in year *t+1* for consumption in year *t*. The rate of social time preference is the excess of the marginal rate of substitution of consumption between the two periods in excess of unity. In the following figure, the *U*'s represent indifferent levels of society's welfare between consumptions in years *t* and *t+1*. The slope at any point on any of this society's time indifference curves gives the marginal rate of substitution between the consumptions of the two periods at that point.

Fig. 6.4. Intertemporal Equilibrium

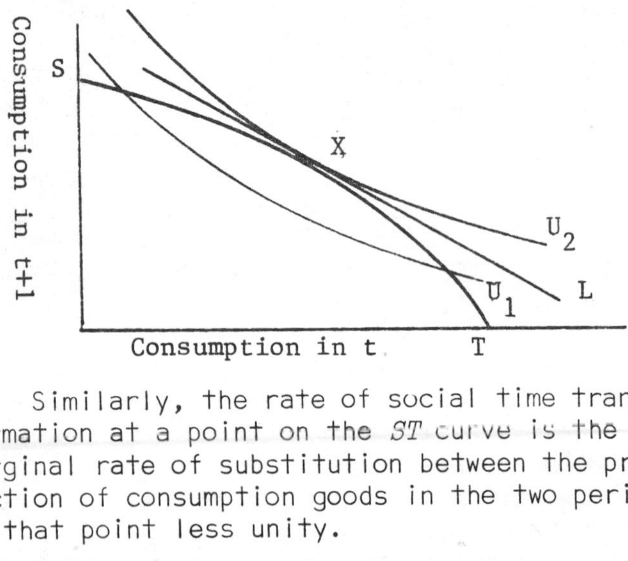

Similarly, the rate of social time transformation at a point on the *ST* curve is the marginal rate of substitution between the production of consumption goods in the two periods at that point less unity.

In equilibrium, the rate of the social time preference would be equal to the rate of the social time transformation. This is shown at point *X*. At point *X* the social transformation curve touches the highest social preference curve between periods *t* and *t+1*. The equilibrium rate of social time discounting at *X* is given by the slope of line *L* less unity; line *L* is tangent to both the social time preference curve and the social time transformation curve.

It is seen that if the social time preference map can be unambiguously constructed and the social time transformation curve is known, then it is possible to derive the rate of social time discounting for each period. Under conditions of perfect competition, this rate might equal some "representative" market interest rate. But the introduction of the market interest rate raises questions of money and monetary policies, besides those of determining what the representative rate of interest is. Moreover, conditions of perfect competition and a perfect money market seldom hold, making the relationship between the rate of social time discounting and the market interest rate rather tenuous.

The central question is whether the rate of social time discounting can be approached without invoking some market rate of interest under presumably perfect and real market conditions. This seems tremendously difficult if not an impossible task. As mentioned before, the difficulties surrounding the construction of a social welfare function are insurmountable. The situation is worsened by the fact that social welfare functions are partly dependent on the investment decisions expected to be made and the investments expected to be undertaken. The usual problems of changes in taste and technology are present here as in all dynamic economics. The most serious failure, however, is the inability of economists and social scientists to overcome the difficulties associated with interpersonal and intertemporal comparisons.

V. SOCIAL DISCOUNT RATE AND THE PRIVATE (MARKET) RATE

V-1 Theoretical Justification for a Lower Social Rate of Discounting

Recently, Marglin[12] has built a theoretical framework on the earlier works of Sen[13] and Steiner,[14] to show that there is a logical justification for the social discount rate to be lower than the market rate. He deals with a model in which provision for the next generation as a group (not for one's heirs) is the only motivation for saving: It is supposed (1) that time is divided into two periods, "present" and "future"; (2) that all members of the community alive now die at the end of the present, their places being taken by individuals who spring into existence fully grown at the beginning of the future; (3) that no investment undertaken in the present yields its fruits until the future; (4) that the same investment opportunities are open to all individuals, and finally (5) that all individuals are alike in the sense that they have similar time-preference maps.

If there are n individuals in the community, then the change in utility from the point of view of each individual if everybody invests one dollar is

$$\delta U_i = -1 + \alpha kn - \beta(n-1)$$

where δU_i is the utility, k the marginal rate of transformation between future and present consumption, α the marginal value an individual places on consumption by members of the next generation relative to his own consumption, and β the marginal value he places on consumption by contemporaries relative to his own.[15]

Each is made better off if $\delta U_i > 0$, $i = 1, 2, \ldots n$. This is when $\alpha kn \geq 1 + \beta(n-1)$. Thus, each is made better off so long as the marginal gross gain from the total investment of n dollars, αkn, exceeds the loss of utility from his personal sacrifice plus the psychic loss he feels because others' sacrifices $1 + \beta(n-1)$.

The marginal private discount rate of individual i is the marginal utility to him of consumption by a member of the next generation, less unity. The marginal private rate of discounting, therefore,

$$r^i_{pri} = \frac{1}{\alpha} - 1.$$

The marginal social rate of discount of individual i, on the other hand, is his net marginal rate of substitution of future for present consumption on the assumption that his sacrifice is accompanied by the sacrifices of everyone else in the community. The marginal social rate of discounting

$$r^i_{soc} = \frac{1 + (n-1)\beta}{n\alpha} - 1.$$

For large n, the above expression becomes approximately

$$r^i_{soc} \cong \frac{\beta}{\alpha} - 1.$$

Since $\beta < 1$, $r^i_{pri} > r^i_{soc}$. The policy implications which Marglin derives from this are that the rate of interest determined in an atomistic competitive market need have <u>no</u> normative significance in the planning of collective investment, and that the market determined rate of investment need <u>not</u> be optimal in any welfare sense. Marglin's conclusion on the basis of his analysis is that in the evaluation of public projects, the social rate of discounting ought to be lower than the market rate of interest.

V-2 Social Rate of Discounting, Some Rebuttals

The inadequacy of Marglin's model and the inadmissibility of the conclusions derived therefrom have been pointed by several writers. Tullock[16] commented that an individual is confronted with a choice among four alternatives. He can (a) consume, (b) save for his own and his posterity's future consumption, (c) make charitable gifts to his contemporaries and (d) make charitable contributions to future generations. Marlgin's equations combine the two present-day alternatives (a) and (c) and put them in opposition to the two future alternatives (b) and (d), also combined. It is easiest to consider first the two private ways in which an individual can use his funds, (a) and (b). In making the standard comparison of present sacrifice and future gain, the individual will invest or disinvest until his personal rate of discount equals the market rate. He will follow similar stipulations in deciding between (c) and (d).

The decision between gifts to contemporaries and gifts to the future must be made within the income allotted to charity. According to Marglin's equations, it appears that the equilibrium for the individual will be reached at one extreme or the other. If $\alpha k > \beta$ all gifts would be made to the future; if $\alpha k < \beta$ all gifts would be made to the present. "In making decisions on whether or not to make charitable gifts, individually or collectively, we normally do not evaluate the value to us of further consumption by "all" members of the community, but only by those who are less well of than ourselves. An increase in the consumption of someone who is already consuming more than we, does not improve our satisfaction."[17]

Dan Usher has also cast similar doubts on the validity of Marglin's conclusions. He argues that altruism alone is not sufficient to cause the actual rate of investment to differ from the socially optimal rate. "For this it is necessary that man be on the whole more future oriented in their altruism than they are in sharing consumption between themselves and their own children."[18]

Lind[19] has extended Marglin's model by introducing elements of realism which go a long way to shake and rebut Marglin's conclusions. Noting that generations overlap, Lind redefines the marginal utility function of the ith individual by

$$\delta U_i = -t_i - \beta_i \sum_{k \neq i} t_k + k\,\gamma_i t_i + k\alpha_i \sum_{k \neq i} t_k$$

where t_k is the change in the level of investment of the kth individual; t_k may be positive, negative or zero. γ_i represents the marginal utility to the ith individual of an additional unit of future cosumption, and β_i the marginal value individual i places on consumption by contemporaries relative to his own, and α_i the marginal value an individual i places on consumption by members of the next generation relative to his own consumption. Assuming all the individual identical, the above equation reduces for $t_i = 1$, to

$$\delta U_i = -1 - \beta(n-1) + k\gamma + k\alpha(n-1).$$

The above equation departs from Marglin's in the fact that the marginal utility of one's own future consumption is separated from the other $n-1$ individuals. It would be appropriate to assume $\gamma > \alpha$. An individual can invest for his own and his children's future or for the future of others. These two investment opportunities are associated with rates of discount which are $1/\gamma - 1$ and $1/\alpha - 1$ respectively. The lower of the two rates, viz., $1/\gamma - 1$, will be the operative rate.

In equilibrium, the marginal rate of substitution between present and future consumption $1/\gamma$ is equal to the marginal rate of transformation k. Each individual would invest one unit of consumption if $\delta U_i \geqq 0$, i.e., if $k(\gamma + (n-1)\alpha) \geqq 1 + (n-1)\beta$. The rate of discount associated with this joint investment opportunity is given by

$$r^* = k-1 = \frac{1 + (n-1)\beta}{\gamma + (n-1)\alpha} - 1,$$

which for large n approximates $\beta/\alpha - 1$. In this extended model, the social rate of discount, $\beta/\alpha - 1$, may be greater than, less than or equal to the private $1/\gamma - 1$.

If $\beta/\alpha > 1/\gamma = k$, everyone will be better off if an agreement is reached that each individual decreases his investment by one unit. This follows from the fact that $\delta U_i = 1 + (n-1)\beta - k(\gamma + (n-1)\alpha) > 0$ for $\beta/\alpha > 1/\gamma = k$. If $\beta/\alpha < 1/\gamma = k$, the reverse will be true. In the first case, the social rate is larger than the private rate, implying that an individual would, given the opportunity, choose to have his neighbors invest <u>less</u> for their future and their children's future than he would himself choose to invest and in the second case, the reverse will be true. However, it seems reasonable to assume that each one of the individuals considers the allocation which is optimal for himself, also to be optimal, from his point of view, for people just like him. This implies that $\beta/\alpha = 1/\gamma$, and thus private and social rates of discount are equal.

When we consider a large society with individuals having different incomes and preferences, it may be that for some i, $\beta_i/\alpha_i < 1/\gamma_i$ and for some others $\beta_i/\alpha_i > 1/\gamma_i$. By assumption $1/\gamma_i = k$ in equilibrium, so that $k\gamma_i t_i - t_i = 0$ for all i. If we further assume

$$\sum_{i=1}^{n} t_i = a > 0,$$

then

$$\delta U_i = t_i - \beta_i \sum_{k\neq 1} t_k + k\gamma_i t_i + k\alpha_i \sum_{k\neq 1} t_k$$

$$= (k\alpha_i - \beta_i)(a - t_i)$$

In order $\delta U_i \geqq 0$, t_i must be greater than a when β_i/α_i is greater than $k = 1/\gamma_i$ and it must be less than a when β_i/α_i is less than $k = 1/\gamma_i$. Clearly we can choose such a set of t_i, but we can also choose t_i's such that

$$\sum_{i=1}^{n} t_i = 0 \text{ or } < 0.$$

The implication of all this is that the utility of every individual can be increased by agreements under which some will increase investment, others will decrease it and still others will leave it unchanged. It is evident that the crucial consideration here is the distribution of investment among individuals rather than the level of total investment.

The two salient points, as Lind rightly claims, which emerge from his analysis are: (1) if each individual, given the market equilibrium, feels that the marginal rate at which he is willing to trade present for future consumption is correct for every other individual, then his private and social discount rate are equal and the market rate of interest is of normative significance. In a society whose members have similar preferences and incomes, it is reasonable to assume that the private rate and social rate will coincide and the market rate will be no different. This is intuitively clear since when all individuals are assumed to have identical preferences, then all the problems of aggregation and interpersonal comparisons cease to exist and social time preference becomes identical with individual private preference. (2) Given a large population with varying incomes and preference maps, it is reasonable to assume that interdependence effects will be such that in equilibrium $\beta_i/\alpha_i - 1$ will be above the market rate for some i individuals and below it for others. In this case the market solution is not Pareto optimal as social agreements are available that will make everyone better off with or without changing the total level of investment as such. Thus <u>it is not possible, in general, to achieve a Pareto optimum by setting the interest rate at any level, and in this sense there is no social rate of discount</u>. Again this assertion is intuitively obvious as it is premised on the circumstance that since a social preference map cannot be constructed from the preference maps of individuals with different incomes and different individual preference maps. Lind concludes, "Thus, in a large community whose members have varied preference maps and incomes, the preference of interdependence effects necessitates a political solution to both the problem of how much of the community's resources should be invested and the problem of how much of this total should be undertaken by each individual."

V.3 Equilization Principle

We have seen that under assumption of perfect competition, the rate of social time preference, the rate of social time transformation, and the market rate of interest are all equal.

If so, the rate of social time discounting which represents the social time preference must equal either the rate of social time transformation or the market rate of interest or both. Many economists have advocated that the rate of social time discounting ought to be determined with reference to these rates.

Stockfish[20] has suggested that in evaluating government projects, the rate of discount should equal the average rate of return before taxes in the private sector. The reasoning is that most resource using activities permit substitution between different kind of resources, and government activities "serve private ends by providing instrumental services and products" and draw upon the same stock of resources as private producers. Therefore the same discount rate that is encountered in the private sector, ought to be employed in the public sector. For if it is not done, it will lead to many anomalies. A low discount rate in the public sector would justify the use of capital intensive production methods, and more durable and longer-lasting buildings and equipments in the public sector than in the private sector. There seems to be no rational justification to promulgate such behavior. And such an allocation of resources is bound to be inefficient.

Some economists criticize the equalization principle on the ground that it assumes that the level and the structure of rates revealed in the private sector of the economy are optimal. It is true that the optimality of rates prevailing in the private sector has not been proved, and may not ever be proved. But the proponents of the equalization principle maintain that this criticism is irrelevant. "To invest resources purposefully in activities where the return is lower than the highest attainable is simply wasteful and inefficient, whether the highest rate of return is optimal or not."[21]

In order to arrive at a rate of social time discounting on the basis of the rate of return in the private sector, a measure of the marginal efficiency of investment is needed. A rate of return concept, however, seems to imply that rates of return are equal in all lines of activity. But in reality no such equality exists. This may be due to lack of perfect equilibrium at any given time or due to differences in the risks encountered.

The rate of return has to be estimated on the basis of earning assets. These include inventory, net plant and equipment, and accounts receivable; they exclude cash and other short-term liquid assets, and securities and long-term debt that a company may hold as an investment.

The rate of return should be estimated before corporate and property taxes. The government does not have to pay taxes. On the other hand, it shares in the yield from private investment and experiences a loss of tax revenues if it causes resources to be diverted from investment in the private sector.

The above paragraphs suggest the derivation of the rate of social time discounting from the rate of return on physical assets and equipment. Some other economists, Baumol[3] among them, while emphasizing the correctness of this line of reasoning, link the rate of social time discounting to the rate of return on a riskless bond. "The correct discount rate is the percentage rate of return that the resources utilized would otherwise provide in the private sector."[4]

When a government withdraws resources from the private sector it must take them from what would have been consumed by consumers or what would have been invested by business firms. Consumers' goods do not provide a rate of return that is directly measurable, but when a consumer voluntarily purchases a bond with a return of say r per cent he indicates that this rate of return compensates him for giving up a dollar's worth of present consumption. But to consumers who do not purchase any bonds, their time preference must be such that the rate of time discounting is higher than percent. This is equally true for a man who fails to purchase bonds because he cannot afford them.

It is not the rate on short-term securities, but the yield of the long-term bonds which is relevant for the purpose of determining the rate of social time discounting. This is because when the resources are withdrawn from the private sector, they are put into projects lasting for 30 to 50 years. However, it is the rate of return on <u>riskless</u> long-term bonds which would reflect the "pure" rate of time discounting. Baumol suggests that for "all practical purposes a government bond can be considered to be such a riskless security."[5]

As for the resources withdrawn from the business firms, Baumol's suggestion is that the rate of return before taxes on public utilities should provide the guidelines for the determination of the discount rate. Baumol falls short of suggesting any specific way of combining the rate on long-term riskless government bonds and the rate of before-tax returns on public utilities. It may be surmised that a weighted average of the two rates would serve as the rate of discounting, the weights being the proportions in which resources are withdrawn from consumption and investment respectively.

The upshot of the discussion in this subsection is that a great many economists are of the opinion that the rate of discounting in the public sector (or rate of social time discounting) must be the same as that in the private sector under conditions of competitive market equilibrium and that it must not be less than the rate of return on long-term government bonds.

V-4 Conditions of Imperfect Competition

When conditions of perfect competition do not hold, the rates of return on bonds and yields in the private sector may not serve as proper guidelines for the determination of the social rate of discounting. A typical situation is that when the lending and borrowing rates differ and the two differ from the rate of return on physical investment. The situation is depicted by the following diagram.

Fig. 6.5. Different Lending and Borrowing Rates

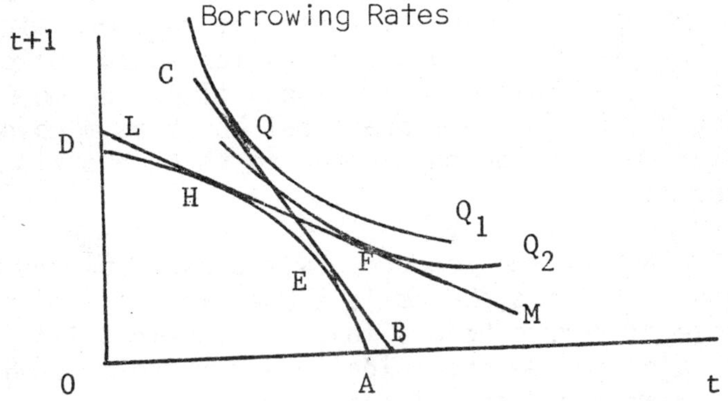

In the diagram above, *LM* and *BC* represent the lending and borrowing rates respectively in the market and the curve, *DA*, is the social time transformation curve. It is only at point *E* that the lending rate and the social rates of return are equal. It is advantageous to an individual to move to point *H* and then move along *LM* by borrowing to point *F* on his (and if all individuals are identical then also on the social) preference curve Q_2. But in this case, the way the diagram has been set up, it will be still more advantageous to the individual to move to point *E* on the transformation curve and then lend along *BC* to reach a still higher point *G* on Q_1.

The point is that when the lending and borrowing rates differ as they do in a less than perfectly competitive market (or in general when there are several market rates) there is no unique point of tangency and it is not certain which rate leads to the point on the social time transformation curve which might lead individuals to the highest social time preference curve. It stands to reason that the real rate of social time discounting ought to be somewhere between the lending and borrowing rates. Where there are several long-term market rates of interest, some average of these rates may be considered as an appropriate rate to be used for discounting in the social evaluation of projects. For instance, if there were only two long-term lending and borrowing rates as in the above figure, then the rate of discounting would be given by a point between E and H on the social time transformation curve. It will be equal to the slope of the curve on that point minus unity.

The discussion here is very simplistic, since it relates only to two periods with constant costs of borrowing and independent investment opportunities. The analysis becomes much more complicated when these assumptions are relaxed and the costs of borrowing are allowed to vary with the size of the loans and dependent investment opportunities are considered. The discussion of these and other aspects of the problem would take us too far afield.[25]

Summary

In non-trivial social choice of projects, basically two methods can be used. One is to derive the internal rate of return of each project and, in comparative choice, to select the project with the highest internal rate of return first and with the second highest internal rate of return next and so on. The main problem with the use of an internal rate of return is that in many cases there are more than one internal rate of return associated with individual projects, and very often the internal rates of return turn out to be imaginary. Therefore, projects can be selected according to an internal rate of return criterion only when each of the projects under consideration has a unique internal rate of return. If this were the case, the criterion of internal rates of return have the great merit that they do not require the knowledge of the social rate of time discounting. However, even when the projects have unique internal rates of return, their use in the selection process would be justifiable only when the social rate of discounting can be assumed to remain constant.

The second criterion is based on the net present value of individual projects. In absolute choice, a project is chosen if its net present value is positive. In comparative choice, the project with the highest net present value is chosen first and with the second highest present value next and so on. The most difficult problem involved in this criterion is that it requires the predetermination of the social rate of time discounting.

Because of the impossibility of interpersonal and intertemporal comparisons, the possibility of constructing an unambiguous social time preference is very remote. if not nil. Hence a social rate of time discounting can hardly be deduced a priori from constructs of social time preferences. Therefore the determination of the social rate of time discounting has to be based on observable indicators and parameters. It has been shown that under conditions of competitive equilibrium, the slope of the market interest rate line, the social time transformation and the social time preference curves, are equal or tend to be equal. Therefore, the social rate of time discounting can either be derived on the basis of the long-term market interest rates or on the basis of the rates of return on productive investments in the market.

Some economists have asserted that the social rate of discounting ought to be lower than the market rate of interest. It has been shown that such assertions are based on either partial or inadequate assumptions. Further it has been argued that in the social evaluation of projects, the application of discount rates which are lower than the market interest rate might lead to inefficiency and waste of resources. It is, therefore, suggested that the rate of social discounting should not differ markedly from the long-term market interest rate.

The fact that conditions of competitive equilibrium are seldom perfect weakens the link between the rate of social time discounting and the market interest rate. In reality, there is no one long-term market interest rate, nor is there one rate of return in each industry. In practice, therefore, a weighted average of these rates will have to be relied upon.

Footnotes

1 These problems have been discussed by J. Hirshleifer, in "On the Theory of Optimal Investment Decision:, Journal of Political Economy, August 1958.

2 These examples are from Hirshleifer (op. cit.) who borrowed them from references cited by him.

3 Martin J. Bailey, "Formal Criteria for Investment Decisions," Journal of Political Economy, October 1959.

4 Hirshleifer, op. cit.

5 A.C. Pigou, Economics of Welfare (1920) 4th edition (London: Macmillan Company, 1932), p. 25.

6 F. P. Ramsay, "A Mathematical Theory of Saving" Economic Journal (December 1928).

7 R. F. Harrod, Toward a Dynamic Economics (London, 1948), p. 48.

8 Otto Eckstein, "Investment Criteria for Economic Development and the Theory of Intertemporal Welfare Economics," Quarterly Journal of Economics (February 1957), p. 75 (footnote).

9 P. A. Samuelson, "An Exact Consumption Loan Model of Interest with or without Social Contrivance of Money," Journal of Political Economy (December 1958).

10 Irving Fisher, The Theory of Interest (New York: Macmillan Co., 1930).

11 J. Hirshleifer, "On the Theory of Optimal Investment Decision," Journal of Political Economy (October 1959); M.S. Feldstein, "The Social Time Preference Discount Rate in Cost-Benefit Analysis," Economic Journal (June 1964).

12 Stephen A. Marglin: "The Social Rate of Discount and the O-timal Rate of Investment," Quarterly Journal of Economics (February 1965).

13 A. K. Sen, "On Optimizing the Rate of Saving: A Note," Economic Journal (December 1956).

14 O. P. Steiner, "Choosing Among Alternative Public Investments in the Water Resource Field," American Economic Review, vol. XLIX (December 1959).

15 The derivation of the formulation is as follows: the utility function of the ith individual can be written formally as $\upsilon_i = \upsilon_i(C_i, C_f, C_p - C_f)$, where C_i is his own consumption, C_f and C_p are the consumption of future and present generations. Marginal utility function of the ith individual is

$$U = \frac{\partial U_i}{\partial C_i} C_i + \frac{\partial U_i}{\partial C_f} C_f + \frac{\partial U_i}{\partial (C_p - \bar{C}_i)} (C_p - C_i).$$

By assumption $\frac{\partial U_l}{\partial C_l} = 1$, $\frac{\partial U_l}{\partial C_f} = \alpha$. This gives $U_l = C_l + \alpha C_f + \beta(C_p - C_l)$.

Investment of one dollar by each individual, means $C_l = 1$, $C_f = kn$,

$C_p - C_l = n-1$.

16 Gordon Tullock, "The Social Rate of Discount and the Optimal Rate of Investment: Comment," Quarterly Journal of Economics, May 1964.

17 Tullock, ibid.

18 Don Usher, "The Social Rate of Discount and the Optimal Rate of Investment: Comment," Quarterly Journal of Economics, May 1964.

19 Robert C. Lind, "Further Comment," Quarterly Journal of Economics, May 1964.

20 Jacob A. Stockfish, "The Interest Rate Applicable to Government Investment Projects," in H. H. Hinricks and G. M. Taylor, (eds.) Program Budgeting and Benefit-Cost Analysis, Goodyear Publishing Co., Inc. (California, 1969).

21 Stockfish, ibid., p. 192.

22 William J. Baumol, "On the Appropriate Discount Rate for Evaluation of Public Projects,: statement from the Planning-Programming-Budgeting System: Progress and Potentials (Hearings before the Sub-Committee on Economy in Government of the Joint Economic Committee, Congress of the United States, 90th Congress, 1st Session, U. S. Government Pringtin Office, Washington D.C., 1967.

23 Baumol, ibid. , Reprinted in H. H. Hinricks and G. M. Taylor (eds.) op. cit. p. 203.

F. P. Ramsay, "A Mathematical Theory of Saving" *Economic Journal* (December 1928).

R. F. Harrod, *Toward a Dynamic Economics* (London, 1948), p. 48.

Otto Eckstein, "Investment Criteria for Economic Developme-t and the Theory of Intertemporal Welfare Economics," *Quarterly Journal of Economics* (February 1957), P. 75 (footnote).

P. A. Samuelson, "An Exact Consumption Loan Model of Interest with or without Social Contrivance of Money," *Journal of Political Economy* (December 1958).

Irving Fisher, *The Theory of Interest* (New York: Macmillan Co., 1930).

J. Hirshleifer, "On the Theory of Optimal Investment Decision," *Journal of Political Economy* (October 1959); MS. Feldstein, "The Social Time Preference Discount Rate in Cost-Benefit Analysis," *Economic Journal* (June 1964).

Stephen A. Marglin: "The Social Rate of Discount and the Optimal Rate of Investment," *Quarterly Journal of Economics* (February 1965).

A.K. Sen, "On Optimizing the Rate of Saving: A Note,: *Economic Journal*

Chapter Seven

RISK AND UNCERTAINTY

I. INTRODUCTION

I-1 Preliminary Remarks

The elements of risk and uncertainty enter into any study whenever the values of variables cannot be measured perfectly, which is almost always the case. In practical affairs, as well as theoretical analysis, it is usual to ignore uncertainty as if the values of variables could be predicted accurately. However, the world is all too dominated by uncertainty and risk, and an analysis that is to be applicable in the real world cannot afford to ignore them. Unfortunately the conceptual difficulties associated with the problems of uncertainty and risk are very great; consequently, cost-benefit investigations generally employ the superficial model of a world of certainty with some rough and ready adjustments made to allow for risk and uncertainty. For example, costs may include an item for contingency for all unexpected and unforeseen costs, but the higher the proportion of the amount set aside for contingency to total cost, the less accurate the evaluation of the project would be. In the same way, benefits may be conservatively or liberally evaluated in the absence of precise information and due to a lack of an adequate analysis of uncertainty. Similarly, instead of arriving at an approximate rate, a higher discount rate than the certainty rate may be used for deriving the present value of a risky project. This again may not be appropriate in all cases. For these reasons, the treatment of risk and uncertainty must be painstakingly pursued, despite all the difficulties of getting adequate solutions.

I-2 Uncertainty Versus Risk

In the literature the terms uncertainty and risk are generally used interchangeably. According to strict definitions, the two terms are not synonymous. Uncertainty describes a situation in which no idea of how events will occur is available. Risk describes a situation in which perfectly accurate information does not exist but some information about the occurrence of the events is available. In particular, from past observation or from some deductive reasoning, probabilities can be ascribed to the occurrence of events. In the case of uncertainty, strictly speaking, there is hardly any scientific method which can be applied to determine the values of variables and parameters. But in risky situations, probability analysis can be used to estimate the approximate values of variables and parameters.

In view of the above, the following discussion should use only the term risk. But, in keeping with the general usage, the two terms will be used interchangeably.

I-3 Plan of the Chapter

Section II of the chapter discusses the conceptual and technical problems associated with the derivation of probabilities of an event or a variable, their expected values and variances. Section III discusses various approaches to handle uncertainty problems, such as the construction of an uncertainty indifference map, the introduction of risk discounting, and the creation of equalization fund. Section IV contains a brief discussion of the game theoretic approach and various criteria of estimation are stated. In section V, the controversy surrounding risky or riskless discount rates in public and private investment projects is dealt with.

II. CONCEPTUAL AND TECHNICAL PROBLEMS[1]

II-1 Basis of Estimation

When an event or variable does not take on some value with certainty, the way to estimate it is first to find the probabilities with which it takes on various values. This can be done from past observations or it can be derived from some theoretical considerations. After the probability distribution of the variable has been established, the next step is to decide the procedure to be used for arriving at the most representative value of the variable. The three most common procedures are the mode, the median and the mean.

The mode is that value of the variable which has the highest probability. The median is the middle value over the range of variation of the variable. The mean is the sum of the values of the variable multiplied by their probabilities. In common practice, the mode and the median are often used to estimate the values of variables which are not known with certainty. But these procedures might not give correct results in a good many cases. The mean, on the other hand, may be off the actual value in some cases, but on the average it gives correct results when the variable to be estimated is involved in many roughly identical projects and its mean is thus based upon repeated sampling and large sample sizes. For illustration consider the following table:

Value of Variable	Probability of Occurrence
10	.09
20	.10
40	.19
60	.17
70	.15
80	.13
90	.11
100	.09

The modal value of the variable is 40 as this is the value which is most frequently occurring. But to evaluate the variable at this figure would be incorrect because the variable will assume this value in 19% cases only. If the variable appears in many identical projects, its realized value will be the mean 60.7. The median value of the variable may be between 60 and 70 and in general may be off from the mean.

To give a concrete example to show how the estimation of variables using modal values may be misleading, consider an example of sales and prices. Suppose it has been determined that there is a 65 per cent chance that the sales will be 80 units and a 35 per cent chance that they will be 40 units. Further it has been predicted that there is a 65 per cent chance that the sales price will be $20 and a 35 per cent chance that the sales price will be $10. If the estimation is based on modal values the value of sales would be $1600. However, a probability appraisal might show that this is not the correct estimate of the most likely revenue. Assuming that the price and sales are not correlated, the probability distribution of the revenue may be as follows:

Price	Sales	Probability	Revenue
20	80	40	$1600
20	40	25	800
10	80	25	800
10	40	10	400

The illustration shows that the most likely revenue is $800 with a probability of 50 per cent rather than $1600 with a probability of 40%. The example shows that when a variable is a product of several different variables, its simple modal value will not give a correct estimate. Nor will the product of the modal values of individual variables give an accurate measure.

It is evident that under conditions of uncertainty the arithmatic mean is a better and safer measure than other procedures. When the variable is involved in many identical projects, the accuracy of its measure will increase with the number of projects.

11-2 Correlated Variables

A crucial consideration in assessing the magnitude of variables is that they are often correlated with one another. If this correlation is not judiciously handled, the estimation may go wrong and the variance of the estimated values may increase. This may be explained by the following example. Suppose there is a 50-50 per cent chance that the sales of a commodity would be 400 units or 200 units. Suppose further that there is a 50-50 per cent chance that the price would be \$20.00 or \$10.00. Suppose the possibility of correlation between the quantity of sales and sale price is ignored, then the mean value of the quantity of sales would be 300 units, the mean value of the sale price would be \$15, and the expected amount of revenue would be \$450. However, if we recognize the correlation possibilities, we might observe that the data show that the amount of sales equals 400 units when the price equals \$10, and that it equals 200 units when the price equals \$20. Now the expected revenue would be

$$\frac{(\$400 \times 10 + \$200 \times 20)}{2} = \$400.$$

It is, therefore, necessary that correlation possibilities be considered when the expected value of a variable is derived.

Discrepancies and biased estimates result when correlation aspects are not completely specified. Therefore, if significant correlations among the variables of a problem are suspected, it would be advisable to recognize and to discover the underlying systematic relationships.

11-3 Probability Distributions of Basic and Dependent Variables

It is essential that the probability distribution of the basic (or explanatory) variables be determined first. Then the probability distribution of the dependent variables should be derived to estimate its expected value. In other words, it is inappropriate to estimate the expected values of the explanatory variables from their probability distributions and then to derive the expected value of the dependent variable, except when the relationship between the explanatory variable and the dependent variable is perfectly linear. To illustrate, suppose the agricultural yield is a nonlinear function of rainfall given by the following relationship:

$$Y = 50 = 10W - .1W^2$$

Suppose that the frequency distribution of rainfall measured in inches is 20" with a probability of .3, 40" with that of .5, and 50" with .2. The mean rainfall would be 36". Substitution of 36" for W in the above equation gives the agricultural yield equal to 280 units.

However, if the probability distribution of the agricultural yield corresponding to the probability distribution of the rainfall is generated, the following yields corresponding to their probabilities result:

Units of Yield	Probability	W
210	.3	20"
290	.5	40"
300	.2	50"

With the above probability distribution of agricultural yields, the mean or expected value would be 210 x .3 + 290 x .5 + 300 x .2 = 268 units. It is evident that the estimate of the yield on the basis of its own probability distribution would give more accurate results than the one based on the mean value of the explanatory variable, rainfall.

The problem can be explained by another example which is of great relevance in project evaluation. This is the estimation of the values of outputs and/or inputs. Suppose the frequency distribution of the quantity and price of a good is as in the table below:

Quantity	Probability	Price	Revenue or Cost
100	.2	25	2500
200	.3	20	4000
300	.4	15	4500
400	.1	10	4000
mean=240		mean=18	mean=3900

If the value of the output or input is estimated by multiplying the mean of the quantity by the mean of the price, the result is 4320. But if the revenue or cost is estimated by multiplying their different levels with their corresponding probabilities and then summing, the result is 3900. Again this latter figure is more accurate and reliable than the first.

In principle it can be stated that the value of a variable ought to be estimated by generating its own probability distribution rather than on the basis of the mean values of its explanatory variables. The estimate will be biased if one is using the means of the probability distributions of the elementary explanatory variables to derive a mean of the aggregate or dependent variable. This is because the dependent variable takes on values corresponding to the values taken on by the elementary variables and because it is not necessary that the elementary variables take on their mean values. Even if they do, it is not necessary that the dependent variable will take on its mean value when the elementary variables do. This is evident from the above examples.

This situation is also the reason why the mean of a variable which is a non-linear function of some elementary variables is not equal to the value of the function when the mean values of the elementary variables are substituted in it. Thus in general, as in the agricultural yield example given above,

$$Y \neq 10 + 5C\overline{W} - .1\overline{W}^2,$$

and in the sales and price example

$$\overline{R} \neq \overline{p}\,\overline{q},$$

where the bars on the top of the variables indicate their mean values.

II-4 Variance of Estimates

The variance of a variable is the sum of the squares of the differences of its values from its mean multiplied by the probabilities of the corresponding values of the variable. Thus the variance of a variable X is given by

$$\Sigma(X_t - \overline{X})^2\, p_t$$

where p_t is the probability of X taking on value X_t and $\overline{X}$ is the mean value of X. The less the actual value of X differs from its mean, the smaller is the variance. Hence it is a good index of the stability and reliability of the estimate. The estimate of a variable is more reliable, the smaller is its variance.

When a variable is a sum of two or more elementary variables, the mean or the expected value of the variable is sum of the mean of the elementary variables. However, the variance of the variable will differ according to the correlation among them. Suppose the benefit of a project is the sum of the two benefits B_1 and B_2. Suppose first that B_1 and B_2 are not correlated and their probability distribution and that of their sum are given as below:

Probability	B_1	B_2	B	Mean and Variance
.25	60	50	110	$\overline{B}$ = 140
.25	60	70	130	
.25	100	50	150	Var (B) = 500
.25	100	70	170	

Suppose however that B_1 and B_2 are correlated and that whenever B_1 takes on the higher value so does B_2, so that the probability distribution of B_1 and B_2 and B are given as below

Probability	B_1	B_2	B	Mean and Variance
.5	60	50	110	$\overline{B}$ = 140
.5	100	70	170	Var (B) = 900

The above shows that when the components are correlated the variance of the total benefit may increase, if the larger values of the components occur together and so do the smaller. On the contrary when the larger value of one component occurs with the smaller value of the other, the variance of the benefit will decrease as is evident from the following table.

Probability	B_1	B_2	B	Mean and Variance
.5	60	70	130	$\overline{B}$ = 140
.5	100	50	150	Var (B) = 100

Obviously, with the mean of the benefit being the same, the project whose benefits are characterized by the second type of correlation would be preferable to the first. It would also be preferable to the case when there is no correlation.

11-5 Variance of Several Variables

In project evaluation, a variable of interest is often the sum or product of several other variables. And the variance of the main variable is a function of the variances of the component variables.

If a variable X is sum of variables Y and Z, then

$$\begin{aligned} V(X) &= V(Y+Z) \\ &= E[(Y+Z)^2] = E[Y^2+Z^2+2YZ] \\ &= E[Y^2] + E[Z^2] + 2E[YZ] \end{aligned}$$

If Y and Z are independent then $E[YZ] = 0$, so that the variance of the aggregate variable is the sum of the variances of its components, i.e.,

$$V(X) = V(Y) + V(Z)$$

If a variable Q is product of two variables Y and Z, then

$$\begin{aligned} V(Q) &= V(YZ) \\ &\simeq [E(Y)]^2V(Z)+[E(Z)]^2V(Y) \\ &\qquad +2E(Y)E(Z)E\{(Y-E(Y))(Z-E(Z))\} \end{aligned}$$

When Y and Z are independent, the exact formulation is

$$V(Q) = V(YZ) = [E(Y)]^2V(Z)+[E(Z)]^2V(Y)+V(Y)V(Z).$$

These formulas can be generalized for larger number of variables.*

To illustrate the formula for variance for the sum of the variables, let the present value of net benefits of a project be represented by

*For the derivation of these formulae refer to Leo A Goodman "On the Exact Variance of Products", Journal of American Statistical Association, 1960

$$R = B_o + aB_1 + a^2B_2 \ldots$$

where R is the present value, B_t is the net benefit in year t with a known probability distribution, and $a = (1 + r)^{-1}$ where r is the constant rate of discount, then the expected present value

$$E(R) = E(B_o) + aE(B_1) + a^2E(B_2) + \ldots$$

and the variance of R,

$$V(R) = V(B_o) + a^2V(B_1) + a^4V(B_2) + \ldots + a^{2t}V(B_t) + \ldots$$

when the annual net benefits are independent of each other. But if the net benefits are correlated then,

$$V(R) = V(B_o) + a^2V(B_1) + a^4V(B_2) + \ldots + a^{2t}V(B_t) + \ldots + 2a^2E(B_oB_1) + 2a^6E(B_1B_2) + \ldots + 2^{2t+2}E(B_tB_{t+1}) + \ldots$$

III. APPROACHES TO THE UNCERTAINTY PROBLEM

III-1 Certainty Equivalents

One of the frequently suggested approaches to deal with uncertainty is based on the concept of 'certainty equivalents'. The idea behind this concept is that to every risky situation there corresponds a riskless situation between which the decision-makers are indifferent. To illustrate, consider two situations. One represents a value of $100 with probability of .8, and of $500 with probability of .2. The expected value of the situations is $180. However, a decision-maker or decision-makers may be risk shy (or risk averters) and they may be indifferent between a situation representing a certain value of $150 (i.e., a value of $150 with probability equal to unity) and the first situation. On the contrary if the decision-makers are risk-takers, they may be indifferent between the risky situation with expected value of $180 and a riskless situation of $200 or more. Thus the certainty equivalent value is one which makes the decision-makers indifferent between this value with probability of unity and a set of other values with probabilities associated with a risky situation.

The certainty equivalent rule is that when a choice is to be made from a number of risky situations, the one with the highest certainty equivalent should be selected.

The concept of certainty equivalent, however, is not very helpful in practice, since it is not easy to determine the certainty equivalent of risky situations. This is because finding a certainty equivalent is nothing other than the evaluation of uncertain situations. Without some explicit criteria for solving the problem on a rational basis, no advance is made just by introducing a new terminology.

III-2 Uncertainty Indifference Map

A slightly explicit consideration of uncertainty is provided by constructing an uncertainty indifference map. The map represents a family of indifference curves, each of which joins points representing combinations of expected value and variance of the variable under study, among which the decision-makers are indifferent. In the following figure, the expected values are measured horizontally and variances vertically, and each point represents a combination of the two. The curved lines drawn join the points which are equally preferred by (or acceptable to) the decision-makers. The indifference curves slope upward to the right which is reasonable. It shows that a decision-maker is indifferent between point

A representing a higher expected value, but a higher variance too and point *B* representing a lower expected value but also a lower variance.

Fig. 7.1. Uncertainty Indifference Map

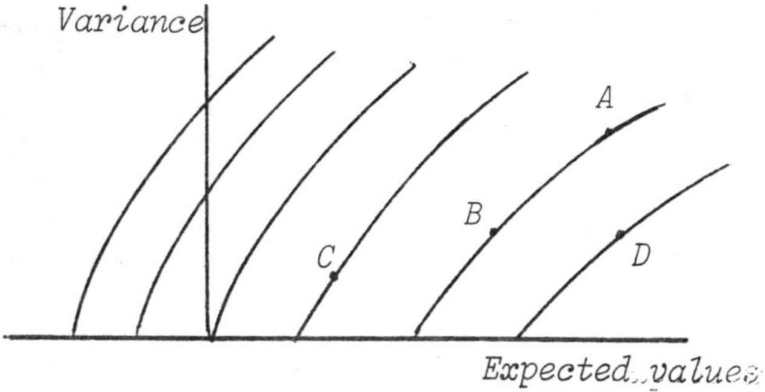

The advantage of this representation is that if such a map can be constructed, it is possible to choose unequivocally among different risky situations, by locating them on the indifference map on the basis of their expected values and variances. This is done by finding their certainty equivalents which are the points where these indifference curves intersect the horizontal axis. The point *C* in the figure is not preferable to *A* and *B*, since its certainty equivalent is lower than that of *A* and *B*, even though it has a lower variance. Point *D* is preferable to *A* and *B*, because its certainty equivalent is greater, though its variance is less than that of *A* and greater than that of *B*.

An uncertainty or a gamblers' indifference map makes the determination of certainty equivalents somewhat explicit in the sense that it includes variances as indices of risks. Thus it is a step forward in the study of uncertain situations.

However, the main difficulties remain. The construction of a gamblers' indifference map rests on striking successive trade-offs between expected value and variance. This implies that variance covers all aspects of risk fully or adequately. In many situations, this may be very hard to believe. The same variance may be obtained for various 'spreads' of risk, among which the decision-maker may not be indifferent. Moreover, there may be discontinuities involved; there may be a minimum value, below which any value taken by a variable may not be acceptable. In some cases, when the probability of failure is very high the trade-off between expected value and variance may be such that no certainty equivalent other than zero may be feasible as shown by R. Dorfman.[1]

III-3 Risk-discounting

Another expedient in arriving at the certainty equivalent to a risky outcome is to multiply the expected value by a risk-discount factor between zero and one, which becomes smaller as the risk becomes larger. A typical risk discount factors is $1/1+c\sigma$, where σ is the standard deviation and c is a constant. If the expected value of an outcome is μ then its certainty equivalent which is obtained by multiplying μ by the risk-discount factor $1/1+c\sigma$, is $\mu/1+c\sigma$. The standard-deviation elasticity of certainly equivalent is

$$d \log \left(\frac{\mu}{1+c\sigma}\right) \div d \log \sigma = - \frac{\sigma c}{1+c\sigma}$$

and the relative marginal decrease in certainty equivalent due to a small increase in the standard deviation is $c/1+c\sigma$. It is thus seen that c represents an additional loss in certainty equivalent due to additional risk represented by the standard deviation.

One desirable characteristic of the risk-discount factor $1/1+c\sigma$ is that it has the same form as the interest rate discounting for a single year, viz., $1/1+r$, where r is the pure interest rate. If the standard deviation of the outcomes in future years remains constant, then the present value of an outcome whose expected value is μ_t in year t is

$$\frac{\mu_t}{(1+c\sigma)(1+r)^t}.$$

However, if it is assumed that the riskiness increases with time, then the rate of time discounting may be taken as $r + c\sigma$ to arrive at what may be called certainty equivalent present value. Thus if the expected value in year t is μ_t, then the certainty equivalent present value is

$$\frac{\mu_t}{(1+r+c\sigma)^t}.$$

This device has the effect of reducing the present value of net benefits that would be obtained under uncertainty in the distant future sharply and of early benefits only mildly. However this implies that the standard deviation of the anticipated annual benefits increases with time, which may be questionable. Moreover, this approach does not show any rationale as to the adjustment in the expected value due to risk or standard deviation. In particular it does not indicate how to determine c of the risk-discount formula.

III-4 Equalization Fund

The above traditional approaches fail to suggest any rational criteria to adjust the expected values for uncertainty. One of the recent attempts to overcome this shortcoming is the creation of an equalization fund suggested by H. A. Thomas. The idea behind this concept is that the cost of a project includes uncertainty, and the cost of uncertainty can be estimated by the size of a fund which obviates the ups and downs in the expected values of net benefits. The size of the fund is to be adequate to cover the shortfall of actual benefits from the expected values of benefits in any year provided that any excess in any year is added to the fund. Thus the fund will be large enough to ensure that the users of the project receive net benefits equal to the expected values in every year. This device is designed to convert a risky situation into a fully insured one. The cost of uncertainty is considered equal to an amount of fund which can equalize the actual benefits with their expected values in each year.

The size of the equilization fund, however, cannot be fixed at a level which covers one hundred per cent of each and every shortfall that might occur. A project may sustain continuous losses in successive years. The equalization fund may not be large enough to cover such extreme eventualities. In general all that is required is that the fund should be large enough so that the probability that it is exhausted over the lifetime of the project does not exceed a certain low percentage say five per cent or one per cent. After the equalization fund has been estimated, it can be added to the cost of the project. If the equalization fund is denoted by EF and the expected net benefits before considering EF by μ, then net benefits after incorporating the cost of uncertainty equal to EF is

$$B = \mu - EF$$

Under some simplifying assumptions, it can be shown that the equalization fund

$$EF = \frac{\nu_\alpha \sigma}{\sqrt{2r}}$$

where σ is the standard deviation of the single year outcome, ν_α is the normal deviate with probability α of being exceeded and r is the rate of interest earned by the equalization fund. To illustrate, if α = 0.05, and r = 0.04, then ν_{α} = 1.645 and $\sqrt{2r}$ = 0.283. Suppose that the standard deviation of the expected net benefit of a project in a year is 100, then

$$EF = \frac{1.645 \times 100}{.283} = 510.$$

If μ is 1,000 then B = 1000-510 = 490.

IV. GAME-THEORETIC APPROACHES

IV-1 Introduction

A whole new approach to risky situations was started by von-Neumann and Morgenstern , known as game theory. In a simple two-person zero-sum game, the two players have alternative strategies and the gain of one player, known as the payoff, depends not only on the strategy which he adopts but also on the strategy adopted by the other player. What one player gains the other loses. To illustrate, in the following table a_{ij}'s represent the payoffs to player I if he adopts strategy i when player II adopts strategy j. If it is positive player I gains a_{ij} if it is negative player II gains the same and player I loses.

TABLE 7.1

Two Person Zero Sum Game

		Strategy of Player II					
		1	2	. . .	j	. . . . . .	n
Strategies of Player I	1	a_{11}	a_{12}		a_{1j}		a_{1n}
	2	a_{21}	a_{22}		a_{2j}		a_{2n}
	.						
	i	a_{i1}	a_{i2}		a_{ij}		a_{in}
	.						
	.						
	m	a_{m1}	a_{m2}		a_{mj}		a_{mn}

In the above game, player I has m strategies and player II has n strategies. If player I plays his ith strategy and II his jth, the payoff to player I from II is a_{ij}, and so on. In usual game theory, the two players employ pure or mixed strategies and play competitive or cooperative games so as to optimize their gains. A number of theories have been developed to solve two person zero-sum games, though search for solutions to non-zero sum more person games has not been always successful.

IV-2 Game Theory in Cost-Benefit Analysis

Game theory in the context of cost-benefit analysis undergoes some modification. Here decision-makers take the place of player I and player II is replaced by nature. Alternative projects represent the different strategies of the decision-makers, and different states represent the strategies of nature. This decision game can be illustrated as below

TABLE 7.2

Nature and Decision Makers

		States of Nature						
		1	2	. . .	j	. . .	. . .	n
Projects	1							
	2							
	. . .							
	i				a_{ij}			
	. . .							
	m							

States of nature may be defined in various ways. To illustrate, if the decision-makers are going to analyze a set of agricultural projects of certain types, the state of nature may represent different levels of rainfall. Or the states may represent a combination of different elements such as rainfall, temperature, world agricultural prices, farm machinery supplies and so on.

Different states of nature may have probabilities associated with them. These probabilities may not change with the choice of projects by the decision-makers. In this sense, the game-theoretic extension to cost-benefit analysis is simple. However when the choice of projects is likely to change the probabilities associated with the states or when it introduces some new states, the states of nature may become more difficult to analyze than the behavior of player II.

IV-3 Some Simple Criteria

The following are some of the frequently suggested criteria.

(i) Maximum criterion. In this criterion, the decision-maker first finds the minimum payoff for each alternative project corresponding to various states of nature. Provided that each state of nature is equally likely, the decision-maker chooses the project with the maximum of these minimum payoffs. To state in symbols, the decision-maker first determines

$$\min_j \{a_{ij}\},$$

for each i and then

$$\max_i [\min_j \{a_{ij}\}].$$

To illustrate in number, consider three alternative projects and three states of nature as given below.

TABLE 7.3

Maximum Criterion

		States of Nature		
		1	2	3
Projects	1	10	5	15
	2	3	6	7
	3	9	8	2

The table shows that the minimum payoff for project 1 is 5, for project 2 is 3 and for project 3 is 2. That is to say

$$\min_j a_{ij} \text{ is } 5$$

for $i = 1$, 3 for $i = 2$, 2 for $i = 3$. The maximum of these is 5 given by project 1. Thus

$$\max[\min_j \{a_{ij}\}] = 5$$

given by project 1. Hence this project ought to be selected. This criterion is useful when the gain from the project has to be above a certain minimum level. Only those projects whose minimum payoffs are above the critical level can be considered for selection.

(ii) Minimax Regret Criterion: In this criterion, the difference between the maximum payoff for each of the states of nature is derived. For instance, if the payoff to project i for the jth state of nature is highest of all other states of nature, then the measure of regret for each of the states is

$$a_{ij} - a_{i1},\ a_{ij} - a_{i2},\ a_{ij} - a_{ij},\ \ldots,\ a_{ij} - a_{in}.$$

Similarly, if the payoff to project k is highest when the state l occurs, then the row of regrets of project k is

$$a_{kl}-a_{k1},\ a_{kl}-a_{k2},\ \cdots,\ a_{kl}-a_{kl},\ \cdots,\ a_{kl}-a_{kn},$$

and so on. The regret matrix is formed of such rows.

The first step in the minimax regret criterion is to pick the maximum regret value in each row for individual projects. Thus for project i, the maximum regret value is

$$\max_k \{a_{ij} - a_{ik}\},$$

if a_{ij} is the greatest payoff value in row i. The next step is to find the project which has the least maximum regret value. This is to find

$$\min_i \ [\max_k \ \{a_{ij} - a_{ik}\}].$$

To illustrate numerically consider the following payoff table

TABLE 7.4

Maximum Row Values

		States of Nature			
		1	2	3	4
Projects	1	10	20	30	40*
	2	15	10	25	35*
	3	16	39*	29	19
	4	11	21	37*	13

In the above payoff matrix elements $\max_j a_{ij}$ have been starred. The regret matrix corresponding to the above payoff matrix is

TABLE 7.5

Regret Matrix

		States of Nature			
		1	*2*	*3*	*4*
Projects	*1*	*30**	*20*	*10*	*0*
	2	*20*	*25**	*10*	*0*
	3	*23**	*0*	*10*	*20*
	4	*20**	*16*	*0*	*24*

In the above regret matrix elements $\max_k \{a_{ij}-a_{ik}\}$ have been starred. The table shows that $\min_i [\max_k\{a_{ij} - a_{ik}\}]$ is 23 given by project 3.

This approach is useful in circumstances when the decision-makers consider that too wide a variation in the net benefits may be intolerable, and there is less concern for the minimum value of benefits that might accrue in any year, or when there may be no critical minimum level of benefits as in the preceding approach.

The approach may be highly applicable in choice among fertilizer and irrigation projects. A fertilizer project may result in a very high yield when the water supply is adequate, but in a very low yield when a drought occurs. The critical minimum level of benefits set by the decision-makers may be such that in conditions of inadequate water supply, the yield may be lower than this level. In this case, the project will be rejected according to the first approach. However, suppose that the fertilizer project succeeds in yielding the critical minimum level of benefits. (In some cases the project may be considered as satisfying the critical minimum requirement, if it can yield more than this level in 95 or 99 per cent of the cases.) So this project will not be rejected according to the first approach, and may well be selected if its minimum possible yield is higher than other projects under consideration.

However, when a fertilizer project is to be selected from a number of projects some of which are irrigation projects, the achievement of critical minimum yield and the choice of the project with the maximum minimum yield may not be an adequate criterion. The maximum minimum benefit may be given by a fertilizer project, but at the same time, the benefits may be highly variable. On the contrary, the maximum minimum benefits of irrigation projects may not be very high, but they may be relatively more stable than those of the fertilizer projects. If less variability of benefits is a consideration, then the minimum regret criterion would be relevant leading to choice of an irrigation project.

(iii) Weighting Index: The above two approaches are very one-sided, the first emphasizes minimum security, the second minimum variability. A third approach purports to combine the maximum and minimum benefits obtainable from a project by a predetermined index.

Suppose the minimum and maximum benefits from a project i for different states are a_{ij} and a_{ik} respectively. The two are weighted by an index to get a value

$$a_i^* = \alpha \; min\{a_{ik}\} + (1-\alpha) \; max\{a_{ik}\}$$

$$or \quad a_i^* = \alpha \, a_{ij} + (1-\alpha) a_{ik}, \quad 0 < \alpha < 1$$

The project i to be chosen is one which has the highest weighted value a_i^*, that is, for which $\max_i \{a_i^*\}$. To illustrate, consider three projects and four states in the following table.

TABLE 7.6 States and Projects

		States			
		1	2	3	4
Projects	1	5	10	12	17
	2	13	11	12	12
	3	10	20	15	11

		α=0	α=1	α=1/2	α=2/3
$a_1^* = \alpha 5+(1-\alpha)17 = 17-12\alpha$	=	17	5	11	9
$a_2^* = \alpha 11+(1-\alpha)13 = 13-12\alpha$	=	13	7	12	12 1/3
$a_3^* = \alpha 10+(1-\alpha)15 = 15-5\alpha$	=	15	10	12½	11 2/3

If $\alpha = 0$, this implies that the decision-makers are interested in the maximum benefits of projects and are not bothered by the lower benefits that might occur. In this case,

$$\max_i \; a_i = 17$$

given by project 1. On the contrary, when $\alpha = 1$, this implies that the decision-makers want to play it safe and consider the minimum benefits only in their choice of projects. Thus when $\alpha = 1$, this approach coincides with the first approach mentioned above. In the above example

$$\max \{a_i{}^*\} = 10$$

given by project 3.

The above two cases represent extreme optimism and extreme pessimism on the part of decision-makers. In a majority of cases, the attitude of the decision-makers (conditioned by the prevailing circumstances) will lie between the extremes. If they are pessimistic, α may be between 0 and $\frac{1}{2}$, if they are optimistic α may be between $\frac{1}{2}$ and 1. The above illustrative table shows that when $\alpha = \frac{1}{2}$, project 3 will be selected, but when $\alpha = 2/3$, project 2 will be selected.

This approach is flexible and is useful when extreme security or stability is not the main consideration. However, the determination of the specific value of the index α would pose problems. Of necessity, it has to be largely arbitrary. The most that can be said is that, when a minimum secure level of benefits is the main consideration α will approach zero, but when the maximum benefits are the main consideration α will approach 1, and that it would vary between 0 and 1 according to the degree of pessimism and optimism.

IV-4 Probability Associated States

When the probabilities associated with the states are known, the choice of projects can be made in the way discussed in sections II and III. However, it may be possible and desirable to combine the approaches of this section with the maximum expected value. To illustrate, it may be added to the criteria discussed above that the project chosen must have a minimum expected value. Then the projects whose expected values are below this minimum value may be deleted, before the above criteria are applied.

In cases when the probabilities associated with the states are not known, it has been suggested that one should assume equal probability for the states. This device, however, is very faulty and irrational, even though one may have to use it as a last resort. The lack of knowledge about the probabilities does not give any indication of their being equal.

V. UNCERTAINTY IN PUBLIC AND PRIVATE INVESTMENTS

V-1 The Controversy

The consideration of the risk element associated with the investment projects of the public sector in contrast to those of the private sector has been a matter of considerable controversy. The analysts have taken several positions on this issue. One is that risk should be treated in the same way for public investments as it is for private investments, and that net benefits of private and public investments should be discounted at the same rate. The proponents of this viewpoint include Hirshleifer, Baumol, and Stockfish. They argue that in perfect capital markets discount rates reflect both time (or waiting) and risk, hence the rates obtaining in these markets should be used to evaluate public as well as private investment projects. It is emphasized that to discount public sector projects at a lower rate than market rates will result in overinvestment in public investments at the expense of private investments yielding relatively higher returns.

The opposing position is that the government can overcome or cope with uncertainty better than private investors and so government investments should not be evaluated by the same criteria used in private markets. This position is supported by the argument that the government invests in a great number of diverse projects and consequently is able <u>to pool risks</u> to a much greater extent than private investors. Another argument put forward in favor of lower rate of risk discounting for public investments than that for private investments is that many of the uncertainties in private sector are related to moral hazards such as fraudulent behavior of the operators in the private sector. Many of such risks are not present in the case of public investments.

This position, especially the first of these lines of argument, is taken by P. A. Samuelson and W. Vickerey, K. J. Arrow, S. A. Marglin, and others.

V-2 Hirshleifer Approach[1]: Risky Interest Rate

Using the concept of "states of the world" at each date Hirshleifer has shown that a risky interest rate will differ from the market interest rate under conditions of certainty. To illustrate the idea, he deals with the elementary case of choice between consumption now and consumption one year from now. There is no uncertainty now but one year from now just one of two alternative states of the world "a" and "b" must come about. There are three objects of choice in this situation: claims to present consumption, claims to future consumption valid if and only if the state "a" obtains and claims to future consumption valid if and only if state "b" obtains.

In the riskless case, the market determines the interest rate r_1 as a discounting factor for future and present claims. Thus if the price of current claims P_0 is taken as unity, the price of claims one year from now,

$$P_1 = \frac{1}{1+r_1}$$

where r_1 is the market interest rate.

The present value for the certainty case can now be written in the form

$$V_o = -P_o i_o + P_1 q_1$$

where i_o is the amount of investment (i.e., consumption forgone) and q_1 is the amount available one year hence.

In the model of risk the market will determine the price ratios among the three objects of choice: claims to present consumption, i_o, claims to future consumption, q_{1a}, if state "a" obtains and claims to future consumption, q_{1b}, if state "b" obtains. Now the present value rule of riskless model can be extended to the risky situation

$$V_o = -P_o i_o + P_{1a} q_{1a} + P_{1b} q_{1b}$$

where P_{1a} and P_{1b} are the prices of future contingent claims depending upon which state, "a" or "b", obtains. In the risky situation, V_o is the present certainty equivalent value (PCEV) and is strictly objective. "It does not depend at all upon the decision-maker's personal time-preference (or even probability beliefs), but only upon the net integration of all individuals' preferences and beliefs as expressed in the market in the form of prices for present and future claims."[2]

In the certainty model the simple relationship $P_1 = 1/(1+r_1)$ holds between tho rate of interest r_1 and the price of future claims P_1. Since a unit of future consumption can be purchased with certainty by combining unit future claims for each state we can write

$$P_1 = P_{1a} + P_{1b} = \frac{1}{1 + r_1}.$$

This is the definition of a riskless rate of interest r_1 in an uncertain world.

Risk can be considered as a social cost or a merely private cost that government ought to ignore. It is argued in support of the latter view that government is in a position to undertake many independent projects and, thus, by pooling risks it can treat the mathematical expectation of yield as certain. The proponents of this view would estimate the present value of a project by discounting the mathematical expectations of the benefits and costs at each date with the riskless rate of interest r_1. In contrast, private risk aversion represents a social cost, then the mathematical expectation of net benefits has to be discounted by a "risky interest rate" $r_1{}^*$ "suitable for the characteristic pattern of risk of the investment in question."

To determine whether the riskless or the risky interest rate is appropriate for discounting, one can make use of the present certainty equivalent value rule which gives correct results, and see which of these rates is consistent with this rule. For a two year and two state project, suppose $P_{1a} = 0.3$, $P_{1b} = 0.5$, $q_{1a} = 3$, $q_{1b} = 0$, and $P_0 = 1$, $q_0 = 1$. The PCEV of this project

$$V_0 = -1 + 0.3 \times 3 + 0.5 \times 0 = -.01 .$$

The riskless interest rate is given by

$$0.3 + 0.5 = \frac{1}{1 + r_1} ,$$

or $\quad r_1 = .25$.

Now let the probabilities of the two states be $\pi_{1a} = \frac{1}{2} = \pi_{1b}$. Then the mathematical expectation of the return of the project in year 1 is $\frac{1}{2} \times 3 + \frac{1}{2} \times 0 = 1.5$, and the present value is $-1 + 1.5/1.25 = 0.2$. But it is known that the PCEV of the project is negative and it should not be adopted. Therefore, the use of the riskless rate in discounting the mathematical expectation of future returns cannot be correct in general. The correct risky rate $r_1{}^*$ is given by the formula

$$1 + r^* = \frac{\pi_{1a} q_{1a} + \pi_{1b} q_{1b}}{p_{1a} q_{1a} + p_{1b} q_{1b}} .$$

The rationale of the formula is immediately seen, when it is noted that r_1^* is the rate which makes the discounted value of the mathematical expectations equal to the present certainty equivalent value. The mathematical expectation of states "a" and "b" is $\pi_{1a}q_{1a}+\pi_{1b}q_{1b}$. The discounted value of this expression at the risky interest rate is

$$\frac{\pi_{1a}q_{1a}+\pi_{1b}q_{1b}}{1+r^*} = (\pi_{1a}q_{1a}+\pi_{1b}q_{1b}) \frac{P_{1a}q_{1a}+P_{1b}q_{1b}}{\pi_{1a}q_{1a}+\pi_{1b}q_{1b}} = P_{1a}q_{1a}+P_{1b}q_{1b}$$

Putting this in the present value formula gives the PCEV. It can be checked that for the values assumed here $r_1^* = 2/3$.

It is noted that a suitable risky discount rate is determined by the consistency of results with those yielded by the PCEV rule. It may be asked that if PCEV is a pre-requisite for determining the risky discount rate r^*, then there is no need for deriving r^*, all projects can be evaluated by estimating their PCEV's from the outlay i_0, receipts q_{1a}, q_{1b} and objective market prices P_{1a} and P_{1b}. In practice this is not feasible. The number of states at a single point of time is too large and there do not exist a complete set of securities whose prices would directly provide the data for the use of PCEV rule.

For practical purposes, Hirshleifer suggests the concept of "risk class." According to him, a proposed government project can be placed in the same risk class as a private project. For instance in evaluating a public power project, it can be assumed that it falls in the same risk class as private power projects. Suppose that these are financed half and half by stocks and bonds, and that market prices for securities are such that the mathematical expectation of yield on the stocks is 8 per cent and the bonds 5 per cent. Then the suitable r_1* for discounting expected returns of the comparable government project would be 6.5 per cent.

The risky discount rate would be usually higher than the riskless rate, but not necessarily in all cases. For instance, if P_{1a} = 0.3 and P_{1b} = 0.5 as before, but q_{1a} = 0 and q_{1b} = 3, then the present certainty equivalent value V_0 = 0.5. The riskless interest rate i = .25 as before, but the risky interest rate of r_1*, for $\pi_{1a} = \frac{1}{2} = \pi_{1b}$ as before, is zero, given by

$$1 + r_1^* = \frac{\frac{1}{2} \times 0 + \frac{1}{2} \times 3}{0.3 \times 0 + 0.5 \times 3}.$$

That the riskless rate is higher than the risky rate is explained by the fact that the riskless rate is calculated in terms of a pattern of returns yielding equally in the two states. But in the present example, the returns fall disproportionately in the more highly valued state. The view that the government should employ a lower rate than private industry would be valid, if it were the case that the returns from government projects fall in disproportionately high valued states in comparison with private industry.

The idea of an adjustment for risk through the discount rate has been criticized even by some of the supporters of the view that "the market reflection of private risk aversion represents a real social cost." However, the alternative to use of the risky interest rate would be to determine at each date the equivalent of the net return at that date. If this could be done then the riskless rate could be used to discount these future certainty equivalents into present certainty equivalents. Hirshleifer states, however, that the calculation of these future certainty equivalent values would require direct knowledge of consumers' utility functions, and so is not a feasible procedure.

V-3 The Public Cost of Risk Bearing-- Arrow-Lind Analysis[3]

Arrow and Lind present an analysis which shows that when the number of individuals is large, the cost to each individual of risks undertaken by public projects is nil. Their analysis is as follows. Consider the case where all individuals have the same preferences and their disposable incomes are identically distributed random variables represented by A. Suppose that the government undertakes an investment with returns represented by B, statistically consisting of a certain part $\overline{B}$, equal to expected returns and a random part X incorporating risk with mean zero.

Consider a specific tax-payer whose fraction of the public investment is denoted by s, $0 \leq s \leq 1.0$, as determined by the taxes he pays. Then the individual's disposable income is equal to $A + sB = A + s\overline{B} + sX$. The individual values the addition to his income with allowance for the cost of risk-bearing associated with the random component sX.

Now introduce the function

$$W(s) = E[U(A + s\overline{B} + sX)]$$

representing the expected utility as a function of s which is his share of B. Assuming W to be differentiable we have,

$$W'(s) = E[U'(A + s\overline{B} + sX)(\overline{B} + X)]$$

Since X is assumed independent of A, therefore $U'(A)$ and X are also independent. Hence

$$E[U'(A)X] = E[U'(X)]\ E[X] = 0.$$

This means that

$$W'(0) = E[U'(A)(\overline{B} + X)]$$
$$= \overline{B}E[U'(A)], \textit{ since } E(X) = 0 .$$

But the above is equivalent to

$$\lim_{s\to 0} \frac{E[U(A + s\overline{B} + sX) - U(A)]}{s} .$$

Now suppose that there are n individuals and all individuals are identical, then $s = 1/n$, then the above becomes

$$\lim_{n\to\infty} nE[U(A + \frac{\overline{B} + X}{n}) - U(A)] = \overline{B}E[U'(A)].$$

If we assume that the individual is a risk-averter, then there exists a unique number, $k(n) > 0$, for each value of n such that

$$E[U(A + \frac{\overline{B} + X}{n})] = EU[(A + \frac{\overline{B}}{n} - k(n)]$$

This implies that the individual would be indifferent between paying an amount equal to $k(n)$ and accepting the risk represented by $1/n\ X$. It is evident that $\lim k(n) = 0$, i.e., the cost of holding the risky asset goes to zero as the amount of this asset held by the individual goes to zero. However, Arrow and Lind have proved a stronger result. From the above two equations it follows that

$$\lim_{n\to\infty} nE[U(A + \frac{\overline{B}}{n} - k(n) - U(A)] = \overline{B}E[U'(A)]$$

In addition, $\overline{B}/n - k(n) \quad 0$, when $n \to \infty$. It follows from the definition of a derivative that

$$\lim_{n\to\infty} \frac{E[U(A + \frac{\overline{B}}{n} - k(n) - U(A)]}{\overline{B}/n - k(n)} = E[U'(A)]$$

Dividing the preceding two equations,

$$\lim_{n\to\infty} [\overline{B} - nk(N)] = \overline{B}$$

$$\text{or} \quad \lim_{n\to\infty} nk(n) = 0 .$$

The above shows that the total of the cost of risk-bearing goes to zero as the number of taxpayers, n, becomes large.* From this it is concluded that if n is large, the expected value of net benefits $\overline{B}$ closely approximates the correct measure of net benefits, and the cost of risk-bearing is negligible. This result will still hold when individuals have different preferences, incomes and taxes, provided that as n becomes larger, the share of the public investment borne by any individual becomes smaller. This is perhaps the most formal statement of the pooling argument.

V-4 Further Review of the Approaches

This basic difference between the two approaches is that one, as demonstrated by Hirschleifer, rests on the premises that the risky

---

* Jim Wilson who has carefully read this manuscript made the following remark:

"But could not the same sort of logic be used to show that as the number of tax payers becomes large, the additional taxation required to finance a given project tends toward zero and that therefore public investments on the margin have a blank check."

This is a valid remark and exposes the weakness of the arguments of Lind and Arrow.

interest rate is different from the riskless rate and that the two will be equal only when the prices of future state-claims are in exact proportion to the probabilities associated with the states. Since individuals are risk-averters, the relative prices of state-claims would, in general, be different. However, it is not necessary that the risky rate would always be higher than the riskless rate. The essence of Hirschleifer's argument seems to be that investment projects, whether private or government, should be evaluated on the basis of utilities of individuals as shareholders or tax-payers, taking into account their risk aversion.

The Arrow-Lind analysis implies that the cost of risk-bearing associated with public investment is so diffused that it is almost zero. Hence, public investments should be evaluated on the basis of a riskless discount rate. This analysis rests on the so-called pooling argument. Hirshleifer contends that the risks of private investment projects are also dispersed through buying and selling of securities and, hence, there is no essential difference between the private and government projects. For concreteness he gives the following illustration. Suppose that individuals can be grouped into equally numerous "even" and "odd" categories. Suppose further that each individual is faced with an investment opportunity where q_{1a} is 3 if state "a" obtains and q_{1b} is zero if state "b" obtains, and define state "a" as the situation where the evens obtain 3 and the odds obtain 0, while state "b" is the reverse situation. Then it may be that "private risk aversion may make every individual disinclined to undertake his personal investment project, whereas, on the social level, there is no risk at all." But this will be true only when the two classes of individuals cannot trade state-a claims for state-b claims. But if they traded, at par, say, they could convert their respective investment opportunities such that $q_{1a} = q_{1b} = 1.5$, a situation which would be privately as well as socially riskless.

The sponsors of the pooling argument, including Arrow and others, counter argue that market imperfections hinder the trading that could eliminate private risks. It is argued that markets for many types of insurance do not exist. The behavior of someone who has insurance may alter, so that the observed outcome may be adverse to the insurer and may not conform to at par trading. Also such markets would require complicated and specialized contracts which are costly.[4]

Hirschleifer concedes that the number of conceivable time-state contingencies is enormous, far greater than the number of distinct securities traded and that the imperfect marketability of state claims is a fact, and so there is a degree of validity in the pooling argument. But he counter-argues that the "imperfect ability of Government to distribute time-scale claims in accordance with consumers' marginal preferences is surely an equally significant fact...The effect of the corporate income tax is very likely greater than imperfection of capital markets in determining private risky markets."[5] As a practical matter, Hirshleifer and Shapiro believe that the use of comparable risky rate of discount from the private sector is the best general guide both for private and government investment projects.

One might also raise the question as to whether risk-spreading associated with large corporations might also not bring about the same result as government projects. If each stockholder's share in the corporation is a small component of his income, the cost of risk-bearing to him will be very small. Therefore, if the managers were acting in the best interests of the shareholders, they would essentially ignore

ADDENDA

Due to pagination errors not discovered until after the book was bound, pages 221,2,3,4 and pages 241,2,3,4 are out of order. Please read in this order: 223,4,1,2 and 244,1,2,3. Text is correct!

Table 6.1 Net Benefits

	Initial Capital Outlay	Net Benefits in Yr. 1	Yr. 2	Yr. 3	Yr. 4
Project One	300	30	39	60	54
Project Two	100	10	15	18	20
Project One Normalized	100	10	13	20	18

Insert Table 6.1 on page 145

Goods

- Private
  - Direct Market Pricing
- Public
  - Direct Market Pricing
  - Indirect Pricing
  - Non-market Pricing
- External
  - Indirect Pricing
  - Non-Market Pricing

Social Goods (Public Indirect Pricing, Public Non-market Pricing, External Indirect Pricing, External Non-Market Pricing)

Insert Table Above On Page 83: Table 4-2.

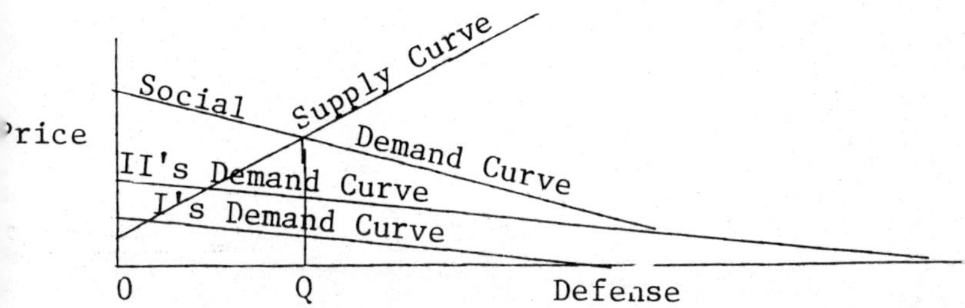

11-2 Marginal Cost Vs Full Cost Pricing

Insert Graph Above On Page 100.

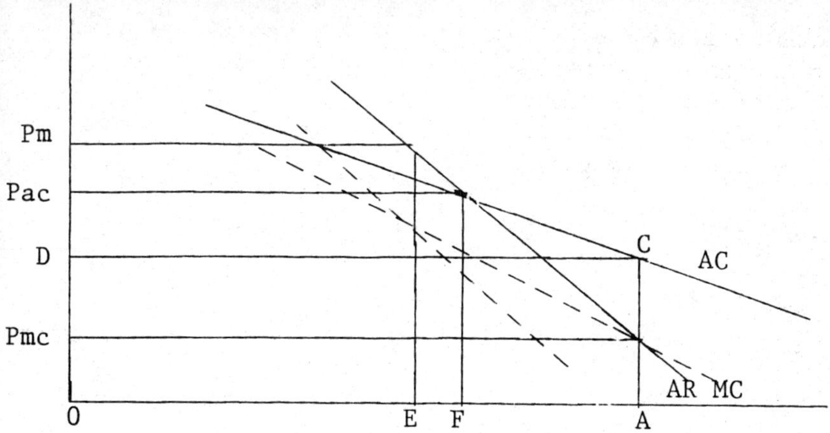

11-2 Marginal Cost Versus Full Cost Pricing

Insert graph above on page 85 over 11-2.

expected values of the independent variables in functions except those in linear functions. The correct procedure is to derive the probability distribution of the dependent variable and then to estimate its expected value.

The expected values of outcomes are not the sole criterion for setting up the order of preference among them. It is also necessary to consider their variances. An outcome with higher expected value but with a higher variance, may be less preferable to another outcome with lower expected value and a lower variance. The concept of "certainty equivalents" has been evolved to deal with situations in which the expected values of outcomes are associated with different variances. The techniques developed to apply the concept of certainty equivalents include the construction of indifference maps, risk discounting and equalization fund.

Another approach to deal with risk and uncertainty is the application of game theory. The two person-zero sum game can be converted into a game between decision makers and nature. The strategies of the decision-makers are taken to be the different projects and the strategies of nature are taken to be the various states of nature. Several simple criteria can be used for project selection through the application of game theory. These criteria are maximum criterion, minimax regret criterion, and criterion using weighting index.

There has been a great deal of debate on the uncertainty and risk associated with projects in the public versus private sectors and the relative rates of time discounting to be used in the two sectors. One group of writers is of the opinion that the public projects are exposed to lower risk than the private sector projects. According to them, the rate of time discounting applied in public sector ought to be lower than that applied in the private sector. The other group does not find any significant difference in this respect. According to this group a uniform rate of time discounting should be applied in both the sectors.

Footnotes

1 This section has been overly influenced by Shlomo Reutlinger, Techniques for Project Appraisal under Uncertainty, The Johns Hopkins Press, Baltimore, 1976.

2 R. Dorfman, "Basic Economic and Technologic Concepts: A General Statement" in A. Mass et al., Design of Water Resource System, Harvard University Press, 1962, pp. 129-58. This section owes very much to this article.

3 H.A. Thomas, referred to in R. Dorfman, "Decision Rules Under Uncertainty" in Richard Layard (ed.), Cost-Benefit Analysis, Harmondsworth, Middlesex, England: Penguin Education, 1972. This is excerpted from R. Dorfman, "Basic Economic and Technologic Concepts: A General Statement," in A. Mass et al., Design of Water Resource Systems, Harvard University Press, 1962.

4 See H.A. Thomas Jr. for deriving the formula and reference.

5 J. von Neumann and O. Morgenstern, Theory of Games and Economic Behavior, Princeton University Press, 1944.

6 Parts of this section are based on Jack Hirschleifer and David L. Shapiro, "The Treatment of Risk and Uncertainty," in the Analysis and Evaluation of Public Expenditures: The PPB System, Volume I, Joint Economic Committee, Congress of the United States, 1969.

risks. Arrow and Lind address themselves to this question and accept the merits of this fact.[6] However they find two reasons why large corporations may behave as risk averters. First, in order to control the firm, some shareholders may hold a large block of stock representing a substantial part of their wealth, making the costs of risk-bearing non-negligible. Secondly, even though from the stockholder's point of view, risk should be ignored, it may not be in the interest of corporate managers to neglect risk, since their careers and incomes are intimately connected with the performance of the firm. It should be pointed out that even governments are not immune from such considerations. A very big investment project, civil or military, which represents a significant fraction of the total budget may have an influence on the prospects of the continuity of the regime, and the promotions and incomes of the managers of government projects are also related with their success, and so they may also be prone to risk aversion to a considerable degree.

The upshot of all these points and counterpoints is that a project need not be evaluated at a lower discount rate just because it is a government project and another at a higher rate just because it is a private project. A consideration will have to be given to the risk class in which the project lies. Further, as has been shown by Hirshleifer, a risky interest rate need not necessarily be lower than the riskless rate. It should also be recognized as has been done by Arrow and Lind[7] that all benefits and costs do not accrue to the government and are not distributed among the taxpayers. Some benefits and costs accrue directly to individuals. In this case it is appropriate to discount these for the risk as these individuals would. The correct procedure would be to separate out the costs borne by and benefits accruing to the government and private individuals and to evaluate them at appropriate rates of discount according to the risks involved or felt by individuals. In practice, however, most costs are borne publicly and should be discounted using the appropriate rate for government investment and at the certainty rate if the pooling argument is accepted. But benefits often accrue to individuals, and hence their expected value should be discounted at an appropriate rate depending on the nature of the uncertainty and the time-risk preferences of individuals. Ironically in a typical case where costs are borne publicly and benefits accrue privately, this procedure will lead to the adoption of fewer public projects than the procedure of using a higher rate to discount both benefits and costs.[8]

To sum up, the criss-cross arguments about risk and uncertainty associated with public versus private investment projects and the discount rates appropriate for their evaluation have not settled the debate, but the differences of viewpoints and practical recommendations have certainly been narrowed. In fact, the implications of the positions held by the opponents have been such that the roles of the policy recommendations have been reversed. In the process, the sharp edges of the controversy have been removed, an outcome not unwelcome in an uncertain world.

Summary

Uncertainty and risk characterize almost all human activities. If information regarding the outcome of an activity is completely nil, no scientific methods can be used to assess the expected value of the outcome. If probabilities can be associated with the occurrences, statistical methods can be used to estimate the expected values of the variables involved in the analysis. It is inappropriate to derive the expected value of a dependent variable by substituting the

7 Jack Hirschleifer and David L. Shapiro: op. cit., p. 522.

8 K.J. Arrow and R.C. Lind, "Uncertainty and the Evaluation of Public Investment Decisions," American Economic Review, Vol. 60, 1970.

9 Arrow and Lind, op. cit. (p. 339).

10 Arrow and Lind, op. cit. (p. 359).

11 Arrow and Lind, op. cit. (p. 356).

12 Arrow and Lind, op. cit. (p. 358).

Appendix to Chapter Two

INTENDED AND UNINTENDED OUTPUTS ACCOUNTED AND UNACCOUNTED INPUTS

In chapter two, the outputs and inputs of a project have been classified according to their nature and characterisitcs. The classification discussed can be summarized as set forth below.

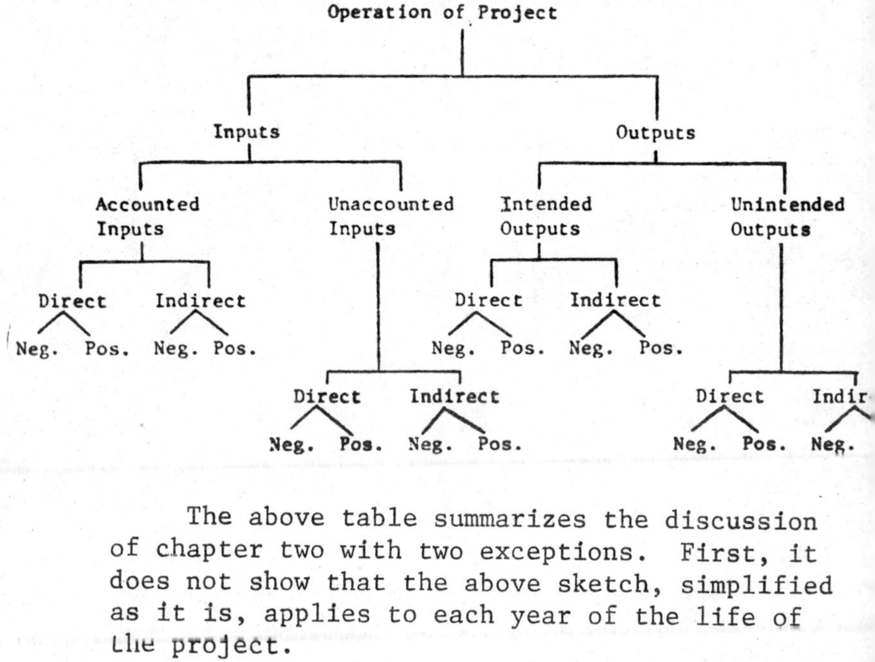

The above table summarizes the discussion of chapter two with two exceptions. First, it does not show that the above sketch, simplified as it is, applies to each year of the life of the project.

The above classification applies to a greater or lesser degree to every project. In case of some projects, the extent of unintended outputs and unaccounted inputs may be small, so that they may have little external (environmental or social) effect. In a majority of cases, however, the unintended outputs and unaccounted inputs have crucial importance for social welfare can be illustrated by a seemingly innocuous project such as forest harvesting.

The harvesting of trees requires the construction of access roads, and the use of expensive capital equipments. It is, therefore, profitable to maximize the cut from any given area in the short run. Therefore, clear-cutting of forests is an efficient and profitable method. However, the picture changes drastically, when the long-run consequences of clear-cutting are taken into account. A brief description of these consequences is given below, labeling them with the categories of input and output classifications.

Clearcutting removes the plant cover which changes the local micro-climate. The plant cover is, thus, <u>unaccounted direct input</u> in clearcutting.

The local climate is greatly determined by the local rainfall. Massive harvesting through clearcutting reduces the local ground level water and CO_2 oxygen recycling. Local ground level water and CO_2 thus become <u>unaccounted indirect input</u>.

Clearcutting also results in compaction of the soil due to the movement of heavy bulldozers and dragging of logs. Soil compaction may be considered <u>unintended direct output</u>. The removal of plant cover along with the compaction of the soil makes it more difficult for the Douglas fir and Lodgepole pine to re-establish themselves. Therefore, reduction in their growth is <u>unaccounted indirect input</u>. Moreover, because of the removal of shade, water in streams is exposed to direct sunlight which raises the water temperature high enough to reduce the reproduction of trout and salmon.

The raising of water temperature may be considered unintended indirect output while the reduction in the reproduction of trout and salmon can be considered unaccounted indirect input. Clearcutting also leads to a reduction in the animal habitat in the area. This is another unaccounted indirect input.

Clearcutting leaves organic debris in the area. This may be unintended direct output. The debris may serve for some time as food for some animals such as elk and deer. The increase in the number of these animals may be considered unintended indirect output (positive).

However, the debris may have to be slash-burned because of fear that it might catch fire by lightning. In either case it would produce air pollution. The air pollution thus caused is unintended indirect output (negative).

It may now be considered whether the debris produced by clear-cutting is a positive output or negative output. If it is not slash-burned and the increase in the supply of elk and deer is considered desirable, then the debris would be a positive output. However, if the debris is burned, then it causes pollution and it would be considered negative output. If the debris is left unburned then it may breed elk and deer (a positive output), but at the same time, there is a danger that it would be burned by lightning producing pollution (negative output). Now it is not clear whether the debris be considered positive or negative output. The classification of the debris as positive or negative will depend on the value attached to the expected increase in the number of elk and deer and the expected chance of the debris being burned by lightning and the negative value attached to the pollution caused by the burning of the debris.

If the expected loss of value caused by the burning of debris by lightning is more than the expected gain of value from elk and deer then the debris is negative output, otherwise positive.

The clearcutting of forests allows the previously shaded forest undergrowth (brush) to receive increased sunlight. This increases the growth of brush which spreads and covers the land previously covered by timber. This brush is permanent food (browse) for deer and elk. The clearcutting may thus result in an increase in the number of deer and elk.

The increased brush is unintended indirect output. It is positive in that it results in increased deer and elk-herds. It is negative in that it grows faster than sapling fir (timber) trees, thus preventing reforestation. The net effect can be determined by comparing the loss due to the stifling of natural reforestation and the benefit from increased numbers of deer and elk.

Since debris can serve as food for deer and elk only for a short time, it may be negative direct unintended output while brush may be negative indirect unintended output. This is because the loss of timber may far outweigh the gain from deer and elk.

Another consequence of clearcutting at an extensive scale is that it causes increased soil erosion due to more rapid water runoff than before. Soil erosion may be considered unaccounted indirect input. The rapid water runoff raises the sediment load of streams and lowers the level of mineral nutrients and humus in the area. The first may be considered unintended indirect output, while the second as unintended indirect input. The organic material that washes into the water supplies requires oxygen for its decomposition while the increased turbidity of the waters reduces the photosynthetic activity in lakes and streams. These may again be treated as indirect input or output depending on the fact whether something is being reduced or produced and increased.

Even though clearcutting results in lower ground level water and CO_2-O_2 recycling (lower rainfall) than before, the rapid water runoff increases the level of water and its fluctuation at downstream locations. With increased fluctuations, the probability of both initial flooding and subsequent drought go up. Increased water level and its fluctuations can be treated as unintended indirect outputs. These will be negative outputs if they cause more harm than good to the affected areas.

Increased downstream flooding can be prevented by building dams. The social cost-benefit analysis of clearcutting may be ended before dam construction is taken up for consideration, and the latter may be considered as a separate project. However, the construction of dams may not have been undertaken in the first instance. If the dam does not have any effects other than preventing harmful effects of clearcutting, then its cost can be considered as the value of the loss due to the clearcutting. And if the value of the gains does not exceed the value of the loss, then the clearcutting should not be undertaken. However, when a dam is constructed, it will start the streams of its own outputs and inputs which will in most cases go beyond just preventing the harmful effects of the clearcutting. It will therefore be necessary to include the analysis of costs and benefits of dam construction as part of the total analysis.

Without going into details of the cost of accounted direct inputs and the value of intended direct outputs of electricity and flood control, some of the indirect inputs and outputs may be mentioned here. As unintended direct outputs, or as unaccounted direct inputs, the dams flood upstream land, act as silt traps, change water temperature, impede commercial traffic and reduce the fish population. As unintended indirect outputs or unaccounted indirect inputs, water is slowed down behind dams, resulting in proliferation of aquatic plant life raising the level of water evaporation and causing stagnant water leading to significant health hazards.

Furthermore, as the dam prevents material from flowing downstream, dredging will have to be undertaken, involving direct and indirect inputs. Also, the sand that is washed away by the action of the ocean is not replaced because of the dam. The dam also causes a reduction in the biological productivity of the estuaries by retarding the flow of minerals to them and by raising the ration of salt to fresh water. All these can be properly labeled indirect unintended outputs and unaccounted inputs.

The above example illustrates the intricacies and complexities involved in tracing the sequences of intended and unintended outputs and accounted and unaccounted outputs. The above description of the consequences of clear-cutting is not exhaustive and in practice, it would seldom be possible to trace all the repercussions of a project. How far the project evaluators will go in analyzing a project will depend on the resources and skills at their disposal. The further they go in identifying, the more accurate their analysis would be. However, after a certain stage, the marginal cost of obtaining accuracy might exceed the value of additional accuracy.

Appendix to Chapter Three

RELATIONSHIP BETWEEN SOCIAL UTILITY AND PRICE-QUANTITY VARIATIONS

The following is a formal statement of the relationship between social utility and price-quantity variations of goods and the underlying assumptions. Social utility U is a function of individual utilities, w^k, k = 1, 2, ... n

$$U = U\left(w^1_k, w^2_k, \ldots\ldots w^n_k\right) \qquad (1)$$

The utility of an individual is a function of the amount of goods he consumes at a particular time.

$$w^k = w^k\left(q^k_1, q^k_2, \ldots\ldots q^k_m\right), \quad k = 1,2, \ldots n \quad (2)$$

Variation in social utility

$$dU = \sum_k U_k \, dw^k$$

$$= \sum_{ki} U_k \, w^k_i \, dq^k_i \ \ldots\ldots\ldots\ldots \quad (3)$$

Since we do not know either the function U or w, the variation of social utility can be obtained if we assume that each individual is a utility maximiser. The individual k purchases the amount q^k_i, i = 1, ..., n with his income y^k at prices p^{ki}_i such that his utility is maximized. His behavior is characterized by

$$\left.\begin{array}{l} \max w^k\left(q^k_1, \ldots, q^k_m\right) \\ \text{subject to } \sum_i p^k_i q^k_i = y^k \end{array}\right\} \qquad (4)$$

The solution to (4) gives

$$w_i^k = \lambda_k p_i^k \tag{5}$$

assuming that the prices are independent of quantities consumed by the individual k. λ_k is the Lagrangian multiplier representing the marginal utility of income of individual k corresponding to his utility function w^k. Putting (5) into (3) we have

$$dU = \sum_{ki} U_k \lambda_k p_i^k dq_i^k \tag{6}$$

$U_k = \frac{\partial U}{\partial w^k}$ is the marginal increase in social utility due to a unit increase in the utility of individual k, hence $U_k\lambda_k$ is the increase in social utility due to an increase of one unit in the income of individual k. If $U_k\lambda_k$ is assumed independent of k, then this constant can be equated to one by a suitable transformation of U. However the independence of $U_k\lambda_k$ from k implies that (1) marginal increase in social utility from a unit increase in the utility of each individual is the same, or (2) the two elements for each individual are such that their product equals a constant. Whichever the interpretation, if we define optimal distribution of income as one which results in the constancy of $U_k\lambda_k$ for all k's, normalized to equal unity, then the variation in the social utility in a marginal transformation can be expressed as

$$dU = \sum_{ki} p_i^k dq_i^k \tag{7}$$

Further if the price system confronting each individual is the same, the variation in social utility can be expressed as

$$dU = \sum_{ki} p_i dq_i^k$$

$$= \sum_i p_i dq_i^k \quad \text{where} \quad \sum_k dq_i^k = dq_i \qquad (9)$$

(9) leads to the basic concept in cost-benefit analysis, one that is taken for granted in most discussions. It is that, under the assumptions of an optimal distribution of income as defined above and a system of prices which is the same for all individuals and is independent of the quantities consumed, then the variation in social utility in a marginal transformation is equal to the variation in total real consumption.

3. Variation in Social Utility in Terms of Productive Activities

In practice, cost-benefit analysis is applied to individual projects and it may be convenient to account for the increase in consumption goods at the production point. The variation in social utility can be studied under three assumptions regarding the state of the economy: (1) The economy is closed and the resources are fully employed before and after the point when the variance in social utility is estimated. (2) The economy is closed but the resources are not fully employed. (3) The economy is open with full employment of resources.

In some problems, it is not the variation in quantities but the variation in prices that are known. This is particularly true in case of government taxes and subsidies and price regulations. The demand for good i by individual k can be written

$$q_i^k = q_i^k\left(p_1, p_2, \ldots, p_n, y_k\right)$$

$$dq_i^k = \sum_j (ij)_k dp_j + (i)_k dU_k \qquad (10)$$

Using notations by Boiteux and Lesourne, we set

$$\frac{\partial q_i^k}{\partial p_j} + q_j^k = (ij)_k \text{ and } \frac{\partial q_i^k}{\partial y_k} = (i)_k .$$

Let the production function be $f(q_1, q_2, \ldots q_n) = 0$ so that

$$\sum_i f_i dq_i = 0$$

We can therefore write

$$dU = \sum_i p_i dq_i = \sum_i \left(p_i - f_i\right) dq_i$$

$p_i - f_i = t_i$ is the levy on the ith good, and is equal to the difference between the consumption price of the good and the marginal productivity of the firm. Now

$$dU = \sum_i p_i dq_i = \sum_{ijk} t_i (ij)_k dp_j + \sum_{ik} t_i (i)_k dU_k$$

If we set $dU_k = \rho_k dU$, $\left(\sum_k \rho_k = 1\right)$, we can write $(i) = \sum_k \rho_k (i)_k$; (i) expresses the increase in total demand for the ith good when social real income increases by one unit, given constant consumption prices. Now we can write

$$dU = \frac{\sum_{ij} t_i (ij) dp_j}{1 - \sum_i t_i (i)}$$

$\left[\rho_k \text{ is certainly a judgmental parameter}\right]$,

In a closed economy with full employment resources, the total output of the ith good in the economy is

$$q_i = \sum_h q_{ih} + q_{io}$$

where q_{ih} is the amount of good i operated by the h_{th} firm and q_{io} is the amount of good i initially available. If good i is output of firm h it is positive, if input it is negative.

$$dq_i = \sum_h dq_{ih}$$

$$\text{and } \sum_i p_i dq_i = \sum_{hi} p_i dq_{ih}$$

It is obvious that $\sum_i p_i dq_{ih}$ is variation in profits of the h_{th} firm.

Under our assumptions then in a closed economy with full employment of resources, the variation in social utility in a marginal transformation equals the variation in the real profits of firms, calculated with the system of consumption prices.

It may be asked: Why should primary and intermediate goods be valued at consumption prices when they are not consumed? The answer is that it is immaterial at what prices the primary and intermediate goods are valued, because the sales of one firm are the purchases of another firm and hence their values cancel out. Hence no contradiction arises if all the goods are uniformly evaluated at the consumption prices.

It should be noted that $\sum_i p_i dq_{ih}$ is the variation in profits of firm h in a marginal transformation since this represents the difference between the values of marginal inputs and marginal outputs, calculated with constant prices P_i. We can then say that the economy is in an optimal state when given a unique price system the firms' real profits are maximum possible. For in this case the firms' profits cannot increase in a marginal transformation and $dU = \sum_i p_i dq_{ih} = 0$. But if the economy is not already in an optimal state then a marginal transformation is desirable for the community if it brings about a positive variation in the real profits of at least one firm without negative variations in real profits of other firms.

This appendix is based on Jaques Lesourne's <u>Cost-Benefit Analysis and Economic Theory</u>, North Holland Publishing Co. (Amsterdam, 1975) Part I.

Appendix to Chapter Five

CUMULATIVE ACCOUNTING PRICES

It is intended to show that factor combination according to cumulative accounting prices can lead to larger level of output than that according to marginal accounting prices.

Let $\tilde{L}_t$ denote the uncommitted labor and $\tilde{K}_t$ the uncommitted capital in year t. Let F denote the production function which does not change over years. Let this be homogeneous of degree one, so that:

$$L \frac{\partial F(L,K)}{\partial L} + K \frac{\partial F(L,K)}{\partial K} = F(L,K).$$

Marginal accounting prices of labor and capital are given by

$$\tilde{w}_t = \frac{\partial F(\tilde{L}_t,\tilde{K}_t)}{\partial \tilde{L}_t}, \quad \tilde{r}_t = \frac{\partial F(\tilde{L}_t,\tilde{K}_t)}{\partial \tilde{K}_t} \qquad (1)$$

Cumulative accounting prices of labor and capital are given by

$$w_t^* = \frac{\partial F(\sum_1^t \tilde{L}_t, \sum_1^t \tilde{K}_t)}{\partial \sum_1^t \tilde{L}_t}, \quad r_t^* = \frac{\partial F(\sum_1^t \tilde{L}_t, \sum_1^t \tilde{K}_t)}{\partial \sum_1^t \tilde{K}_t}. \qquad (2)$$

Now it is supposed that the supplies of uncommitted labor and capital grows at constant rates λ and k respectively, so that

$$\tilde{L}_t = L_1 e^{\lambda(t-1)}, \quad \tilde{K}_t = K_1 e^{k(t-1)} \quad \text{where } \lambda \gtreqless k.$$

For the sake of simplicity of exposition, suppose that the projects last two years and the production function is of Cobb-Douglas type,

$$P = L^{\alpha}K^{\beta}, \quad \alpha + \beta = 1$$

In year 1, the ratio of the amounts of factors combined according to cumulative accounting prices is given by

$$\frac{L_1^*}{K_1^*} = \frac{\tilde{L}_1}{\tilde{K}_1} z \text{ where } z = \frac{1 + \left(\frac{1 + e\lambda}{1 + e^k}\right)^{\alpha}}{1 + \left(\frac{1 + e^k}{1 + e^{\lambda}}\right)^{\beta}} \tag{3}$$

If $\lambda < k$, then $z < 1$, so in year 1, $\tilde{L}_1$ cannot be fully utilized, but $\tilde{K}_1$ can be fully utilized, so $K_1^* = \tilde{K}_1$.

Therefore $L_1^* = \tilde{L}_1 z$

and $\tilde{\tilde{L}}_2 = \tilde{L}_2 + \tilde{L}_1 - L_1^* = \tilde{L}_1(e\lambda - 1 - z)$

where $\tilde{\tilde{L}}_2$ is the uncommitted labor in year 2, including the labor which could not be utilized in year 1. Hence the total output that can be produced with the uncommitted supplies of labor and capital available in years 1 and 2 according to cumulative accounting prices using it only in year 1 is

$$2(P_1^* + P_2^*) = 2\left[(\tilde{L}_1 z)^{\alpha}\tilde{K}_1^{\beta} + \tilde{L}_1^{\alpha}(e\lambda - 1 - z)^{\alpha}K_2^{\beta}\right] \tag{4}$$

The total output using the marginal accounting prices would be

$$2(\tilde{P}_1 + \tilde{P}_2) = 2\left[\tilde{L}_1^{\alpha}\tilde{K}_1^{\beta} + \tilde{L}_2^{\alpha}\tilde{K}_2^{\beta}\right] \tag{5}$$

The difference between (4) and (5) is

$$2\left(P_1^* + P_2^*\right) - 2\left(\widetilde{P}_1 + \widetilde{P}_2\right) = \qquad (6)$$

$$2\widetilde{L}_1^{\alpha}\widetilde{K}_1^{\beta}\left[z^{\alpha} - 1 + (e^{\lambda} + 1 - z)^{\alpha}e^{k\beta} - e^{\lambda\alpha}e^{k\beta}\right] = 2\widetilde{L}_1^{\alpha}\widetilde{K}_1^{\beta}\left[-\alpha\epsilon + \left(\frac{e^k}{e^{\lambda}}\right)\alpha\epsilon\right]$$

where z has been replaced by $1-\epsilon$, ϵ being a small positive number.

As $\lambda < k$, the quantity within the bracket is definitely positive; hence the proof that the cumulative accounting prices lead to a higher level of output than the marginal accounting prices.

If $\lambda = k$, i.e., when L and K increase at the same rate, (6) reduces to zero and there is no difference in results according to the two approaches.

Turning now to the case when $\lambda > k$,

$$\frac{L_1^*}{K_1^*} = \frac{\widetilde{L}_1}{\widetilde{K}_1} z \quad \text{where } z = \frac{1 + \left(\frac{1+e^{\lambda}}{1+e^{k}}\right)^{\alpha}}{1 + \left(\frac{1+e^{k}}{1+e^{\lambda}}\right)^{\beta}} > 1 . \qquad (7)$$

In this case $\widetilde{K}_1$ will not be fully utilized and $\widetilde{L}_1$ will be fully utilized in year 1 according to cumulative accounting prices. Thus

$$L_1^* = \widetilde{L}_1 \text{ and } K_1^* = \widetilde{K}_1 \cdot \frac{1}{z} = \widetilde{K}_1(1-\epsilon)$$

where ϵ is a small positive number and

$$\widetilde{\widetilde{K}}_2 = \widetilde{K}_2 + \widetilde{K}_1 - K_1^* = \widetilde{K}_1\{e^k + 1 - (1 - \epsilon)\} ,$$

Appendix to Chapter Five

JOHANSEN'S DYNAMIC ACCOUNTING PRICES

$$\text{Min } L = \sum_{t=1}^{T} a^t \left[\sum_{\tau = t-\theta_1+1}^{t} n_1^\tau + \sum_{\tau = t-\theta_2+1}^{t} n_2^\tau + \sum_{\tau = t-\theta_x+1}^{t} n_x^\tau \right]$$

Subject to

$$x^\tau = g^\tau\left(n_x^\tau, k_x^\tau, v_1^\tau \; v_2^\tau\right)$$

$$k^t = z_1^t, k_1^t, + z_2^t k_2^t + z_x^t k_x^t$$

$$v_1^\tau = f_1^\tau\left(n_1^\tau, k_1^\tau\right)$$

$$v_2^\tau = f_2^\tau\left(n_2^\tau, k_2^\tau\right)$$

Where n_1^τ, n_2^τ, and n_x^τ are the labor inputs in sectors 1, 2, and x; a^t is the weight attached to labor in year t; θ_1, θ_2, and θ_x are the physical life of capital equipment in sector i; x^τ is output of sector x in vear τ: f_1^τ, f_2^τ, and g^τ are the production functions in sectors 1, 2, and x; k_1^τ, k_2^τ, and k_x^τ are the amounts of capital inputs in sectors 1, 2, and x; v_1^τ, v_2^τ are the ouputs produced in sectors 1, and 2 and used in sector x; z_1^t, z_2^t, and z_3^t are the prices of capital equipment for sectors 1, 2, and x in year t.

Forming the Lagrangian expression we have

$$\Phi = \sum_{t=1}^{T} a^{t} \left[\sum_{\tau = t-\theta_1+1}^{t} n_1^{\tau} + \sum_{\tau = t-\theta_2+1}^{t} n_2^{\tau} + \sum_{\tau = t-\theta_x+1}^{t} n_x^{\tau} \right]$$

$$- \sum_{t=1}^{T} \lambda^{t} \left[\sum_{\tau = t-\theta_x+1}^{t} g^{\tau}\left(n_x^{\tau}, k_x^{\tau}, v_1^{\tau}, v_2^{\tau}\right) - x^{\tau} \right]$$

$$- \sum_{t=1}^{T} \mu^{t} \left[k^{t} - z_1^{t} k_1^{t} - z_2^{t} k_2^{t} - z_x^{t} k_x^{t} \right]$$

$$- \sum_{t=1}^{T} \gamma_1^{t} \left[\sum_{\tau = t-\theta_1+1}^{t} f_1^{\tau}\left(n_1^{\tau}, k_1^{\tau}\right) - \sum_{\tau = t-\theta_x+1}^{t} v_1^{\tau} \right]$$

$$- \sum_{t=1}^{T} \gamma_2^{t} \left[\sum_{\tau = t-\theta_2+1}^{t} f_2^{\tau}\left(n_2^{\tau}, {}_2^{\tau}\right) - \sum_{\tau = t-\theta_x+1}^{t} v_2^{\tau} \right]$$

Minimization conditions are obtained by equating the partial derivatives of the above Lagrangean expression with respect to n_1^t, n_2^t, n_x^t, k_1^t, k_2^t, k_x^t, v_1^t, and v_2^t for i = 1, 2, ..., T, to zero. In general it is not easy to eliminate the Lagrangean multipliers to obtain simple efficiency conditions from the eight equations corresponding to the eight partial derivatives. However when we set the lifetime of capital in all sectors equal, i.e., $\theta_1 = \theta_2 = \theta_x = \theta$, the eight equations can be solved to give

$$f_{1n}^t g_{v1}^t = f_{2n}^t g_{v2}^t = g_n^t$$

$$\frac{f_{1k}^t}{z_1^t} g_{v1}^t = \frac{f_{2k}^t}{z_2^t} g_{v2}^t = \frac{g_k^t}{z_x^t}$$

where $f_{1n}^t = \dfrac{\partial f_1^t}{\partial n_1^t}$ and similarly for other symbols.

When the lifetime of capital in individual sectors is not equal, the above simple relationships do not hold. However the Lagrangean multipliers can be used as prices to achieve efficiency. It is seen that λ^t is the marginal cost in terms of increases in L of an increase in k^t; γ_i^t (i = 1, 2) is the marginal value in terms of decreases in L of a given increase in the supply of goods of the type produced by primary sector i. The solution of the eight where K is the uncommitted capital in year 2 including that unutilized in year 1.

As before the total output due to the cumulative and marginal accounting prices is,

$$2(P_1^* + P_2^*) = 2\left[\tilde{L}_1^{\alpha}\tilde{K}_1^{\beta}(1-\epsilon)^{\beta} + \tilde{L}_1^{\alpha}e^{\lambda\alpha}\tilde{K}_1^{\beta}(e^k + \epsilon)^{\beta}\right].$$

The difference between the outputs due to cumulative and marginal accounting prices is,

$$2(P_1^* + P_2^*) - 2(\tilde{P}_1 + \tilde{P}_2) = 2\tilde{L}_1^{\alpha}\tilde{K}_1^{\beta}\Big[(1-\epsilon)^{\beta} - 1 + e^{\lambda\alpha}e^{\beta k}\Big\{(1 + \frac{\epsilon}{e^k})^{\beta} - 1\Big\}\Big] = 2L_1^{\alpha}K_1^{\beta}\left[-\epsilon\beta + \left(\frac{e^{\lambda}}{e^k}\right)^{\alpha}\epsilon\beta\right] \quad (8)$$

It is positive, since $\lambda > k$. Thus factor combination according to cumulative accounting prices leads to higher value of output than that due to marginal accounting prices, even when cumulative accounting price is used in one year only. When the life of a project is not two years but any θ years, the proposition applies with greater force, the larger θ is. In this case

$$\frac{1 + \left(\frac{1+e^{\lambda}}{1+e^{k}}\right)^{\alpha} + \ldots + \left(\frac{1+e^{\lambda}}{1+e^{k}}\right)^{(\theta-1)\alpha}}{1 + \left(\frac{1+e^{k}}{1+e^{\lambda}}\right)^{\beta} + \ldots + \left(\frac{1+e^{k}}{1+e^{\lambda}}\right)^{(\theta-1)\beta}} = z$$

when $\lambda < k$, and

$$\frac{1 + \left(\frac{1+e^{\lambda}}{1+e^{k}}\right)^{\alpha} + \ldots + \left(\frac{1+e^{\lambda}}{1+e^{k}}\right)^{(\theta-1)\alpha}}{1 + \left(\frac{1+e^{k}}{1+e^{\lambda}}\right)^{\beta} + \ldots + \left(\frac{1+e^{k}}{1+e^{\lambda}}\right)^{(\theta-1)\beta}} = z$$

when $\lambda > k$, and so z or $\frac{1}{z} < 1$ more strongly than in case when $\theta = 2$.

equations derived from equating the partial derivatives equal to zero is

$$\frac{a[t,t+\theta_x-1]}{g_n^t} = \frac{\mu^t z_x^t}{g_k^t} = \frac{\gamma_1[t,t+\theta_x-1]}{g_{v_1}^t} = \frac{\gamma_2[t, t+\theta_x-1]}{g_{v_2}^t}$$

$$= \lambda(t, t+ {}_x-1),$$

$$\frac{a[t, t+ \theta_1-1]}{f_{in}^t} = \frac{\mu^t z_i^t}{f_{ik}^t} = \gamma_i[t, t+ \theta_1-1], \; (i = 1, 2)$$

Where $a[t, t+\theta_x-1] = \sum_{t=t}^{t+\theta-1} a_t$ and similarly for other parentheses [ ] following the Lagrangian multipliers.

The physical optimization conditions have a dual in profit maximization conditions. Consider sector 1, and let the product price be q_1^t, wage rate w^t and the accounting price of capital be Z_1^t which may be different from z_1^t. The whole investment project will appear as consisting of an initial investment outlay of $Z_1^t k_1^t$, wage outlay of $w^t n_1^t$, $w^{t+1} n_1^t$ ..., $w^{t+ \,1-1} nt$, and intakes $q_1^t v_1^t$, $q_1^{t+1} v_1$, ..., $q_1^{t+ \,1-1} v_1^t$. Total profits for the project will be

$$\pi_1^t = f_1^t\,(n_1^t, k_1^t)q\;\;[t, t+\theta_1-1] - n_1^t\,w[t, t+\theta_1-1] - Z_1^t\,k_1^t$$

Differentiating the above for profit maximization with respect to n_1^t, k_1^t, we have

$$w[t, t+\theta_1-1]/f_{1n}^t = Z_1^t/f_{1k}^t = q_1[t, t+\theta_1-1]$$

We shall get similar profit maximization conditions for sectors 2 and x. Comparing these conditions with the physical optimization conditions stated above, that the efficiency requirements are fulfilled if the prices are, for t = 1, 2, ... T:

$w^t = a^t$ = the wage rate in year t;

$Z_i^t = \mu^t z_i^t$ = the accounting price of capital to sector i in year t (i = 1, 2, x);

$p^t = \lambda^t$ = the output price for the secondary sector in year t;

$q_i^t = \gamma_i^t$ = the output price for the ith primary sector in year t (i = 1, 2).

The physical efficiency conditions can now be restated by replacing the parameters and multipliers by the corresponding prices which they equal.

The efficiency conditions can then be written as below by replacing the Lagrangian multipliers by the prices.

$$\frac{w[t, t+\theta_x-1]}{g_n^t} = \frac{Z_x^t}{g_k^t} = \frac{q_1[t, t+\theta_x-1]}{g_{v_1}^t} = \frac{q_2[t, t+\theta_x-1]}{g_{v_2}^t}$$

$$= p[t, t+\theta_x-1],$$

$$\frac{w[t, t+\theta_i-1]}{f_{in}^t} = \frac{Z_i^t}{f_{ik}^t} = q_i[t, t+\theta_i-1] \quad (i=1,2)$$

Under the restrictive assumptions stated above, Professor Johansen has been able to derive the accounting prices of factors in a dynamic set up. These prices are determined only up to a factor of optimality. The accounting prices for capital goods are formed by multiplying all capital prices by a common factor μ^t. We may interpret this as a correction to bring total demand for investment goods in harmony with the available amount, without distorting relative capital good prices. a entering the preference function (total labor input) may reflect a discounting of the future. Then we might interpret w^t as a discounted wage rate rather than as the current wage rate in year t.

BIBLIOGRAPHY

Chapter One

Dupuit, J. "On the Measurement of Utility of Public Works," _International Economic Papers_, Vol. 2 (translated from French, "De la Measure de l'Utilite des Travaux Publiques," _Annales des Ponts et Chaussees_, 2nd Series, Vol. 8, 1844).

Chenery, Hollis B. "The Application of Investment Criteria," _Quarterly Journal of Economics_, Vol. 67, 1953.

Ciriacy-Wantrup, Siegfried von "Benefit-Cost Analysis and Public Resource Development," _Journal of Farm Economics_, Vol. 37, 1955.

Kahn, Herman, and Mann, Irwin "Techniques of Systems Analysis," Santa Monica, CA: 1946, Rand Corporation, Research Memorandum RM-1829-I.

Eckstein, Otto _Water-Resource Development_, Cambridge, MA: Harvard University Press, 1958.

Hirshleifer, Jack "On the Theory of Optimal Investment Decision," _Journal of Political Economy_, Vol. 66 (August, 1958).

McKean, Ronald N. _Efficiency in Government Through Systems Analysis, with Emphasis on Water Resources Development_, New York, NY: John Wiley & Sons, 1958.

U.S. Federal Inter-Agency River Basin Committee, Proposed Policies for Economic Analysis of River Basin Projects (known as the

Green Book). Report by the Subcommittee on Benefits and Costs. Washington, DC: Government Printing Office, 1950. Revised in Inter-Agency Committee on Water Resources, Subcommittee on Evaluation Standards, Proposed Practices for Economic Analysis of River Basin Projects (also known as the Green Book) 1958.

Steiner, Peter O. "Choosing Among Alternative Public Investments in the Water Resource Field," _American Economic Review_, Vol. 49, (December, 1959).

U.S. Bureau of the Budget, _Standards and Criteria for Formulating and Evaluating Federal Water Resources Developments_ (known as the Consultant's Report). Report of Panel of Consultants to the Bureau of the Budget. Washington, DC: Bureau of the Budget, 1961.

Kurtilla, John V. "Welfare Aspects of Benefit Cost Analysis," _Journal of Political Economy_, Vol. 69, 1961.

National Bureau of Economic Research, _Public Finances: Needs, Sources, and Utilization_. Princeton, NJ: Princeton University Press, 1961.

Rothenberg, Jerome _The Measurement of Social Welfare_, Englewood Cliffs, NJ: Prentice-Hall, Inc., 1961.

Hines, Lawrence G. "The Hazards of Benefit Cost Analysis as a Guide to Public Investment Policy," _Public Finance_, 1962.

Masse, Pierre Optimal Investment Decisions: Rules for Action and Criteria for Choice, Englewood Cliffs, NJ: Prentice-Hall, 1962.

Mass, Arthur, and Others Design of Water-Resource Systems, Cambridge, MA: Harvard University Press, 1962.

Peacock, Alan T., and Robertson, D. J. (eds.) Public Expenditures: Appraisal and Control, Edinburg, IL: Oliver and Boyd, 1963.

Borus, M. E. "A Benefit Cost Analysis of the Economic Effectiveness of Retraining and the Unemployed," Yale Economic Essays, Vol. 4, No. 2, Fall, 1964.

Marglin, Stephen A. Approaches to Dynamic Investment Planning, Amsterdam, Netherlands: North Holland Publishing Co., 1963.

Turvey, Ralph "On the Divergence Between Social Cost and Private Cost," Economics, N. S. Vol. 30, (August, 1963).

McKean, Ronald N. "Cost-Benefit Analysis and British Defence Expenditure," Scottish Journal of Political Economy, Vol. 10, (February, 1963).

Feldstein, Martin S. "Opportunity Cost Calculation in Cost-Benefit Analysis," Public Finance, 1969.

Prest, R. A., and Turvey, R. "Cost-Benefit Analysis: A Survey," Economic Journal, Vol. 75, 1965.

Novik, David (ed.) Program Budgeting, Cambridge, MA: Harvard University Press, 1965, Second Edition, New York, NY: Holt, Rinehart and Winston, Inc., 1967.

United Nations, Department of Economic and Social Affairs, A Manual for Programme and Performance Budgeting, Sales No. 66, XVI. I., New York, NY: United Nations, 1965.

Dorfman, Robert (ed.) "Measuring Benefits of Government Investments," Washington, DC: Brookings Institution -- Studies of Government Finance, 1965.

Kantorovich, Leonid V. The Best Use of Economic Resources, Cambridge, MA: Harvard University Press, 1965.

Pearman, Elizabeth H. Bibliography on Cost-Benefit Analysis and Planning -- Programming -- Budgeting, McLean, VA: Research Analysis Corporation, 1966.

Peterson, Robert L. "The Use and Misuse of Cost Effectiveness," Air University Review, (March-April, 1966) 17.

U.S. Bureau of the Budget, Program Analysis Techniques: A Selected Bibliography, Revised Edition, Washington, DC: Government Printing Office, 1966.

Gross, Robert N. Principles of Cost Effectiveness Analysis, Washington, DC: U.S. Industrial College of the Armed Forces, Publication No. L66-24, 1966.

Haldi, John "Issues of Analysis in Cost-Effectiveness Studies for Civilian

Agencies of the Federal Government," paper presented at the Institute of Management Sciences, Philadelphia, PA: (September 7, 1966); Washington, DC: Bureau of the Budget, 1966.

Mass, Arthur "Benefit-Cost Analysis: Its Relevance to Public Expenditute Decisions," Quarterly Journal of Economics, (May, 1966).

Quade, E. S. "Systems Analysis Techniques for Planning -- Programming -- Budgeting," Santa Monica, CA: Rand Corporation, Paper P-3322, 1966.

Marglin, Stephen A. Public Investment Criteria: Benefit-Cost Analysis for Planned Economic Growth, Cambridge, MA: M.I.T. Press, 1967.

Ward, J. T. "Cost-Benefit Analysis," Journal of Public Administration, New Zealand, 1967.

Haveman, Robert H. "Benefit-Cost Analysis: Its Relevance to Public Investment Decisions: Comment," Quarterly Journal of Economics, Vol. 81, 1967.

Leyden, Fremont J., and Miller, Ernest G. (eds.) Planning Programming Budgeting, Chicago, IL: Markham Publishing Co., 1968.

Musgrave, R. A. "Cost-Benefit Analysis and the Theory of Public Finance," Journal of Economic Literature, 1969.

Hinrich, Harley H., and Taylor, Graeme M. Program Budgeting and Benefit-Cost Analysis, Pacific Palisades, CA: Goodyear

Publishing Co., 1969.

Joint Economic Committee, Congress of the United States The Analysis and Evaluation of Public Expenditures: The PPB System. A Compendium of Papers, Submitted to the Subcommittee on Economy in Government of the Joint Economic Committee, Congress of the United States, Vol. I, II, and III.

United Nations Industrial Development Organization Guidelines for Project Evaluation, United Nations, New York, NY, 1972.

Harberger, A. Project Evaluation, London, England: Macmillan, 1972.

Little, I. M. D., and Mirrlees, J. A. Project Appraisal and Planning for Developing Countries, New York, NY: Basic Books, Inc., Publishers, 1974.

Steiner, Peter O. "Public Expenditure Budgeting," The Studies of Public Finance, The Brookings Institution, Washington, DC, 1974.

Mishan, E. J. Cost-Benefit Analysis and Economic Theory (Studies in Mathematical and Managerial Economics) Amsterdam, Netherlands: North-Holland Publishing Co., 1975.

Marglin, Stephen A. Value and Price in the Labour-Surplus Economy, Oxford, CT: Clarendon Press, 1976.

Chapter Two

Streeter, H. W., and Phelps, E. B. "A Study of the Pollution and Natural Purification of the Ohio River," Public Health Service Bulletin No. 146, Washington, DC, 1923.

Scitovsky, T. "Two Concepts of External Economies," Journal of Political Economy, 1954.

Coase, H. "The Problem of Social Cost," Journal of Law and Economics, 1960.

Buchanan, J. M., and Stubblebine, W. C. "Externality," Economica, Vol. XXIX, (November, 1962).

Davis, O. A., and Whinston, A. B. "Externality, Welfare and the Theory of Games," Journal of Political Economy, 1962.

Meade, J. E. "External Economies and Diseconomies in a Competitive Situation," Economic Journal, 1962.

Bohm, Peter External Economies in Production, Stockholm, Sweden: Almquist and Wiksells, 1966.

Strotz, R. H. "Urban Transportation Parables," in Margolis (ed.), The Public Economy of Urban Communities, Baltimore, MD: The Johns Hopkins Press, 1965.

Sobel, M. J. "Water Quality Improvement Programming Problems," Water Resources Research, Vol. 1, No. 4, 1965.

Mishan, E. J. "Reflections on Recent Developments in the Concept of External Effects," The Canadian Journal of Economics and Political Science, February, 1965.

Wolozin, Harold The Economics of Air Pollution, New York, NY: W. W. Norton and Company, Inc., 1965.

Davidson, P., Adams, F. G., and Seneca, J. "The Social Value of Water Recreation Facilities Resulting from an Improvement in Water Quality: The Delaware Estuary," In Kreese, A. V., and Smith, S. C. (eds.), Water Research, Baltimore, MD: Johns Hopkins Press, 1966.

Federal Water Pollution Control Administration, Report on the Effluent Charge Study, F. W. P. C. A., Mimeo, 1966.

Schaumberg, G. W., and Mills, E. S. "Water Pollution Control in the Delaware Estuary" Harvard University Water Program, Mimeo, 1967.

Johnson, E. L. "A study in the Economics of Water Quality Management," Water Resources Research, Vol. 3, No. 2, 1967.

Fiering, M. B. Streamflow Synthesis, Cambridge, MA: Harvard University Press, 1967.

Ridker, Ronald G. Economic Costs of Air Pollution, New York, NY: Praeger Publishers, Inc., 1967.

Hayden, Boyd J. "Collective Facilities in Water Quality Management," appendix to Chapter 10 in Kneese, A. V., and Bower,

B. T. Managing Water Quality: Economics, Technology, Institutions, Baltimore, MD: Johns Hopkins Press, 1968.

Johansen, L. "Explorations in Long-term Projections for the Norweigan Economy," Economics of Planning, Vol. 8, No. 1-2, 1968.

Martin, D. O., and Tikvart, J. A. "A General Atmospheric Diffusion Model for Estimating the Effects on Air Quality of One or More Sources," Air Polution Control Association Journal, 1968.

Fair, G. M., Geyer, J. C., and Okum, D. A. Water and Wastewater Engineering, Vol. 2, New York, NY: John Wiley & Sons, Inc., 1968.

Davis, R. K. The Range of Choice in Water Management, Baltimore, MD: Johns Hopkins Press, 1968.

Smith R. "Costs of Conventional and Advanced Treatment of Waste Water," Journal of the Water Pollution Control Federation, 1968.

Black, R. J., et. al. "The National Solid Wastes Survey." An interim report, presented at the 1968 Annual Meeting of the Institute for Solid Wastes of the American Public Works Association, Miami Beach, FL, (October, 1968).

Upton, C. "Optimal Taxing of Water Pollution," Water Resources res., Vol. 4, No. 5, 1968.

Ayres, Robert U., and Kneese, Allen V. "Environmental Pollution," U.S. Congress, Joint Economic Committee, Federal Programs for the Development of Human Resources, Vol. 2, Proceedings of symposium on Human Ecology, Washington, DC, Department of Health, Education and Welfare, 1968.

Buchanan, J. "External Diseconomies, Corrective Taxes, and Market Structure," American Economic Review, 1969.

Combustion Engineering, Inc. "Technical Economic Study of Solid Waste Disposal Needs and Practices," IV, U.S.D.H.E.W., Bureau of Solid Waste Management, Rockville, MD, 1969.

Dorfman, R., and Jacoby, H. "A Model of Public Decisions Illustrated by Water Pollution Policy Problem," in the Analysis and Evaluation of Public Expenditures: The P.P.B. System, Joint Economic Committee, Washington, DC, U.S.G.P.O., 1969.

Kohn, R. "Linear Programming Model for Air Pollution Control: A Pilot Study of the St. Sois Airshed," Second Air Pollution Control Association, New York, NY, 1969.

Ayres, Robert U., and Kneese, Allen V. "Production, Consumption and Externalities," American Economic Review, 1969.

Mishan, E. J. "The Relationship Between Joint Products, Collective Goods, and External Effects," Journal of Political Economy, 1969b.

Bohm, Peter, and Kneese, Allen V. (eds.) *The Economics of Environment*, London, England: St. Martin's Press, 1971.

Carter, A. P., and Brady, A. (eds.) *Contributions to Input-Output Analysis*, Vol. I and II, New York, NY: Elsevier, 1971.

Forsund, F. R. "Allocation in Space and Environmental Pollution," *Swedish Journal of Economics*, Vol 74, No. 1, 1972.

Peskin, Henry M. "National Accounting and the Environment," Article No. 50, Statistical Central Bureau, Oslo, Norway, 1972.

Russel, C. S., and Spofford, W. O., Jr. "A Quantitative Framework for Residuals Management Decisions," in Kneese, A. V., and Bower, B. (eds.) *Environmental Quality Analysis*, Baltimore, MD: Johns Hopkins Press, 1972.

Smith, V. L. "Dynamics of Waste Accumulation: Disposals Versus Recycling," *Quarterly Journal of Economics*, 1972.

Strom, S. "Dynamics of Pollution and Waste Treatment Activities," Memorandum from Institute of Economics, University of Oslo, (10 May 1972).

Baumol, W. "On Taxation and the Control of Externalities," *American Economic Review*, 1972.

Mohring, H., and Kraus, M. "The Role of Pollutee Taxes in Externalities Problems," (Notes for Dalhousie and Toronto University Seminars), 1972.

Isard, W., et. al. Ecologic-Economic Analysis for Regional Development, New York, NY: Free Press, 1972.

U.S. Environmental Protection Agency, Office of Air Programs, Compilation of Air Pollution Emission Factors, Research Triangle Park, NC, (February, 1972).

Wright, W. H. "Alternative Approaches to Water Quality Management in the Trent River Basin," Unpublished Dissertation, University College, Oxford, 1972.

Debon, J. K., and Frankel, R. "Residuals Management in the Coal-Energy Industry," unpublished MS, Resources for the Future, Inc., 1972.

Haefele, E. T. "Environmental Quality as a Problem of Social Choice," in Knease, A. V., and Bower, B. T. (eds.) Envrionmental Quality Analysis: Theory and Methods in the Social Sciences, Baltimore, MD: Johns Hopkins Press, 1972.

Holzworth, G. C. Mixing Heights, Wind Speeds, and Potential for Urban Air Pollution Throughout the Continuous United States, Publ. No. AP-101 E.P.A., Office of Air Programs, Research Tiangle Park, NC, 1972.

Dorfman, Robert, and Dorfman, Nancy S. (eds.) Economics of the Environment, New York, NY: W. W. Norton and Company, Inc., 1972.

d'Arge, R. C., and Kogiker, K. C. "Economic Growth and the Environment," Review of Economic Studies, Vol. 12, 1973.

Dorfman, R., Jacoby, H., and Thomas, H. A. (eds.) Models for Managing Regional Water Quality, Cambridge, MA: Harvard University Press, 1973.

Russel, C. S. "Municipal Evaluation of Regional Water Management Proposals," in Dorfman, R., Jacoby, H., and Thomas, H. A. (eds.), Models for Managing Regional Water Quality, Cambridge, MA: Harvard University Press, 1973.

Rothenberg, J., and Heggie, Ian G. (eds.) The Management of Water Quality and the Environment, New York, NY: John Wiley & Sons, Inc., 1974.

Forsund and Strom, Steiner "Industrial Structure, Growth and Residual Flows," in Rothenberg and Heggie (eds.), The Management of Water Quality and the Environment, New York, NY: John Wiley & Sons, Inc., 1974.

Miernyk, William H., and Sears, John T. Air Pollution Abatement and Regional Economic Development, Lexington, MA: D. C. Heath and Co., 1974.

Kneese, Allen V., and Schultz, Charles L. Pollution, Prices and Public Policy, Washington, DC: The Brookings Institute, 1975.

Chapter Three

Hotelling, Harold "Stability in Competition," Economic Journal, Vol. 39, (March, 1929).

Pigou, Arthur C. The Economics of Welfare, 4th Edition, New York, NY: The Macmillan Co., 1932.

Bergson, A. "A Reformulation of Certain Aspects of Welfare Economics," Quarterly Journal of Economics, (February, 1938).

Kaldor, Nicholas "Welfare Proposition of Economics and Inter-Personal Comparisons of Utility," Economic Journal, 1939.

Hicks, J. R. "The Foundation of Welfare Economics," Economic Journal, 1939.

------- "The Valuation of Social Income," Economica, 1940.

Scitovsky, Tiber "A Note on Welfare Propositions in Economics," Review of Economic Studies, Vol. 9, (November, 1941).

Black, D. "On the Rationale of Group Decision Making," Journal of Political Economy, (February, 1948).

Friedman, M. "The Marshallian Demand Curve," Journal of Political Economy, 1949.

Little, I. M. D. A Critique of Welfare Economics, Oxford, CT, 1950.

Samuelson, P. A. The Foundations of Economic Analysis, Cambridge, MA, 1950.

Schumpeter, Joseph A. Capitalism, Socialism, and Democracy, 3rd Edition, New York, NY: Harper & Row Publishers, Inc., 1950.

Little, Ian Malcolm David "Social Choice and

Individual Values," Journal of Political Economy, 1952.

Little, I. M. D. "Social Choice and Individual Values," Journal of Political Economy, 1952.

Hildreth, C. "Alternative Conditions for Social Orderings," Econometrica, (January, 1953).

Harsanyi, J. C. "Cardinal Utility in Welfare Economics and in the Theory of Risk-Taking," Journal of Political Economy, 1953.

Kennedy, Charles F. "The Economic Welfare Function and Dr. Little's Criterion," Review of Economic Studies, Vol. 20, No. 2, 1953.

Rothenberg, Jerome "Conditions for a Social Welfare Function," Journal of Political Economy, Vol. 61, (October, 1953).

Kemp, M. C. "Arrow's General Possibility Theorem," Review of Economic Studies, Vol. 21, 1953-54.

Baldwin, Robert E. "A Comparison of Welfare Criteria," Review of Economic Studies, Vol. 21, No. 2, 1954.

Lewis, W. A. "Economic Development with Unlimited Supplied of Labour," Manchester School of Economics and Social Sciences, 22, 1954.

Buchanan, James M. "Individual Choice in Voting and the Market," Journal of Political Economy, Vol. 62, (August, 1954).

------------- "Social Choice, Democracy, and Free Markets," Journal of Political Economy, Vol. 62, (April, 1954).

Bergson, A. "On the Concept of Social Welfare," Quarterly Journal of Economics, (May, 1954).

Bauer, P. T. West African Trade, Cambridge, MA, 1954.

Meade, J. E. The Theory of International Economic Policy, Vol. II, Oxford, CT, 1955.

Majumdar, T. "Choice and Revealed Preference," Econometrica, 1956.

Lipsey, Richard G., and Lancaster, Kelvin "The General Theory of Second Best," Review of Economic Studies, Vol. 24, No. 1, 1956.

Hicks, J. R. A Revision of Demand Theory, Clarendon, TX, 1956.

Little, Ian Malcolm David A Critique of Welfare Economics, 2nd Edition, Oxford, CT, 1957.

Eckstein, Otto "Investment Criteria for Economic Development and the Theory of Intertemporal Welfare Economics," Quarterly Journal of Economics, Vol. 71, (February, 1957).

Graaff, Johannes de Villiers Theoretical Welfare Economics, Cambridge, MA, 1957.

Galbraith, John Kenneth The Affluent Society, Boston, MA: Houghton Mifflin Co., 1958.

Bator, F. "The Anatomy of Market Failure," *Quarterly Journal of Economics*, 1958.

Eckstein, O. *Water Resource Development*, Cambridge, MA, 1958.

Qayum, A. *Theory and Policy of Accounting Prices*, North Holland, 1960.

Mishan, E. J. "Survey of Welfare Economics, 1939-59," *Economic Journal*, 1960.

Stigler, George J. "The Economics of Information," *Journal of Political Economy*, Vol. 69, (June, 1961).

Chenery, H. B. "Comparative Advantage and Trade Policies," *American Economic Review*, 1961.

Balog, T. "Economic Policy and the Price System," *U.N. Economic Bulletin for Latin America*, 1961.

Rothenberg, Jerome *The Measurement of Social Welfare*, Englewood Cliffs, NJ: Prentice-Hall, 1961.

Telser, Lester G. "How Much Does it Pay Whom to Advertise?" *American Economic Review*, Vol. 51, (May, 1961).

Green, H. A. J. "The Social Optimum in the Presence of Monopoly and Taxation," *Review of Economic Studies*, 1961.

Kurtilla, John V. "Welfare Aspects of Benefit-Cost Analysis," *Journal of Political Economy*, Vol. 69, (June, 1961).

Hines, Lawrence G. "The Hazards of Benefit-Cost Analysis as a Guide to Public Investment Policy," _Public Finance_, Vol. 17, No. 2, 1962.

Buchanan, J. M., and Fullock, G. _The Calculus of Consent_, Ann Arbor, MI, 1962.

McKean, Ronald N. "Cost Benefit Analysis and British Defence Expenditure," _Scottish Journal of Political Economy_, Vol. 10, (February, 1963).

Mishan, Edward J. _Welfare Economics; Five Introductory Essays_, New York, NY: Random House, Inc., 1964.

Davis, Otto A., and Whinston, Andrew "Welfare Economics and the Theory of Second Best," _Review of Economic Studies_, Vol. 32, (January, 1965).

Prest, Alan R., and Turvey, Ralph "Cost-Benefit Analysis: A Survey," _Economic Journal_, Vol. 75, (December, 1965).

Bruno, M. "The Optimal Selection of Export Promoting and Import Substituting Projects," Paper delivered at the First United Nations International Seminar on Development Planning, Ankara, Turkey, 1965.

Pearman, Elizabeth H. _Bibliography on Cost-Benefit Analysis and Planning-Programming-Budgeting_, McLean, VA: Research Analysis Corporation, 1966.

Kruger "Some Economic Costs of Exchange Control: The Turkish Case," _Journal of Political Economy_, 1966.

Marglin, S. A. "Industrial Development in the Labour Surplus Economy," mimeo, Harvard University, 1966.

------------ *Public Investment Criteria*, Allen and Unwin, 1967.

Scott, M. F. G. "Rationalle of the Method to be Used to Evaluate a Project," OECD Memorandum, 1967.

Mohring, Herbert "Consumer's Surplus Benefit Measures," Harvard University Seminar on Political Economy Decisions, (March, 1967).

Tullock, Gordon "The General Irrelevance of the General Impossibility Theorem," *Quarterly Journal of Economics*, Vol. 81, (May, 1967).

Hansen, B. *Long and Short-Term Planning in Underdeveloped Countries*, North Holland Publishing Co., 1967.

Nelson, James R. "The Value of Travel Time," in Samuel B. Chase, Jr. (ed.), *Problems in Public Expenditure Analysis*, Washington, DC: Brookings Institution, 1968.

Little, I. M. D., Scitovsky, T., and Scott, M. F. G. *Industry and Trade in Some Developing Countries*, Paris, London, 1970.

Joshi, Vijay "Foreign Trade and Investment Criteria," in Eltis, W. A., Scott, M. F. G., and Wolfe, J. N., *Induction, Growth, and Trade*, Clarendon Press, 1970.

Arron, K. J., and Kurz, M. Public Investment, the Rate of Return and Optimal Fiscal Policy, Baltimore, MD: Johns Hopkins Press, 1970.

Rudra, A. "Use of Shadow Prices in Project Evaluation," Paper presented at the Second World Econometric Congress, Cambridge, MA, 1970.

Sen, A. K. "Interrelation Between Project Planning and Aggregate Planning," Paper presented at the Conference on Economic Development at Dushambe, 1970.

------------ Collective Choice and Social Welfare, London, 1970.

Harberger, A. C. "Three Basic Postulates of Applied Welfare Economics," Journal of Economic Literature, 1971.

------------ The Social Opportunity Cost of Labour," International Labour Review, 1971.

Dixit, A. K. "Short-Run Equilibrium and Shadow Prices in the Dual Economy," Oxford Economics Papers 23, 1971.

Dasgupta, P. "Public Sector Pricing Rules," Economic and Political Weekly, Annual Number, (January, 1971).

Mirrlees, J. A., and Diamond, P. A. "Optimal Taxation and Public Production," American Economic Review, (March-June, 1971).

Dasgupta, P., and Stiglitz, J. E. "Benefit-Cost Analysis and Trade Policies," mimeo (forthcoming), 1971.

Dasgupta, P., and Stiglitz, J. E. "Valuation of Tradeables in Benefit-Cost Analysis," mimeo, 1971.

Stiglitz, J. E., and Dasgupta, P. "Differential Taxation, Public Goods, and Economic Efficiency," Review of Economic Studies, Symposium on Public Finance, (April, 1971).

Currie, J. M., Murphy, J. A., and Schmitz, A. "The Concept of Economic Surplus and Its Use in Economic Analysis," Economic Journal, 1971.

Little, I. M. D. "On Measuring the Value of Private Direct Overseas Investment," in Ranic, G. (ed.), The Gap Between Rich and Poor Nations, New York, NY: The Macmillan Co., 1972.

Harberger, A. C. Project Evaluation Markham Publishing Co., 1972.

Sen, A. K. "Control Areas and Accounting Prices: An Approach to Economic Evaluation," Economic Journal, 1972.

Reuber, G. L., Crooknell, H., Emerson, M. R., and Gallais-Hamonno, G. Private Foreign Investment in Development, Fair Lawn, NJ: Oxford University Press for OECD Development Center, 1973.

Khan, A. R., and Mirrlees, J. A. "Optimal Prices for a Developing Economy," Oxford, CT: Nuffield College, 1973.

Lal, D. Appraising Foreign Investment in Developing Countries, Heinemann, 1974.

Zacherhauser, _et_. _al_. (eds.) _Benefit-Cost and Policy Analysis_, Chicago, IL: Aldine Publishing Co., 1975.

Qayum, A. "Evaluation of Public Sector Projects, Assessment Little-Mirrlees Manual," _Economic and Political Weekly_, (February, 1976).

Mishan, E. J. _Cost-Benefit Analysis_, New York, NY: Praeger Publishers, Inc., 1976.

Chapter Four

Little, Ian Malcolm David "Social Choice and Individual Values," _Journal of Political Economy_, Vol. 60, (October, 1952).

Bowen, Howard R. "The Interpretation of Voting in the Allocation of Economic Resources," _Quarterly Journal of Economics_, Vol. 58, (November, 1953).

Chenery, Hollis B. "The Application of Investment Criteria," _Quarterly Journal of Economics_, Vol. 67, (February, 1953).

------------ "Social Choice, Democracy and Free Markets," _Journal of Political Economy_, Vol. 62, (April, 1954).

Buchanan, James M. "Individual Choice in Voting and the Market," _Journal of Political Economy_, Vol. 62, (August, 1954).

Ciriacy-Wantrup, Siegfried von "Benefit-Cost Analysis and Public Resource Development," _Journal of Farm Economics_, Vol. 27, (November, 1955).

------------ "Welfare Criteria, Pricing, and Decentralization of a Public Service," Quarterly Journal of Economics, Vol. 71, (August, 1957).

------------ "An Economic Theory of Political Action in a Democracy," Journal of Political Economy, Vol. 65, (April, 1957).

Downs, Anthony An Economic Theory of Democracy, New York, NY: Harper, 1957.

Eckstein, Otto "Investment Criteria for Economic Development and the Theory of Intertemporal Welfare Economics," Quarterly Journal of Economics, Vol. 71, February, 1957.

Black, Duncan The Theory of Committees and Elections, New York, NY: Cambridge University Press, 1958.

------------ Water-Resource Development, Cambridge, MA: Harvard University Press, 1958.

------------ "On the Theory of Optimal Investment Decision," Journal of Political Economy, Vol. 66, (August, 1958).

Samuelson, Paul A. "Aspects of Public Expenditure Theories," Vol. 40, (November, 1958).

Strotz, Robert H. "Two Propositions Related to Public Goods," Review of Economics and and Statistics, Vol. 40, (November, 1958).

Steiner, Peter O. "Choosing Among Alternative Public Investments in the Water Resource

Field," American Economic Review, Vol. 49, (December, 1959).

Coase, Ronald H. "The Problem of Social Cost." Journal of Law Economics, Vol. 3, (October, 1960).

------------ "A Survey of the Theory of Public Expenditure Criteria," in Public Finances: Needs, Sources, and Utilization, Princeton, NJ: Princeton University Press for National Bureau of Economic Research, 1961.

Buchanan, James M., and Stubblebine, William C. "Externality," Economica, N.S. Vol. 29, (November, 1962).

------------, and Tullock, Gordon The Calculus of Consent, Ann Arbor, MI: The University of Michigan Press, 1962.

Hines, Lawrence G. "The Hazards of Benefit-Cost Analysis as a Guide to Public Investment Policy," Public Finance, Vol. 17, No. 2, 1962.

Masse, Piere Optimal Investment Decisions: Rules for Action and Criteria for Choice, Englewood Cliffs, NJ: Prentice-Hall, 1962.

------------, and Kafoglis, Milton Z. "A Note of Public Goods Supply," American Economic Review, Vol. 53, (June, 1963).

Johansen, Leif "Some Notes on the Lindhal Theory of Determination of Public Expenditures," International Economic Review, Vol. 4, (September, 1963).

Marglin, Stephen A. Approaches to Dynamic Investment Planning, Amsterdam: North Holland Publishing Company, 1963.

------------ "The Opportunity Costs of Public Investment," Quarterly Journal of Economics, Vol. 77, (May, 1963).

------------ "The Social Rate of Discount and the Optimal Rate of Investment," Quarterly Journal of Economics, Vol. 77, (February, 1963). See also comment by Lind, Robert C. "The Social Rate of Discount and the Optimal Rate of Investment: Further Comment," Quarterly Journal of Economics, Vol. 78, (May, 1964), Usher, Dan "The Social Rate of Discount and the Optimal Rate of Investment: Comment," Quarterly Journal of Economics, Vol. 78, (November, 1964).

McKean, Ronald N. "Cost-Benefit Analysis and British Defense Expenditure," Scottish Journal of Political Economy, Vol. 10, (February, 1963).

Thomas, Harold A. Jr. "The Animal Farm: A Mathematical Model for the Discussion of Social Standards for Control of the Environment," Quarterly Journal of Economics, Vol. 77, (February, 1963).

Turvey, Ralph "On Divergences Between Social Cost and Private Cost," Economica N.S., Vol. 30, (August, 1963).

------------ "Net Social Benefit Calculation and the Public Investment Decision," Oxford Economic Papers, Vol. 16, (March, 1964).

------------ "Opportunity Cost Calculations in Cost-Benefit Analysis," Public Finance, Vol. 19, No. 2, 1964.

------------ "The Social Time Discount Rate in Cost-Benefit Analysis," Economic Journal, Vol. 74, (June, 1964).

Jorgenson, Dale "Review: Approaches to Dynamic Investment Planning by Stephen A. Marglin," American Economic Review, Vol. 4, (June, 1964).

Wellisz, Stanislaw "On External Diseconomies and the Government-Assisted Invisible Hand," Economica N.S., Vol. 31, (November, 1964).

Birdsall, William C. "A Study of the Demand for Public Goods," in Musgrave, Richard A. (ed.), Essays in Fiscal Federalism, Washington, DC: Brookings Institution, 1965.

Dorfman, Robert (ed.) Measuring Benefits of Government Investment, Washington, DC: Brookings Institution, 1965.

Feldstein, Martin S. "The Derivation of Social Time Preference Rates," Kykos, Vol. 18, Fasc. 2, 1965.

------------ "Investment Decision Under Uncertainty: Choice Theoretic Approaches," Quarterly Journal of Economics, Vol. 79, (November, 1965).

Olson, Mancur Jr. The Logic of Collective Action, Cambridge, MA: Harvard University Press, 1965.

Prest, Alar R., and Turvey, Ralph "Cost-Benefit Analysis: A Survey," Economic Journal, Vol. 75, (December, 1965).

------------- "The Role of Alternative Cost in Project Design and Selection," Quarterly Journal of Economics, Vol. 79, (August, 1965).

Hirshleifer, Jack "Investment Decision Under Uncertainty Application of State Preference Approach," Quarterly Journal of Economics, Vol. 80, (May, 1966).

Maass, Arthur "Benefit-Cost Analysis: Its Relevance to Public Investment Decisions," Quarterly Journal of Economics, Vol. 80, (May, 1966).

Pearman, Elizabeth H. Bibliography on Cost-Benefit Analysis and Planning-Programming-Budgeting, McLean, VA: Research Analysis Corporation, 1966.

U.S. Bureau of the Budget, Program Analysis Techniques: A Selected Bibliography, Revised Edition, Washington, DC: Government Printing Office, 1966.

Williams, Alan "The Optimal Provision of Public Goods in a System of Local Government," Journal of Political Economy, Vol. 74, (February, 1966).

Haveman, Robert H. "Benefit Cost Analysis: Its Relevance to Public Investment Decisions: Comment," Quarterly Journal of Economics, Vol. 81, (November, 1967).

Mishan, Edward J. "Criteria for Public Investment: Some Simplifying Suggestions," Journal of Political Economy, Vol. 75, (April, 1967).

Harberger, Arnold C. "Survey of Literature on Cost-Benefit Analysis for Industrial Project Evaluation," in Evaluation of Industrial Projects, U.N., 1968.

Nelson, James R. "The Value of Travel Time," in Chase, Samuel B., Jr. (ed.), Problems in Public Expenditure Analysis, Washington, DC: Brookings Institution, 1968.

Steiner, Peter O. "Public Expenditure Budgeting" in The Economics of Public Finance, Washington, DC: The Brookings Institution, 1974.

Weisbord, Burton A. "Collective-Consumption Services of Individual Consumption Goods," Quarterly Journal of Economics, Vol. 78, (August, 1969).

Air and Water Pollution

Herfindahl, Orris C., and Kneese, Allen V. Quality of the Environment, Baltimore, MD: Hopkins Press of Resources of the Future, 1965.

Michelson, Irving, and Tourin, Boris "Comparative Method for Studying Costs of Air Pollution," Public Health Reports, Vol. 81, (June, 1966).

Ogden, Delbert C. "Economic Analysis of Air Pollution," Land Economics, Vol. 42, (May, 1966).

Johnson, E. "A Study in the Economics of Water Quality Management," Water Resource Res., Vol. 3, No. 2, 1967.

Ridker, Ronald G. Economic Costs of Air Pollution, New York, NY: Praeger Publishers, 1967.

Schaumberg, G. Water Pollution Control in the Delaware Estuary, Cambridge, MA: Harvard Water Program, 1967.

Dales, J. H. Pollution Poverty and Prices, Toronto, ON: University of Toronto Press, 1968.

Kneese, A. V., and Bower, B. T. Managing Water Quality: Economics, Technology, Institutions, Baltimore, MD: The Johns Hopkins University Press, 1968.

Smith, R. "Costs of Conventional and Advanced Treatment of Waste Water," J. Water Pollution Control Fed., (September, 1968).

Dorfman, R., and Jacoby, H. "A Model of Public Decisions Illustrated by a Water Pollution Policy Problem," in The Analysis and Evaluation of Public Expenditures: The PPB System, Joint Economic Committee, Washington, DC: U.S. Government Printing Office, 1969.

Zerba, R. D. Jr. The Economics of Air Pollution: A Cost-Benefit Approach, Toronto, Ontario, Department of Public Health, 1969.

Kneese, Allen V., Ayres, Robert U., and d'Arge, Ralph C. Economics and Environment: A Materials Balance Approach, Washington, DC: Johns Hopkins Press for Resources for the Future, Ind., 1970.

Barret, Larry B., and Waddell, Thomas H. "The Cost of Air Pollution Damages: A Status

Report," Environmental Protection Agency, mimeo, 1971.

Crocker, Thomas D. "Urban Air Pollution Damage Functions," presented at the Econometric Society Meetings, New Orleans, LA: (December, 1971).

Currie, J. M., Murphy, J. A., and Schmitz, A. "The Concept of Economic Surplus and Its Use in Economic Analysis," Economic Journal, LXXXI, (December, 1971).

Freeman, A. Myrick III "Air Pollution and Property Values, A Methodological Comment," Review of Economics and Statistics, (November, 1971).

Kneese, A. V. "Environmental Pollution: Economics and Policy," American Economic Association, Papers and Proceedings, 1971.

President's Council on Environmental Quality, Environmental Quality, the Second Annual Report of the Council on Environmental Quality, (August, 1971).

U.S. Environmental Protection Agency, Cost of Clean Water and Cost of Clean Air, Washington, DC: Government Printing Office, 1971.

Gerhard, Paul H. "Air Pollution Control: Benefits, Costs, Inducements," in Mushkin, Selma (ed.), Public Prices for Public Projects, Washington, DC: The Urban Institute, 1972.

Kneese, V., and Bower, B. T. (eds.) Environmental Quality Analysis, Baltimore, MD: Johns Hopkins Press, 1972.

Langham, Max R., Headley, Joseph C., and Edwards, W. Frank "Agricultural Pesticides: Productivity and Externalities," in Kneese and Bower op. cit., 1972.

Lave, Laster B. "Air Pollution Damage: Some Difficulties in Estimating the Value of Abatement," in Kneese, Allen V., and Bower, Blair T. (eds.), Environmental Quality Analysis, Baltimore, MD: Johns Hopkins Press for Resources for the Future, 1972.

Organization for Economic Cooperation and Development, Environmental Damage Costs, Record of a Seminar held at the OECD in August, 1972.

Dorfman, R., Jacoby, H., and Thompson, H. A. (eds.) Models for Managing Regional Water Quality, Cambridge, MA: Harvard University Press, 1973.

Pearce, D. W. Environmental Economics, New York, NY: Longman, 1976.

Freeman, A. M., Haveman, Robert H., and Kneese, Allan V. The Economics of Environmental Policy, New York, NY: John Wiley and Sons, 19 .

Outdoor Recreation

Trice, Andrew H., and Wood, Samuel E. "Measurement of Recreation Benefits," Land Economics, Vol. 34, (August, 1958).

Clawson, Marion "Methods of Measuring the Demand for and Values of Outdoor Recreation," Papers presented at a meeting of the Taylor-Hibbard Club, University of Wisconsin, January 13, 1959, Resources for the Future Reprint No. 10, Washington, DC: RFE, (February, 1959).

Knetsch, Jack L. "Outdoor Recreation Demands and Benefits," Land Economics, Vol. 39, (November, 1963).

Wennergren, . "Valuing Non-market Priced Recreational Resources," Land Economics, 1964.

Mack, Ruth, and Myers, S. "Outdoor Recreation" in Dorfman, R., Measuring Benefits of Government Investments, Washington, DC: Brookings Institution, 1965.

Mack, Ruth P., and Myers, Sumner "Outdoor Recreation" in Dorfman, Robert (ed.) Measuring Benefits of Government Investments, Washington, DC: Brookings Institution, 1965.

Clawson, Marion, and Knetsch, J. L. Economics of Outdoor Recreation, Baltimore, MD: Johns Hopkins Press, 1966.

Dainte, Robert J. "Methods for Determination of Demand for Outdoor Recreation," Land Economics, Vol. 42, (August, 1966).

Davidson, P., Adams, F. G., and Seneca, J. "The Social Value of Water Recreation Facilities Resulting from an Improvement in Water Quality: The Delaware Estuary," Kneese, Allen V. and Smith, Stephen C. (eds.), Water Research, Baltimore, MD: Johns Hopkins Press, 1966.

Stevens, J. "Recreational Benefits from Water Pollution Control," Water Resource Research 2, 1966.

Pearse, P. H. "A New Approach to the Evaluation of Non-Priced Recreational Resources," Land Economics, (February, 1968).

Seneca, J. J. "A Generalized Approach to Estimating Recreation Benefits," University of Pennsylvania, Ph.D. Thesis, 1968.

Cicchetti, C. J., Seneca, J., and Davidson, A. The Demand and Supply of Outdoor Recreation, Bureau of Economic Research, Rutgers University, (March, 1969).

Burt, O. R., and Brewer, D. "Estimation of Net Social Benefits from Outdoor Recreation," Econometrica, 1971.

Maler, Karl-Goran "A Method of Estimating Social Benefits from Pollution Control," The Swedish Journal of Economics, 1971.

Bohm, P. "A Note on the Problem of Estimating Benefits for Pollution Control," Problems of Environmental Economics, OECD, Paris, 1972.

Cicchetti, C. J. "A Review of the Empirical Analyses That Have Been Based Upon the National Recreational Surveys," Journal of Leisure Research, 1972.

Education and Training

Swift, W. J., and Burton, A. "The Valuation of Human Capital," Journal of Political Economy, Vol. 69, (October, 1961).

Bowman, Mary Jean "Social Returns to Education," International Social Science Journal, Vol. 14, No. 4, 1962.

Schultz, Theodore W. The Economic Value of Education, New York, NY: Columbia University Press, 1963.

Becker, Gary S. Human Capital: A Theoretical and Empirical Analysis, with Special Reference to Education, New York, NY: Columbia University Press for National Bureau of Economic Research, 1964.

Borus, Michael E. "A Benefit-Cost Analysis of the Economic Effectiveness of Retraining the Unemployed," Yale Economic Essays, Vol. 4, 1964.

Hirsch, Werner Z., and others Spillover of Public Education: Costs and Benefits, Los Angeles, CA: University of California, Institute of Government and Public Affairs, 1964.

Page, David A. "Retraining Under the Manpower Development Act: A Cost-Benefit Analysis," Public Policy, Vol. 13, 1964.

Somers, Gerald G., and Stromsdorfer, Ernst "Benefit-Cost Analysis of Manpower Retraining," Proceedings of the Seventeenth Annual Meeting, Industrial Relations Research Association, 1964.

Swift, W. J., and Burton, A. External Benefits of Public Education: An Economic Analysis, Princeton, NJ: Princeton University, Department of Economics, Industrial Relations Section, 1964.

Hirsch, Werner Z., and Segelhorst, Elbert W. "Incremental Income Benefits of Public Education," Review of Economics and Statistics, Vol. 47, (November, 1965).

Swift, William J., and Weisbrod, Burton A. "On the Monetary Value of Education's Intergeneration Effects," Journal of Political Economy, Vol. 73, (December, 1965).

------------ "Preventing High School Dropouts," in Dorfman, Robert (ed.), Measuring Benefits of Government Investments, Washington, DC: Brookings Institution, 1965.

Beker, G. S., and Chiswick, B. R. "Education and the Distribution of Earnings," American Economic Review Process, (May, 1966).

Beker, G. S. "Human Capital and the Personal Distribution of Income: An Analytical Approach," Inst. Public Administration, University of Michigan, 1967.

Hanoch, G. "An Economic Analysis of Earnings and Schooling," Journal of Human Resources, 1967.

Ben-Porath, Y. "The Production of Human Capital Over Time," In Hansen, W. L. (ed.), Education, Income, and Human Capital, New York, NY, 1970.

Johnson, T. "Returns from Investment in Human Capital," American Economic Review, (September, 1970).

Chiswick, B. "Income Inequality and Schooling: A Cross-Sectional Study," mimeo, National Bureau of Economic Research, (August, 1972).

Griliches, Z., and Mason, W. M. "Education, Income, and Ability," Journal of Political Economy, (May/June, 1972).

Hause, J. "Earnings Profile: Ability and Schooling," Journal of Political Economy, (May/June, 1972).

Haley, W. J. "Human Capital: The Choice Between Investment and Income," American Economic Review, (December, 1973).

Taubman, P. "Schooling, Ability, Non-Pecuniary Rewards, Socioeconomic Background ...," National Bureau of Economic Research, working paper no. 17, (November, 1973).

Anderson, L. W. "Student Involvement in Learning and School Achievement," paper presented to the American Educational Research Association, Chicago, IL, (April 15-19, 1974).

Leibowitz, A. "Family Investments in Human Capital," Journal of Political Economy, (March/April, 1974).

Solomon, L. C. "The Definition and Impact of College Quality," Explor. Economic Research, 1974.

Wallace, S., and Ihnen, L. A. "Full Time Schooling in Life Cycle Models of Human Capital Accumulation," Journal of Political Economy, (February, 1974).

Wachtel, P. "The Returns to Investment in Higher Education: Another View," in Juster, F. T. (ed.), Education, Income, and Human Behavior, New York, NY, 1975.

Chapter Five

Kahn, R. F. "Some Notes on Ideal Output," Economic Journal, 1935.

Subcommittee on Benefits and Costs (Federal Inter-Agency River Basin Committee) Proposed Practices for Economic Analysis of River Basin Projects, Washington, DC, 1950.

McKenzie, L. W. "Ideal Output and the Interdependence of Firms," Economic Journal, 1951.

Alchian, A. "The Rate of Interest, Fisher's Rate of Return over Costs, and Keynes Internal Rate of Return," American Economic Review, 1955

Galenson, W., and Leibenstein, H. "Investment Criteria, Productivity and Economic Development," Quarterly Journal of Economics, 1955.

Lorie, J., and Savage, L. J. "Three Problems in Rationing Capital," Journal of Business, 1955.

Robinson, R. "The Rate of Interest, Fisher's Rate of Return over Costs and Keynes' Internal Rate of Return: Comment," American Economic Review, 1956.

Lipsey, R. L., and Lancaster, K. "The General Theory of Second Best," Review of Economic Studies, 1956-57.

Eckstein, O. "Investment Criteria for Economic Development," _Quarterly Journal of Economics_, 1957.

Sen, A. K. "Capital-Intensity in Development Planning," _Quarterly Journal of Economics_, 1957.

Eckstein, O. _Water Resource Development -- The Economics of Project Evaluation_, Cambridge, MA: Harvard University Press, 1958.

Hirschleifer, J. "Theory of Optimal Investment Decision," _Journal of Political Economy_, 1958.

McKean, R. N. _Efficiency of Government Through Systems Analysis_, New York, NY: John Wiley & Sons, Inc., 1958.

Samuelson, P., Dorfman, R., and Solow, R. _Linear Programming and Economic Analysis_, New York, NY, 1958.

Bailey, M. J. "Formal Criteria for Investment Decisions," _Journal of Political Economy_, 1959.

Margolis, J. "The Economic Evaluation of Federal Water Resource Development," _American Economic Review_, 1959.

Steiner, P. O. "Choosing Among Alternative Public Investment in the Water Resource Field," _American Economic Review_, 1959.

Qayum, A. _Theory and Policy of Accounting Prices_, Amsterdam, 1960.

Masse, P. _Optimal Investment Decisions: Rules for Action and Criteria for Choice_,

Englewood Cliffs, NJ: Prentice-Hall, Inc., 1962.

Marglin, S. "The Opportunity Costs of Public Investment," Quarterly Journal of Economics, 1963.

------------ "The Social Rate of Discount and the Optimal Rate of Investment," Quarterly Journal of Economics, 1963.

Feldstein, M. "Net Social Benefit Calculation and the Public Investment Decision," Oxford University Press, 1963.

Lind, R. C. "The Social Rate of Discount and the Optimal Rate of Investment: Further Comment," Quarterly Journal of Economics, 1964.

Mishan, E. J. "The Opportunity Costs of Public Investment: Comment," Quarterly Journal of Economics, 1964.

Usher, Dan "The Social Rate of Discount and the Optimal Rate of Investment: Comment," Quarterly Journal of Economics, 1964.

Prest, A., and Turvey, R. "Cost-Benefit Analysis: A Survey," Economic Journal, (December, 1965).

Agarwal, Ramgopal "Shadow Prices and Planning in Underdeveloped Countries," The Manchester School of Economics and Social Studies, (May, 1966).

Tinbergen, J. Economic Policy, Principles and Design, Amsterdam, 1966.

Johansen, Leif "Some Problems of Pricing and Optimal Choice of Factor Proportions in a Dynamic Setting," Economica, (May, 1967).

Marglin, S. A. "The Rate of Interest and the Value of Capital with Unlimited Supplies of Labor," in Shell, K., Essays on the Theory of Optimal Economic Growth, Cambridge, MA: Massachusetts Institute of Technology, 1967.

Marglin, S. A. Public Investment Criteria, George Allen and Unwin, London, 1967.

Sen, A. K. "General Criteria of Industrial Project Evaluation," in Evaluation of Inducstrial Projects, U. N., 1967.

McKean, R. "Shadow Prices," in Chase, S. B. (ed.), Problems in Public Expenditure Analysis, Washington, DC: Brookings Institution, 1968.

Rees, R. "Second Best Rules for Public Enterprise Pricing," Economica, (August, 1968).

Turvey, R. Optimal Pricinq and Investment in Electricity-Supply, London, 1968.

Mishan, E. J. Cost-Benefit Analysis, New York, NY: Praeger Publishers, 1971.

Dasgupta, P. "An Analysis of Two Approaches to Project-Evaluation in Developing Countries," Industrialization and Productivity, Oxford Bulletin, (February, 1972).

Dasgupta, P. "A Comparative Analysis of the UNIDO Guidelines and the OECD Mannual," Bulletin of the Oxford University Institute of Economics and Statistics, (February, 1972).

Dasgupta, A. K., and Pearce, D. W. Cost-Benefit Analysis, New York, NY: Macmillan Co., 1972.

Prest, A. R. "The Role of Labor Taxes and Subsidies in Promoting Employment in Developing Countries," International Labor Office, Geneva, 1972.

Scott, M. "Estimates of Accounting Prices for Mauritius," Nuffield College, mimeo, Oxford, (April, 1972).

Sen, A. K. "Accounting Prices and Control Areas: An Approach to Project Evaluation," Economic Journal, 1972.

Seton, F. Shadow Wages in the Chilean Economy, OECD Development Center, Paris, 1972.

Stern, N. H. An Appraisal of Tea Production on Small-Holdings in Kenya, OECD Development Center, Paris, 1972.

UNIDO, Guidelines for Project Evaluation, written by Dasgupta, P. A., Marglin, S. A., and Sen, A. K., U. N. New York, 1972.

Khan, A. R., and Mirrlees, J. A. "Optimal Prices for a Developing Economy," mimeo, Nuffield College, Oxford, 1973.

Little, I. M. D., and Mirrlees, J. A. Project Appraisal and Planning for Developing Countries, New York, NY: Basic Books, Inc. Publishers, 1974.

Marglin, S. A. Value and Price in the Labour-Surplus Economy, Oxford: Clarendon Press, 1976.

Mishan, E. J. Cost-Benefit Analysis, New York, NY: Praeger Publishers, 1976.

Chapter Six

Fisher, Irving The Rate of Interest, New York, NY: Macmillan Co., 1907.

Ramsay, R. P. "A Mathematical Theory of Saving," Economic Journal, (December, 1928).

Fishter, Irving The Theory of Interest, New York, NY: Macmillan Co., 1930.

Hart, A. G. "Anticipations, Business Planning, and the Cycle," Quarterly Journal of Economics, 1937.

Dean, Joel Capital Budgeting, New York, NY: Columbia University Press, 1951.

Dean, Joel Managerial Economics, Englewood Cliffs, NJ: Prentice-Hall, 1951.

Lutz, Friedrich and Vera The Theory of Investment of the Firm, Princeton, NJ: Princeton University Press, 1951.

Scitovsky, T. Welfare and Competition, Chicago, IL: Richard D. Irwin, Inc., 1951.

Alchian, A. "The Rate of Interest, Fisher's Rate of Return over Costs, and Keynes Internal Rate of Return," American Economic Review, 1955.

Lorie, James H., and Savage, Leonard J. "Three Problems in Rationing Capital," Journal of Business, (October, 1955).

Strotz, R. "Myopia and Inconsistency in Dynamic Utility Maximization," Review of Economic Studies, 1955056.

Robinson, R. "The Rate of Interest, Fisher's Rate of Return Over Cost, and Keynes' Internal Rate of Return: Comment," American Economic Review, 1956.

Sen, A. K. "On Optimizing the Rate of Saving," Economic Journal, (December, 1956).

Solomon, E. "The Arithmetic of Capital Budgeting Decisions," Journal of Business, 1956.

Eckstein, Otto "Investment Criteria for Economic Development and the Theory of Intertemporal Welfare Economics," Quarterly Journal of Economics, (Febru (February, 1957).

Roberts, Harry V. "Current Problems in the Economics of Capital Budgeting," Journal of Business, (January, 1957).

Samuelson, Paul A. "The Pure Theory of Public Expenditure," Review of Economics and Statistics, (November, 1957).

Sen, A. K. "Capital Intensity in Development Planning," Quarterly Journal of Economics, 1957.

Eckstein, Otto Water Resource Development: The Economics of Project Evaluation, Cambridge, MA: Harvard University Press, 1958.

Hirshleifer, J. "On the Theory of Optimal Investment Decision," Journal of Political Economy, (August, 1958).

Pritchford and Hagger "A Note on the Marginal Efficiency of Capital," Economic Journal, 1958.

McKean, R. Efficiency in Government through Systems Analysis, New York, NY: John Wiley and Sons, 1958.

-------------, and Kurtilla, J. V. Multiple Purpose River Development, Baltimore, MD: Johns Hopkins Press, 1958.

Bailey, Martin J. "Formal Criteria for Investment Decisions," Journal of Political Economy, (October, 1959).

Margolis, Julius "The Economic Evaluation of Water Resource Development," American Economic Review, (March, 1959).

Steiner, P. O. "Choosing Among Alternative Public Investments in the Water Resource Field," American Economic Review, (December, 1959).

Bain, Joe "Criteria for Undertaking Water-Resource Development," American Economic Review, (May, 1960).

Hirshleifer, J. De Haven, J. C., and Milliman, J. W. Water Supply: Economics, Technology and Policy, Chicago, IL: University of Chicago Press, 1960.

Hitch, Charles J., and McKean, Roland N. Economics of Defense in the Nuclear Age, Cambridge, MA: Harvard University Press, 1960.

Eckstein, "A Survey of the Theory of Public Expenditure Criteria," in Buchanan, James M. (ed.), Public Finances: Needs, Sources and Utilization, Princeton, NJ: Princeton University Press, 1961.

Shackle, G. L. S. "Recent Theories Concerning the Nature and Role of Interest," Economic Journal, (June, 1961).

Kuhn, Tillo E. Public Enterprise Economics and Transport Problems, Berkeley and Los Angeles, CA: University of California Press, 1962.

Marglin, Stephen A. "Economic Factors Affecting System Design," in Maass, A., et. al., Design of Water Resource Systems, Cambridge, MA: Harvard University Press, 1962.

Mass, P. Optimal Investment Decisions: Rules for Action and Criteria for Choice, Englewood Cliffs, NJ: Prentice-Hall, 1962.

Marglin, Stephen A. Approaches to Dynamic Investment Planning, Amsterdam: North Holland Publishing Co., 1963.

Turvey, R. "Present Value Versus Internal Rate of Return - An Essay in the Theory of the Third Best," Economic Journal, March, 1963.

Wright, J. F. "Notes on the Marginal Efficiency of Capital," Oxford Economic Papers, (June, 1963).

------------ "The Opportunity Costs of Public Investment," Quarterly Journal of Economics, (May, 1963).

------------ "The Social Rate of Discount and the Optimal Rate of Investment," Quarterly Journal of Economics, (February, 1963).

Feldstein, Martin S. "Net Social Benefit Calculation and the Public Investment Decision," <u>Oxford Economic Papers</u>, (March, 1964).

Feldstein, M. S. "The Social Time Preference Discount Rate in Cost-Benefit Analysis," <u>Economic Journal</u>, (June, 1964).

Lind, R. C. "The Social Rate of Discount and the Optimal Rate of Investment: Further Comments," <u>Quarterly Journal of Economics</u>, 1964.

Nichols, A. "The Opportunity Cost of Public Investment: Comment," <u>Quarterly Journal of Economics</u>, 1964.

Tullock, Gordon "The Social Rate of Discount and the Optimal Rate of Investment: Comment," <u>Quarterly Journal of Economics</u>, 1964.

Usher, Dan "The Social Rate of Discount and the Optimal Rate of Investment: Comment," <u>Quarterly Journal of Economics</u>, 1964.

Mishan, E. J. "A Normalization Procedure for Public Investment Criteria," <u>Economic Journal</u>, 1967.

Mabro, R. "Normalization Procedure for Public Investment: A Comment," <u>Economic Journal</u>, 1969.

Nichols, A. "Normalization Procedure for Public Investment Criteria: A Further Comment," <u>Economic Journal</u>, 1970.

Chapter Seven

Pigou, A. C. The Economics of Welfare, 4th Edition, London, 1932.

Marshak, J. "Money and the Theory of Assets," Econometrica, Vol. 6, 1938.

von Neumann, J., and Morgenstern, O. Theory of Games and Economic Behavior, Princeton, NJ: Princeton University Press, 2nd Edition, 1947, (3rd Edition, 1953).

Friedman, M., and Savage, L. T. "The Utility Analysis of Choice Involving Risk," Journal of Political Economy, Vol. 56, (August, 1948).

Shackle, G. L. S. Expectations Economics, Cambridge, MA: University Press, 1949.

U. S. Congress, Subcommittee on Benefits and Costs of the Federal Inter-Agency River Basin Committee, Proposed Practices for Economic Analysis of River Basin Projects: Report to the Federal Inter-Agency River Basin Committee, Washington, DC: Government Printing Office, (May, 1950).

Arrow, K. J. "Alternative Approaches to the Theory of Choice in Risk-Taking Situations," Econometrica, Vol. 19, (October, 1951).

Arrow, K. J., Harris, T., and Marshak, J. "Optimal Inventory Policy," Econometrica, Vol. 20, (July, 1951).

Markowitz, H. "The Utility of Walth," Journal of Political Economy, Vol. 60, (April, 1952).

von Neumann, J., and Morgenstern, O. Theory of Bames and Economic Behavior, Princeton, NJ: Princeton University Press, 3rd Edition, 1953, (2nd Edition, 1947).

Williams, J. D. The Compleat Strategyst, New York, NY: McGraw-Hill, 1954.

Cramer, H. The Element of Probability, New York, NY: John Wiley & Sons, Inc., 1955.

Lipsey, R., and Lancaster, K. "The General Theory of the Second Best," Review of Economic Studies, 1956.

Bellman, R. Dynamic Programming, Princeton, NJ: Princeton University Press, 1957.

Carter, C. F., and others (eds.) Uncertainty and Business Decisions, Liverpool: University Press, 1956.

Churchman, C. W. Introduction to Operations Research, New York, NY: John Wiley & Sons, Inc., 1957.

Dorfman, R., Samuelson, P. A., and Solow, R. M. Linear Programming and Economic Analysis, Hightstown, NJ: McGraw-Hill, 1958.

Eckstein, O. Water Resource Development, Cambridge, MA: Harvard University Press, 1958.

Krutilla, J. V., and Eckstein, O. Multipurpose River Development, Baltimore, MD: Johns Hopkins Press, 1958.

McKean, R. N. Efficiency in Government Through Systems Analysis, New York, NY: John Wiley & Sons, Inc., 1958.

Modigliani, F., and Cohen, K. J. "The Significance and Uses of Ex Ante Data," Chapter IV in Bowman, M. J. (ed.), Expectations, Uncertainty and Business Behavior, New York, NY: Social Science Research Council, 1958.

Boreh, K. "The Safety Loading of Reinsurance," Skandinavisk Aktuarietid-Skrift, 1960.

Goodman, L. A. "On the Exact Variance of Products," Journal of American Statistical Association, Vol. 55, 1960.

Mirshleifer, J., Denaven, J. C., and Milliman, J. W. Water Supply: Economics, Technology, and Policy, Chicago, IL: University of Chicago Press, 1960.

Pigou, A. C. The Economics of Welfare, 4th Edition, New York, NY: Macmillan, 1960.

Bellman, R. Adaptive Control Processes: A Guided Tour, Princeton, NJ: Princeton University Press, 1961.

Eckstein, O. "A Survey of the Theory of Public Expenditure," and "Reply," in Buchanan, J. M. (ed.), Public Finances: Needs, Sources, and Utilization, Princeton, NJ; Princeton University Press, 1961.

Eckstein, Otto Water Resources Development: The Economics of Project Evaluation, Cambridge, MA: 1961.

------------ Introduction to Statistics for Business Decisions, New York, NY: McGraw-Hill, 1961.

Orcutt, G. H. "Simulation of Economic Systems," American Economic Review, Vol. 50, 1961.

Dorfman, R. "Basic Economic and Technological Concepts," in Maass and others, Design of Water Resources Systems, London, Macmillan, 1962.

Farrar, D. E. The Investment Decision Under Uncertainty, Englewood Cliffs, NJ: Prentice-Hall, 1962.

Maas, A. Design of Water Resource Systems, Cambridge, MA: Harvard University Press, 1962.

Masse, Pierre Optimal Investment Decisions, Englewood Cliffs, NJ: Prentice-Hall, 1962.

Burt, O. R., and Allison, D. R. "Farm Management Decisions with Dynamic Programming," Journal of Farm Economics, Vol. 45, 1963.

Hillier, F. S. "The Drivation of Probabilistic Information for the Evaluation of Risky Investments," Management Science, Vol. 9, 1963.

Marglin, S. A. "The Social Rate of Discount and the Optimal Rate of Investment," Quarterly Journal of Economics, (February, 1963).

Arrow, K. J. "The Role of Securities in the Optimal Allocation of Risk-Bearing," Review of Economic Studies, Vol. 31, 1964.

Feldstein, M. S. "The Social Time Preference Discount Rate in Cost Benefit Analysis," Economic Journal, Vol. 74, (June, 1964).

Hertz, D. B. "Risk Analysis in Capital Investment," Harvard Business Review, (January/February, 1964).

Marglin, S. A. "The Social Rate of Discount and the Optimal Rate of Investment," Quarterly Journal of Economics, Vol. 78, (May, 1964).

Marshall, A. Principles of Economics, 8th Edition, London: Macmillan, 1964.

Samuelson, P. A., and Vickrey, W. "Discussion," American Economic Review Proceedings, Vol. 59, 1964.

Samuelson, P. A. "Principles of Efficiency: Discussion," American Economic Review Proceedings, (May, 1964).

Sharpe, W. F. "Capital Asset Prices: A Theory of Market Equilibrium Under Conditions of Risk," Journal of Finance, Vol. 19, (September, 1964).

Tullock, Gordon "The Social Rate of Discount and the Optimal Rate of Investment: Comment," Quarterly Journal of Economics, 1965.

Vickrey, W. "Principles of Efficiency -- Discussion," American Economic Review, Vol. 54, Papers and Proceedings, (May, 1964).

von Neumann, J., and Morgenstern, O. Theory of Games and Economic Behavior, 2nd Edition, New York, NY: John Wiley & Sons, Inc., 1964.

Adelman, R. M. "Criteria for Capital Investment," Operational Research Quarterly,

(March, 1965).

Fellner, William Probability and Profit, Homewood, IL: Richard D. Irwin, Inc., 1965.

Haveman, R. H. Water Resource Investment and the Public Interest, Nashville, TN: Vanderbilt University Press, 1965.

Hirshleifer, J. "Investment Decision Under Uncertainty: Choice-Theoretic Approaches Approaches," The Quarterly Journal of Economics, Vol. 79, (November, 1965).

Howard, R. A. "Dynamic Inference," Operations Research, Vol. 13, (September, 1965).

Knight, F. N. Risk, Uncertainty, and Profit, New York, NY: Harper & Row, 1965.

Lamberton, D. M. The Theory of Profit, Oxford, Basil Blackwell & Mott, Ltd., 1965.

Ozga, S. Andrew Expectations in Economic Theory, Chicago, IL: Aldine Publishing Company, 1965.

Prest, A. R., and Turvey, R. "Cost-Benefit Analysis: A Survey," Economic Journal, Vol. 75, (December, 1965).

Savage, L. J. The Foundations of Statistics, New York, NY: John Wiley & Sons, Inc., 1965.

Zusman, P., and Amaid, A. "Farm Planning Under Weather Uncertainty," Journal of Farm Economics, Vol. 14, (August, 1965).

Arrow, K. J. "Discounting and Public Investment Criteria," in Kneese, A. V. and Smith, S. C. (eds.), Water Resources Research, Baltimore, MD: Johns Hopkins Press, 1966.

Bain, J. S., Caves, R. E., and Margolis, J. Northern California's Water Industry, Baltimore, MD: Johns Hopkins Press, 1966.

Hirshleifer, J. "Investment Decision Under Uncertainty: Applications of the State-Preference Approach," Quarterly Journal of Economics, Vol. 30, (May, 1966).

Swalm, Ralph O. "Utility Theory -- Insights into Risk Taking," Harvard Business Review, (November-December, 1966).

Diamond, P. A. "The Role of a Stock Market in a General Equilibrium Model with Technological Uncertainty," American Economic Review, Vol. 57, (September, 1967).

Haveman, R., and Krutilla, J. V. "Unemployment, Excess Capacity, and Benefit-Cost Investment Criteria," Review of Economics and Statistics, Vol. 49, No. 3, (August, 1967).

Luce, R. D., and Raiffa, H. Games and Decisions: Introduction to Critical Survey, New York, NY: Wiley, 1967.

Arrow, K. J. "The Economics of Moral Hazard: Further Comment," American Economic Review, Vol. 58, 1968.

Baumol, W. J. "On the Social Rate of Discount," American Economic Review, 1968.

Hirshleifer, J. "Preference Sociale a l'Egard du Temps," Recherches Economiques De Louvain, Vol. 34, 1968.

Joint Economic Committee, Economic Analysis of Public Investment Decisions: Interest Rate Policy and Discounting Analysis, Washington, DC, 1968.

King, W. R. Probability for Management Decisions, New York, NY: John Wiley & Sons, 1968.

Moore, P. G. Basic Operation Research, London: Pitman & Son, 1968.

Pauley, H. V. "The Economics of Moral Hazard: Comment," American Economic Review, Vol. 58, 1968.

Ramsey, D. D. "On the Social Rate of Discount: Comment," (unpublished), 1968.

Staats, E. B., Statement of Hon. Elmer B. Staats, Comptroller General of the United States, Joint Economic Committee, Subcommittee on Economy in Government, Interest Rate Guidelines for Federal Decisionmaking, 90th Congress, 2nd Session, 1968.

------------ "The Discount Rate in Public Investment Evaluation" (unpublished), (December, 1968).

U. S. Congress, Joint Economic Committee, Subcommittee on Economy in Uovernment, Interest Rate Guidelines for Federal Decisionmaking, 90th Congress, 2nd Session, 1968.

Schlaiffer, R. Probability and Statistics for Business Decisions, New York, NY: McGraw-Hill, 1969.

Arrow, K. J., and Lind, R. C. "Uncertainty and the Evaluation of Public Investment Decisions," American Economic Review, 1970.

Reutlinger, S. Techniques for Project Appraisal Under Uncertainty, World Bank Staff Paper No. 10, Baltimore, MD: Johns Hopkins Press, 1970.

Fisher, A. "Environmental Externalities and the Arrow-Lind Public Investment Theorem," American Economic Review, 1973.